The Culture of Prison Violence

The Culture of Prison Violence

James M. Byrne, PhD

Professor, Department of Criminal Justice and Criminology
University of Massachusetts Lowell

Don Hummer, PhD

Assistant Professor of Criminal Justice
School of Public Affairs
Penn State Harrisburg

Faye S. Taxman, PhD

Professor, Wilder School of Government and Public Affairs
Virginia Commonwealth University

With a Foreword by Todd Clear, Distinguished Professor
John Jay College of Criminal Justice

Boston   New York   San Francisco
Mexico City   Montreal   Toronto   London   Madrid   Munich   Paris
Hong Kong   Singapore   Tokyo   Cape Town   Sydney

Acquisitions Editor: *Dave Repetto*
Editorial Assistant: *Jack Cashman*
Senior Marketing Manager: *Kelly May*
Production Supervisor: *Roberta Sherman*
Production Service and Electronic
Composition: *GGS Book Services, Inc.*
Composition Buyer: *Linda Cox*
Manufacturing Buyer: *Debbie Rossi*
Cover Designer: *Elena Sidorova*

For related titles and support materials, visit our online catalog at www.ablongman.com.

Between the time website information is gathered and then published, it is not unusual for some sites to have closed. Also, the transcription of URLs can result in typographical errors. The publisher would appreciate notification where these errors occur so that they may be corrected in subsequent editions.

Library of Congress Cataloging-in-Publication Data

The culture of prison violence/edited by James Byrne, Faye S. Taxman,
   and Don Hummer.—1st ed.
     p. cm.
   Includes bibliographical references.
   ISBN 978-0-205-54296-3 (alk. paper)
   1. Prison violence—United States. I. Byrne, James II. Taxman, Faye S.
III. Hummer, Donald C. (Donald Charles)
HV9025.P76 2007
365'.973—dc22   2007001174

Printed in the United States of America

10   9   8   7   6   5   4   3   2   1   11   10   09   08   07

Contents

Foreword

Looking back at the last 35 years of American penology, we might fairly conclude that in the overarching U.S. mind-set, there is a deep-seeded belief in prisons. In fact, with the exception of the in-many-ways aberrant decade of the 1960s, belief in prisons has been a long-standing, uniquely American value, arising in the late 1700s (about the same time we won our freedom) and continuing dauntlessly, in one way or another, through civil war, industrialization, and into our current information age. We now use prisons more than ever before, more than any other democratic society (or dictatorship or autocracy, for that matter). Among our cultural exports, we can now count this faith in imprisonment, as other Western nations seem to now emulate us in this regard. Around the world, English-speaking nations and many other democracies grow their prison populations with some of the same optimism about the wisdom of this practice that we have exhibited now for over two centuries. They have a long way to go, of course, before they will catch up in numbers, but some of them have already matched us in the rhetoric of confinement.

There are ironies in the love affair with incarceration. The most obvious irony is the amount of *forgetting* we have to do to maintain the faith. In the United States, for example, there is no single study showing that people who leave prison are by and large (or even marginally) lucky to have had the experience. To the contrary, the effusive interest these days in the topic of reentry has as its foundational assumption that people who leave prisons bring most of their problems back to the community, intact or amplified by what happened to them behind bars. When encountering a person who is coming back from prison time, only the naive assume they are confronted with someone for whom prison has done what it was supposed to do, and the result is a new homeostasis of the social contract. Common sense tells us that people who do time are hit hard by it, altered in uncertain ways, and in need of "support" as they try to return to civilian life. Our knee-jerk belief in prison seems never to be challenged by our equally somatic senses that people who have gone there are not the better for it.

In the face of these contradictions, faith in prison has remained high. The extremely high rate of return to prison, a phenomenon not unique to the United

States, spawns conclusions about the intractability of deviance rather than the irrelevance of confinement. With any other correctional treatment, we would treat the high failure rate as evidence challenging the assumptions and techniques of the treatment program. Prison gets a pass: Surely these failures are the result of incorrigibility rather than a faulty intervention.

The high rate at which people, once exposed to prison, behave as though its lessons were not taken to heart, does not go unnoticed, however. In a nation of pragmatists, few are satisfied with the fact that so many of those to whom we give the "lesson" of prison fail to learn it. Therefore, running alongside the two-century long, faithful belief in the use of prisons as a penal method has been an equally sincere call for reforming the prison experience.

Prison reform agendas can be divided into two broad camps. There are those who seek to reduce prison failure by making prisons harsher experiences. The simple, logic of this camp is that if prisons are nasty enough, people will not want to come back. The alternative is to make prisons more wholesome places, where people are changed in ways that make them better citizens when they leave. The logic here is a bit more complex, but holds that the missing piece for those who are to be released from prison is not a healthy fear of it, but a workable toolbox for staying out.

For those who want to make prisons worse, there is easy advice. No credible study exists anywhere suggesting that harder treatment is superior to less-hard treatment in reforming the minds of those who have committed crimes. Indeed, what little evidence there is on the question suggests that being harder leads to *worse* outcomes overall, not better ones. To that problematic empirical foundation may be added a further difficulty: There is no principled, morally sustainable position from which to argue on behalf of intentionally increasing the brutality of confinement. The case against hard treatment is so strong that I am tempted to classify its advocates with those who believe in Santa Claus: The source of the belief lives on in the face of contrary evidence because of the good feelings it gives to the believer. Staying with this metaphor, I would suggest it is time for the believers in hard time to "grow up" and start to live in the real world of evidence rather than the fantasy world of intention. No more needs to be said.

For those who belong to the second group of reformers, there are two comforts. First, they are joined by a very large group of expert professional penologists and lay reformers, going back to humanitarian luminaries such as Benjamin Franklin and John Howard and continuing to virtually every serious writer about prison today. They are in very good company. Secondly, there is a small, but impressive, empirical literature to support their case. The size of the effects is not great, admittedly, nor is there any guarantee that any program designed to make prison more humane will be useful in teaching lessons of life to those who are confined. Questions of effectiveness are, after all, empirical matters, and studies sometimes confirm the value of new programs and sometimes fail to do so.

Within the programmatic reform tradition, there are two subclasses. Some people study prison programs to see if they "rehabilitate" people who are exposed to them—that is, to see if people who engage in those programs return to criminal behavior less frequently. These are true pragmatists in the grand American tradition, for they seek social tools to make a better society, beginning where the need is arguably greatest. They have not only a long American tradition behind them; they also stand on a firm moral foundation.

The other subgroup looks into prisons and sees places where brutal treatment is much too frequent—among those who have been confined by law, and between them and the people who keep them while they are behind bars. This group sees the brutality itself as a moral wrong perpetrated on those who are behind bars against their will. They seek to reduce prison brutality. While their aims may be less utilitarian than the programmatic reformers, their project is just as much an empirical one. The question they face is, which kinds of prison strategies brutalize less, and what is the evidence for that conclusion?

I classify penal reform efforts, partly to situate the essays, studies really, in this insightful book. On the one hand, these chapters are undeniably concerned with the problem posed by the contemporary prison: too violent, too likely to lead to failure. In that line of thinking, they take the prison problem seriously, as one of evidence and careful thought. But, they are not the only way one might think about the problem of prison. Abolitionists, for example, solve the problems addressed in these papers by a different strategy. That said, what is to be made of the research offered here by Byrne, his colleagues and contributors? Three terms arise repeatedly in the chapters of this volume, and they provide a useful window from which to view the research presented: programming, legitimacy, and culture.

Programming is a centerpiece of liberal penal reform. Usually, the call for a renewed emphasis on treatment programs is straightforwardly utilitarian; these programs are seen as the way to increase the adjustment of formerly incarcerated to their communities, when they return. In the chapters of this volume, there is that commonsense quality to the question of prison programs, to be sure, but there is an added dimension. These authors think about programs for the way they effect the prison as a place where people live and work. The authors think about programs as a context for doing time, offering a case for more programs that is *not* tied to the (too often meager) way they affect post-release outcomes, but rather to reduction of various forms of prison violence and disorder. The addition of a second criterion—the way programs affect the incarceration experience for the confined *and* the people who work in prisons—is an additional benefit that should not be taken lightly. A case can be built for prison programs *even if* they have little impact on post-release behavior of the formerly incarcerated, if they make the prison context better. If they do so for *both* those who are being punished and those who are carrying out the punishment, then all the better.

In that sense, the case for programs is tied closely to the problem of **legitimacy.** Prison is, by all accounts, a stressful and artificial environment. In too many ways, it mocks the lives of those who spend time there, turning prisoners into initiative-less wards and guards into managers of cruelty. It is hard too see that such an enterprise could ever be legitimate. Yet there is an abiding need for prison to be legitimate, not only in the eyes of the broader society relying upon it but also, and especially, in the eyes of those caught up in the daily drama of confinement. When the way a prison expresses its mission is seen as legitimate by those enmeshed in its daily life, it begins to have a purpose that gives meaning to their lives and has the possibility of becoming a contribution to social life outside the walls. These are simple words to write, but ever-so-difficult to document.

The target of programs built on a foundation of legitimacy is **culture.** Prison culture has been the topic of much research and even more fascinating speculation. The classic works in penology describe prison culture. There are far fewer attempts to change culture. Yet there could hardly be a more important agenda in prison reform than to change the way it feels to live and work there. If prison culture can be changed, then people who spend time there become cultural change agents, and there is a new measure of hope for the institution itself.

This book, then, is a practical book. Its goal is to change practice; to make prisons different. It expresses that goal through an examination of the evidence regarding a number of critical questions about the operation of prisons, as well as the effectiveness of programs designed to reduce prison violence and disorder, increase legitimacy and address the problems associated with negative inmate, staff, and management culture. Each of the following questions are addressed in the chapters that follow:

- How violent are prisons, what is the link between prison and community violence, and what does a careful evidence-based review reveal about what can be done to reduce the level of violence?
- What is the link between prison culture and community culture?
- How legitimate are prison regimes, what difference does it make, and assuming moral performance/legitimacy matters, what do we have to do to improve the performance of prisons in these areas?
- And finally, what is wrong with prison culture, how do we know, and what can we do about it?

For people who seek a penology of which we can be proud, these are crucial questions, essential for the next generation of penal methods. There is no more current, more insightful collection of empirically based essays on the topic than those contained in this volume.

The Culture of Prison Violence

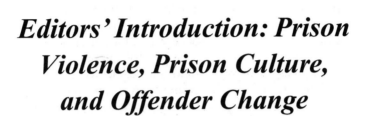

Editors' Introduction: Prison Violence, Prison Culture, and Offender Change

James M. Byrne, PhD

Professor, Department of Criminal Justice and Criminology
University of Massachusetts Lowell

Don Hummer, PhD

Assistant Professor, School of Public Affairs, Criminal Justice Program,
Penn State Harrisburg

Faye S. Taxman, PhD

Professor, Wilder School of Government and Public Affairs
Virginia Commonwealth University

Introduction: A Brief Revisionist History of Prison Reform

Since the mid-1970s, there have been a number of significant changes in the social, legal, political, and administrative character of U.S. prisons: *socially,* there is a greater proportion of minorities in prison, there are more violent offenders in prison, there are more offenders with significant, life-threatening health problems in prison, there are more recent (and illegal) immigrants in prison, and there are more mentally ill offenders in prison; *legally,* the courts now play a much more prominent role in the maintenance of prison standards and in the protection of prisoners' rights; *politically,* crime control has emerged as a major campaign issue, not only influencing the outcome of elections, but also fueling the drive toward incarceration-centered

1

offender control strategies; and (administratively) there have been significant, (though small) changes in the gender, race, and education levels of both prison guards and prison administrators, structural changes in prison organization and administration, and the privatization of many (and in some prisons, all) prison functions (e.g., health care, programs) is becoming increasingly more common (Byrne, 2006).

At the same time, recent increases in prison populations, along with pressure both to *"do more with less"* (in terms of resources, and staffing levels) and to *"do less with more"* (by eliminating and/or restricting access to programs for offenders in prison, reducing access to "unnecessary" recreation, restricting visitation, and limiting inmate movements by expanding both the use of administrative segregation and the number of "supermax" prisons) have put us back to precisely that point in the recent history of prisons where we do not want to be: the weeks and months immediately preceding the Attica riot. In a recent review of prison management trends, Riveland (1999) offered a similar assessment: "In many ways prisons have come full circle from twenty-five years ago . . .

> Today, many of the positive changes that have occurred in the nation's prisons during this quarter decade are in some jeopardy" (174). He goes on to argue that a variety of factors—including inmate idleness, inadequate work and educational programs, limited access to courts, changes in state laws, crowding's effect on inmate—staff ratios, a new breed of get tough prison administrators, and of course, public sentiment toward prisoners—have converged in a manner that mirrors "the volatile conditions that existed in the 1970s" (Riveland, 1999: 175)

While the Attica riot was certainly a watershed event in the history of U.S. prison management, it is disconcerting to consider the possibility that despite the major post–Attica reforms that were initiated, today's prisons are still plagued by yesterday's problems: collective violence, interpersonal violence, intrapersonal violence, and institutional violence (Byrne, 2006; Bottoms, 1999). However, there is currently disagreement over whether the level and/or rate of prison violence is increasing or decreasing as a consequence of both our recent incarceration binge and our expanded utilization of the technology of control in prison settings (Commission on Safety and Abuse, 2006; Useem and Piehl, 2006). Indeed, there are those who would argue that in terms of risk of violent victimization, prisons are actually *safer* than an inmate's home community (Mumola, 2005). Despite this disagreement, most observers agree that (1) the current level of prison violence and disorder is unacceptably high, and (2) violence in prison in many respects mirrors violence in our communities, due to the influence of gangs and the link between institutional culture and community culture (Byrne, 2006; Stowell and Byrne, this volume).

Faced with this grim reality, it appears that prison administrators have two policy choices: (1) wait for the next galvanizing "event" to occur in our federal and/or state prison system and then use this event to gain support for the "next" wave of prison reform; or (2) develop policy based on a proactive strategy that attempts to target the underlying cause(s) of prison disorder (e.g., inmate culture, staff culture, lack of programming, crowding, inadequate classification) and to design a plan of action that *prevents* such a negative occurrence. Regardless of whether new prison reform initiatives are reactive or proactive, it makes sense—given the 60 billion dollar investment in the United States alone on corrections last year—to demand that these initiatives be based on "what works" according to the available research evidence. The problem with this strategy is that we have not conducted the necessary independent, quality research on the cause, prevention, and control of prison violence to provide policy makers and corrections administrators with the answers to questions about what works in this critical area. Each of the chapters included in our volume addresses this issue directly by presenting a detailed examination of the prison violence problem based on the latest empirical research on a wide range of inmate-focused, staff-focused, and management-focused violence prevention strategies.

An Overview of the Special Volume

The collection of original research studies included in this special volume focuses on an array of theoretical, empirical, and policy issues related to the cause, prevention, and control of prison violence and disorder. The authors—including researchers from both the United States and Great Britian—share a common interest in understanding the link between various forms of prison culture (inmate culture, staff culture, and/or management culture) and the level of violence and disorder in prison. In exploring this relationship, the authors delve into a wide range of issues related to prison violence, prison culture, and offender change. Separate chapters focus on the following: (1) an examination the nature and extent of the prison violence and victimization, focusing on the difference between official and unofficial estimates of various forms of prison violence (Byrne and Hummer); (2) identification of new conceptual frameworks for understanding prison violence and disorder (Sparks and Bottoms; Crawley and Crawley), and the potential application of new dynamic conceptions of culture in both institutional and community settings (Stowell and Byrne); (3) presentation of a rationale for examining prison culture, studying its effect on the treatment and control of mentally ill offenders (Lurigio and Snowden) and developing new methods to identify staff culture (positive and negative) as a necessary first step toward improving the "moral performance" of prisons (Liebling); (4) research on new inmate-centered (Edgar) and staff-centered (Byrne, et al.) violence reduction strategies; and (5) an evidence-based review of the research on the impact of institutional culture (and several other factors) on prison violence and disorder (Byrne and Hummer).

We begin with a chapter by James Byrne and Don Hummer, *The Nature and Extent of Prison Violence,* which examines both official and unofficial estimates of interpersonal, intrapersonal, collective, and institutional violence in prison. Clearly, much of the debate over the nature and extent of the prison violence problem can be linked to decisions made by researchers and policy makers about how to use (and interpret) official versus unofficial (self-report, victimization) data on prison violence and disorder. Byrne and Hummer provide a nuanced view of the prison violence problem that draws on both data sources.

The second chapter included in this collection, *Does What Happens in Prison Stay in Prison? Examining the Reciprocal Relationship between Community and Prison Culture,* by Jacob Stowell and James Byrne, presents a model of prison violence and victimization that views prison violence—and prison culture, from an interactionist perspective. Given the wealth of community level research on the social ecology of crime generally, and the importance of person–environment interactions in understanding community violence in particular (Pattavina, Byrne, and Garcia, 2006; Sampson and Bean, 2006), it certainly makes sense to examine person–environment interactions in prison settings. In the concluding section of their article, the authors argue that the field needs to move beyond discussions about the relative merits of strategies based on either importation theory (see, e.g., Irwin and Cressey, 1962), which emphasizes the characteristics of offenders (and to a lesser extent, staff), or deprivation theory (see, e.g., Sykes, 1958), which focuses on the negative conditions and consequences of living in prison. Utilizing a new, dynamic cultural paradigm developed by Sampson and Bean (2006) to help explain community violence, the authors consider the impact of culture on individual behavior in both institutional and community settings.

In Chapter 3, *Examining The Impact of Institutional Culture on Prison Violence and Disorder: An Evidence-Based Review,* Byrne and Hummer present the results of the authors' exhaustive review of the research conducted over the past twenty years on a wide range of factors linked to prison violence, including: (1) prison culture, (2) prison crowding, (3) staffing levels, characteristics, and quality, (4) prison programming, availability, and quality, (5) prison classification practices, (6) prison management practices, (7) situational context, and (8) inmate profiles and gang membership. The authors found that although most of the research on the link between many of the factors just identified (including prison culture) and prison violence is too weak methodologically to draw conclusions, there are two review areas for which more definitive statements can be offered: prison programming and prison classification. According to the authors, "First, inmate programming designed to focus on a number of dimensions of individual change (education, vocational training, treatment for mental health problems and/or drug, alcohol addiction, lifestyle/life-course decisions, and physical health problems) has been directly linked to lower levels of violence and disorder in prison. . . Second, contrary to the general perception, there is no evidence that current prison classification schemes result in safer prisons, primarily because placement in a particular custody level—by itself—does not appear to reduce the "risk" of inmate misconduct (overall, and violent) while in prison" (*this volume*). The authors conclude by emphasizing the importance of conducting independent, quality research in federal and state prisons, not only on prison culture, but also on a wide range of other factors linked to prison violence. They argue that until the necessary research studies are completed, prison managers will not be able to argue that their management strategies are based on an evidence-based review of "best practices" in this 60 billion dollar business (*this volume*).

The next chapter, *Legitimacy and Imprisonment Revisited: Some Notes on the Problem of Order Ten Years After,* is written by Richard Sparks and Anthony Bottoms, co-authors of one of the most comprehensive and critically acclaimed examinations of the prison violence problems conducted in recent years, *Prisons and the Problem of Order* (Sparks, Bottoms, and Hay, 1996). It has been a decade since the release of this book, and the passing of time offers a unique opportunity, both to look *back* at the major research findings and policy recommendations included in this review and to look *forward* and consider the relevance of this study in the current context of prison conditions, policies, and practices, not only in the two high security English prisons examined in the original study (Albany and Long Lartin), but also in prisons in the United States and other countries. Sparks and Bottoms argue persuasively that their main finding about the importance of legitimacy in prisons is as relevant today as it was a decade ago. Indeed, they present a compelling case for developing mechanisms to monitor the level of legitimacy in prison, based on the notion that legitimacy should be viewed as one of the prison system's primary goals. As they observe, "Legitimacy is a term that has both descriptive and normative dimensions. It directs attention to how things work and fail to work. But it should also make us more sharply aware of the gap between things as they are and as they might be" (Sparks and Bottoms, *this volume*). Perhaps most importantly, Sparks and Bottoms's research establishes an important link between the level of legitimacy in a particular prison and the levels of various forms of violence and disorder reported in these facilities.

In Chapter 5, *Why Prison Staff Culture Matters,* Allison Liebling presents new empirical evidence that staff culture can be defined and measured, and that its effects—both positive and negative—on prison violence and disorder can be identified. According to Liebling, unless issues related to negative staff culture are addressed, any new initiatives implemented in these prisons will be undermined. Liebling found that "Culture is related to the likelihood of implementation of new policies, as well as to their outcomes for prisoners. Where large proportions of staff hold negative attitudes toward senior managers and prisoners, they are unlikely to embrace or implement new policies." The consequences for inmates of negative staff culture are also described by Liebling, including its effect on inmate perceptions of safety, and the level of intra-personal violence in prison (e.g., suicide attempts, other forms of self-injury). Liebling's research certainly supports the argument presented by Sparks and Bottoms that *legitimacy* is an important goal for prisons. In addition, her research raises the possibility that there may be a direct link between the "moral performance" of prisons and the moral performance of prisoners, not only while in prison but also upon reentry to the community. If Liebling is correct, then improvements in a prison's moral performance may affect inmate behavior, both while in prison and upon release (Liebling, 2005).

The sixth chapter in this collection, *Culture, Performance, and Disorder: The Communicative Quality of Prison Violence,* by Elaine and Peter Crawley, considers the problem of prison violence from a decidedly different perspective, focusing on the positive effects of both individual and collective violence in prisons (a rare event in even the worst prison settings) on subsequent inmate, staff, and management interactions (and the resulting quality of life) in these prisons. The authors contend that "violence, in addition to being instrumental and expressive, is also *communicative* in that a violent episode can transmit meaning to an audience far wider than its intended recipient" (*this volume*). When considering the cause of both individual and collective violence in prison, the authors echo Sparks and Bottoms's view that "in prisons, both individual and collective disorder tends to occur when prisoners do not perceive the regime (including the behavior of staff) to be legitimate" (*this volume*). Based on data collected in a large ethnographic study of prison officers in six prisons in England, Crawley and Crawley found that in many instances a riot can actually have positive effects on both inmates and staff, because "participation in such events, whether as prison officer or prisoner, provide opportunities for the construction of a courageous identity through stories of endurance and resilience in the face of danger and risk" (*this volume*). In addition, the incident often focuses attention on the underlying "legitimacy" issues that resulted in the act of individual/collective disorder; in many instances, the aftermath of these incidents is "a period of relative calmness in the prison, and a process of 'taking stock' by prison staff" (*this volume*).

While Crawley and Crawley offer a different perspective on the (positive) consequences of individual and collective violence in prison on both inmates and staff, they have emphasized a common theme among the first set of articles included in this volume: Violence in prison appears to be directly related to the legitimacy of the control strategies used to regulate activities and to maintain order and control in prison. The policy implications of these findings for prison management are straightforward: We need to consider new strategies for managing, controlling, and—hopefully—changing offenders sent to prison, based on the notion that concepts such as legitimacy, procedural justice, and moral performance can be applied to prisons in concrete ways that transform the prison experience for both prison staff and inmates.

One problem that limits the utilization of research by corrections managers is that very few new initiatives conducted in prison settings are independently evaluated by external, independent evaluation researchers. In fact, most evaluations of prison programs and initiatives are either in-house evaluations or self-evaluations conducted by the *same* organization responsible for the initiative. For a variety of reasons (e.g., accuracy, quality, financial self-interest), this type of research is bad for the field. Because corrections policy and practice has not been grounded in quality evaluation research (Farabee, 2005), it is certainly open to criticism from all fronts. However, the movement toward evidence-based practice in policing and in the courts is slowly moving into the corrections arena, first in community corrections and now, grudgingly, in the evaluation of institutional corrections programs (Byrne and Taxman, 2006).

The chapter by James Byrne, Don Hummer, and Faye Taxman, *The National Institute of Corrections' Institutional Culture Change Initiative: A Multisite Evaluation,* highlights the findings from their external, independent examination of the initial implementation of NIC's Culture Change Initiative. Their evaluation identifies critical issues related to the design and implementation of staff-focused culture change initiatives that must be addressed by NIC, in conjunction with the private sector service providers they selected to run the projects in several state prison systems across the country. Unfortunately, only preliminary estimates of the impact of the initiative are included in this review, because of NIC's decision to discontinue the external evaluation component of the initiative. Importantly, their analyses (utilizing a pre-post implementation interrupted time series design) do provide support for a link between the initiation of staff-focused culture change initiatives and subsequent reductions in the overall level of disorder reported in prison. However, much more research is needed before the underlying assumption of NIC program developers (i.e., *if staff culture changes, inmate culture will follow*) can be fully tested. Finally, Byrne and his colleagues found no link between the NIC initiative and the reduction of violence (a rare event) in prison. The authors suggest that if violence reduction is your desired goal, then a different array of intervention strategies (at higher dosage levels) may be needed, perhaps targeting *both* staff culture and inmate culture.

The eighth chapter in this volume examines the effects of prison violence and prison culture on mentally ill inmates. Nationally recognized mental health expert Arthur Lurigio, and his colleague, psychologist Elizabeth Snowden, offer their assessment, *Prison Culture and the Treatment and Control of Mentally Ill Offenders.* According to Lurigio and Snowden, "The most reliable studies of mental illness among state prisoners have found that 15 percent suffer from an SMI. . . . based on the 15 percent estimate, at midyear 2004, 224,494 state and federal prison inmates were suffering from an SMI" (*this volume*). The authors review the most likely causes for such a high prevalence rate (e.g., deinstitutionalization and the war on drugs), and then examine the link between prison culture, the social structure of prison, prison discipline, prison employees, and the level/quality of mental health care provided in the U.S. prison system today. They conclude that "inadequate mental health treatment for prisoners with mental illness guarantees that these individuals are going to face the same problems at release as they did when entering prison, which leads to an increased risk for recidivism and reincarceration" (*this volume*).

Next, Kimmett Edgar, the Head of Research at the Prison Reform Trust, Oxford University, focuses on a new inmate-focused culture change strategy (the conflict-centered approach) currently being field-tested in a handful of prisons in England and Wales. His article, *Cultural Roots of Violence in England's Prisons: An Exploration of Inter-Prisoner Conflict,* draws on previous research conducted by the author on prison victimization (O'Donnell and Edgar, 1998), as well as interviews with guards (Edgar and Martin, 2000) and interviews with inmates (Edgar, O'Donnell, and Martin, 2003) on the nature and circumstances of prison violence. In this groundbreaking article, Edgar begins by demonstrating that the "vast majority of incidents in which one prisoner harms another goes unreported" (*this volume*), and he estimates that the reporting rates are about 14 percent for assault, 13 percent for threats, and 12 percent for verbal abuse. Edgar goes on to argue that the reactive control strategies employed in most prisons (e.g., sanctioning known offenders, classifying high-risk inmates, developing staff policies for the use of force) are ineffective because they are not based on an examination of the underlying *cause of* the problem.

Drawing on the principles of restorative justice, Edgar details the key features of a proactive, conflict-centered violence reduction strategy that would utilize an alternative reporting and problem-solving strategy for inmate victimization, focusing on four "spheres of action for promoting personal safety: (1) fulfilling prisoners' basic human needs; (2) ensuring personal safety; (3) providing opportunities for the exercise of personal autonomy; and (4) building in mechanisms for prisoners to resolve their conflicts" (*this volume*). Advocates of restorative justice will be particularly interested in how Edgar describes the conferencing strategies, "facilitated by external, trained mediators, and including each party's supporters" (*this volume*), which are being used in select prisons to understand the cause of the conflict and develop an effective problem-solving strategy. Because Edgar does *not* present independent evidence of the impact of the conflict-centered approach he describes, it must be emphasized that this model has not been subject to external, independent evaluation review. At this point, it is perhaps best described as a promising strategy in need of independent, external review.

We conclude this volume with a brief chapter, *New Directions: An Agenda for Theory, Research and Policy,* where we consider what we know and don't know about the impact of the prison experience on both offenders and communities. Given the negative consequences of incarceration for offenders' subsequent life-course events (e.g., family, work, marriage, location) and desistance from crime, we contend that it is time to "rethink" our approach to offender control and to offender change.

Concluding Comments: New Directions and an Agenda for Change

The articles included in this volume will provide readers with a detailed examination of the problem of prison violence and disorder. By focusing attention on the effects of inmate, staff, and management culture on the behavior of offenders sent to and released from prisons, the authors move the discussion of prison violence beyond the typical debate between advocates of importation theory and advocates of deprivation theory. While prison culture has a place in both theories of prison violence, we suspect that the best explanation for the current levels of prison violence and disorder is found in explorations of person–environment interactions in prison settings. Not surprisingly, person–environment interactions *also* offer the most widely accepted and empirically based explanation for the current levels of *community* violence and disorder (Byrne, 2006; Sampson and Bean, 2006).

In addition, the articles included in this volume provide the reader with an empirically based review of new approaches to the prevention and control of prison violence, including *inmate*-focused (restorative justice) conflict resolution strategies, *staff*-focused culture change strategies, and *management*-focused initiatives that foster legitimacy, increased access to programs/treatment, and a recognition that offender change should replace offender control (e.g., through gang identification, offender segregation) as the primary focus of inmate classification.

Taken together, the articles represent the current "state of the art" in thinking about the cause, prevention, and control of prison violence. While there are certainly a number of important policy issues raised by the authors of these articles, three policy recommendations come immediately to mind: (1) demand transparency from prison management, (2) mandate evidence-based program development in prison settings, and (3) develop and implement strategies emphasizing legitimacy and measuring the moral performance of prisons, in recognition of the simple premise that there is a link between the moral performance of *prisons* and the moral performance of *prisoners* when they return to our communities. Each of the three policy recommendations highlighted below is described in more detail in our final chapter:

- ***Strategy 1: Demand Transparency***—One basic tenet underlying the institutional control of "disruptive" members of our community is "out of sight; out of mind." As a growing number of prisoners reenter the community after experiencing prison violence (as both offenders and victims), we are beginning to understand that these prison "experiences" have negative consequences for both offenders and communities. For this reason, it is critical to develop a system of "oversight" that includes an external review of what happens in prison, and a mechanism for informing the "public" about the level of violence and disorder in prison. One possible approach would be to implement the national performance measurement system recommended by the Association of State Correctional Administrators (Wright, 2005). The underlying assumption of this strategy is simple to articulate: *"What gets measured gets done."* Corrections administrators will know that the performance of their prison will be assessed based on these "outcome measures," and they will respond to this public performance review by developing strategies to address problem areas in their prison's performance review (see Gaes, Camp, Nelson, and Saylor, 2004, for a detailed discussion).

- ***Strategy 2: Require Evidence-Based Practice***—The institutional corrections system lags far behind community corrections in the application of "best practices" to the problem of prison violence and disorder. We need to design a national prison violence reduction initiative that (1) conducts systematic, evidence-based reviews of specific prison problems; (2) field tests various strategies designed based on these reviews; and (3) evaluates these strategies using rigorous evaluation designs (experiments and quasi-experiments).

- ***Strategy 3: Measure the Moral Performance of Prisons***—In addition to monitoring prison performance based on traditional measures of violence and disorder (interpersonal, intrapersonal, institutional, and collective violence/disorder), a new set of outcome measures needs to be introduced, which recognizes the importance of changing the "culture" of prisons (inmate, staff, and management culture) and improving the "quality of life" for both inmates and staff in prison. These outcome measures would focus on the legitimacy (or the "moral performance") of prisons in a variety of areas (inmate–staff relations, daily routines, procedural justice, access to treatment, etc.), based on the assumption that improvements in the moral performance of prisons will ultimately affect the moral performance of prisoners when they return to the community.

References

Beck, A, Hughes, and Harrison (2004). "Data Collection for the Prison Rape Elimination Act of 2003." *Bureau of Justice Statistics Status Report* (June 30, 2004). Washington, D.C.: U.S. Department of Justice, Office of Justice Programs.

Bottoms, A. E. (1999). "Interpersonal Violence and Social Order in Prisons." In M. Tonry and J. Petersilia (Eds.), *Prisons.* Chicago, Illinois: The University of Chicago Press.

Bureau of Justice Statistics (BJS) (2000). *Correctional Populations in the United States, 1997.* Washington, D.C.: U.S. Department of Justice, Office of Justice Programs, Bureau of Justice Statistics.

Byrne, J. M. (2006). Testimony before the Commission on Safety and Abuse in America's Prisons. Public Hearing #4: Oversight, Accountability, and Other Issues. Los Angeles, CA, February 8–9.

Byrne, J., F. Taxman, and D. Hummer. (2005). *An Evaluation of the Implementation and Impact of NIC's Institutional Culture Initiative: Year 2 Update.* Prepared for the National Institute of Corrections, Federal Bureau of Prisons, U.S. Department of Justice. Project #S10002750000006.

Byrne, J. and F. Taxman (2006). "Crime Control Strategies and Community Change–Reframing. The Surveillance vs. Treatment Debate." *Federal Probation,* June: 3–12.

Carroll, L. (2003). "Institutional Culture." Unpublished paper.

Center for Civic Innovation (2000). *Transforming Probation Through Leadership: The Broken Windows Model.* New York, NY: Center for Civic Innovation at the Manhattan Institute and the Robert A. Fox Leadership Program at the University of Pennsylvania.

Commission on Safety and Abuse in America's Prisons (2006). *Confronting Confinement.* Washington D.C.: Vera Institute of Justice.

Corrections Compendium (2002). "Riots, Disturbances, Violence, Assaults, and Escapes." *Corrections Compendium, 27,* 6–19.

Dumond, R. (2000). "Inmate Sexual Assault: The Plague That Persists." *The Prison Journal, 80,* 407–414.

Edgar, K. "A Culture of Violence in England's Prison System: An Assessment of Causes and Solutions." *Journal of Offender Rehabilitation, this issue.*

——— (2005). "Bullying, Victimization and Safer Prisons." *Probation Journal, 52,* 390–400.

Edgar, K., I. O'Donnell, and C. Martin (2003). *Prison Violence: The Dynamics of Conflict, Fear and Power.* Devon, UK: Willan Publishing.

Farabee, D. (2005) *Rethinking Rehabilitation: Why Can't We Reform Our Criminals?* Washington, D.C.: AEI Press, American Enterprise Institute.

Gaes, G., S. Camp, J. Nelson, and W. Saylor (2004). *Measuring Prison Performance.* Walnut Creek, CA: Alta Mira Press.

Gilligan, J. (1996). *Violence: Reflections on a National Epidemic.* New York: Random House.

Hensley, C., R. Tewksbury and T. Castle (2003). "Characteristics of Prison Sexual Assault Targets in Male Oklahoma Correctional Facilities." *Journal of Interpersonal Violence, 18,* 595–606.

Irwin, J. and R. Cressey (1962). "Theives, Convicts, and the Inmate Culture." *Social Problems, 10,* 142–155.

Liebling, A. (1999). "Prison Suicide and Prisoner Coping." In M. Tonry and J. Petersilia, eds., *Prisons.* Chicago, Illinois: The University of Chicago Press, pp. 283–359.

Liebling, A. (2004). *Prisons and Their Moral Performance: A Study of Values, Quality, and Prison Life.* Oxford: Oxford University Press.

Mair J. S., S. Frattaroli, and S.P. Teret (2003). "New Hope for Victims of Prison Sexual Assault." *The Journal of Law, Medicine & Ethics, 31,* 602–606.

Mumola (2005). Suicide and Homicide in State Prisons and Local Jails: Special Report. Washington, DC: Bureau of Justice Statistics, Office of Justice Programs.

National Center for State Courts (2003). *Health Insurance Portability and Accountability Act of 1996; Standards for Privacy of Individually Identifiable Health Information. Applicability to the Courts: An Initial Assessment.* Denver, CO: National Center for State Courts in conjunction with the National Governors Association Center for Best Practices.

National Institute of Corrections (NIC) (2003). Institutional Culture Initiative, Program Meeting, Washington, D.C.

National Research Council (2004). *Fairness and Effectiveness in Policing.* Washington, D.C.: National Academy Press.

O'Donnell, I. and K. Edgar (1998). "Routine Victimization in Prisons." *Howard Journal of Criminal Justice, 37,* 266–279.

Pattavina, A., J. M. Byrne, and L. Garcia (2006). "An Examination of Citizen Involvement in Crime Prevention in High-Risk versus Low-to-Moderate Risk Neighborhoods." *Crime and Delinquency, 52,* 203–231.

Riveland, C. (1999) "Prison Management Trends, 1975–2025." In M. Tonry and J. Petersilia, eds., *Prisons.* Chicago, Illinois: The University of Chicago Press, pp. 163–203.

Sampson, Robert and Lydia Bean (2006). "Cultural Mechanisms and Killing Fields: A Revised Theory of Community-Level Racial Inequality." In Peterson, Krivo, and Hagan, eds., *The Many Colors of Crime: Inequalities of Race, Ethnicity and Crime in America.* New York: New York University Press (retrieved from Robert Sampson's web page).

Sampson, R. J., H. MacIndoe, D. McAdam, and S. Weffer-Elizondo (2005). "Civil Society Reconsidered: The Durable Nature and Community Structure of Collective Civic Action." *American Journal of Sociology, 111,* 673–714.

Sparks, R., A. Bottoms, and W. Hay (1996). *Prisons and the Problem of Order.* Oxford: Clarendon.

Stephan, J. and J. Karberg (2003). *The Census of State and Federal Correctional Facilities.* Washington, D.C.: U.S. Department of Justice.

Struckman-Johnson, C. J. and D. L. Struckman-Johnson (2000). "Sexual Coercion Rates in Seven Midwestern Prison Facilities for Men." *Prison Journal, 80,* 279–390.

Sykes, G. (1958). *The Society of Captives: A Study of a Maximum Security Prison.* Princeton, NJ: Princeton University Press.

The Lifers Public Safety Steering Committee of the State Correctional Institution (2004). "Ending the Culture of Street Crime." *The Prison Journal, 84* (supp.), 48s–68s.

Useem, B. and A. M. Piehl (2006). "Prison Buildup and Disorder." *Punishment and Society, 8,* 87–115.

Welch, M. (2004). *Corrections: A Critical Approach* (Second Edition). New York: McGraw-Hill.

Wortley, R. (2002). *Situational Prison Control: Crime Prevention in Correctional Institutions.* Cambridge, UK: Cambridge University Press.

Wright, K. N. (2005). "Designing a National Performance Measurement System." *The Prison Journal, 85* (3): 368–393.

Wright, K. N., with J. Brisbee and P. Hardyman (2003). *Defining and Measuring Corrections Performance: Final Report.* Washington, D.C.: U.S. Department of Justice.

1

The Nature and Extent of Prison Violence

James M. Byrne, PhD
University of Massachusetts Lowell

Don Hummer, PhD
Penn State Harrisburg

Introduction and Overview: Violence and Disorder in Prison

In this chapter, we examine the major problems facing prison administrators at the state and federal level from three perspectives (1) the official picture of prison problems, drawn from the available nationwide reviews of our state and federal system (Mumola, 2005; Bureau of Justice Statistics, 2000; Corrections Compendium, 2002; Stephan and Karberg, 2003); (2) the wardens, and/or DOC director's, perception of prison problems; and (3) the prisoner's view, based on self-report studies and interviews conducted during the same period (e.g., Mair, Frattaroli, and Teret, 2003; Hensley, Tewksbury, and Castle, 2003; Dumond, 2000).

Violence and Disorder in Prison: The Official View

There are a number of data sources that can be examined to estimate the extent of violence and disorder in our prison system; but our focus in this section will be on the official reports of prison violence and disorder. We begin by examining the annual reviews conducted by the Bureau of Justice Statistics on the number of people who die in our prisons due to some form of violence, including homicide, suicide, and other forms of violence, such as drug overdoses, accidents, and executions. Figure 1.1

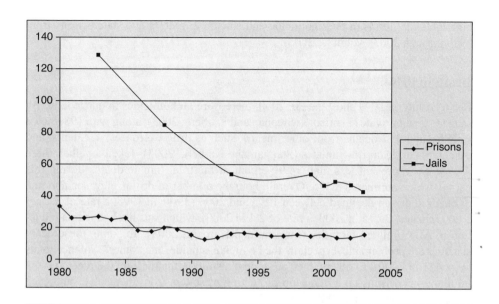

FIGURE 1.1   Suicide Rate, 1980–2003 (Suicides per 100,000 inmates)

Source: Mumola (2005:1). Bureau of Justice Statistics (http://www.ojp.usdoj.gov.bjs/glance/shipj.htm)

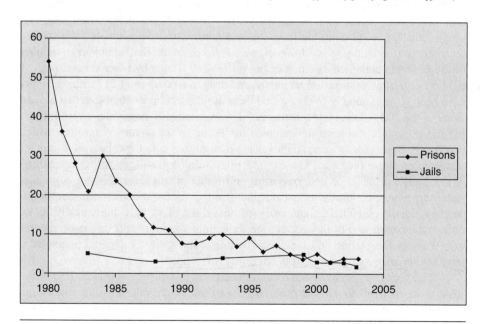

Homicide Rate, 1980–2003 (Homicides per 100,000 inmates)

Source: Mumola (2005:1). Bureau of Justice Statistics (http://www.ojp.usdoj.gov.bjs/glance/shipj.htm)

highlights the trends in both homicide and suicide in federal and state prisons from 1980 through 2003 (Mumola, 2005).

Death in Prison

Between July 1, 1999 and June 30, 2000, there were 56 homicides in our federal (3), state (51), and private (2) prisons (Stephan and Karberg, 2003), along with 198 known suicides and 217 deaths from other means, such as drug overdoses, accidents, and executions of death row inmates (Stephan and Karberg, 2003). Taken together, these 471 deaths represent less than 14.9 percent of the total inmate deaths during this period, which numbered 3,175. Overall, both the number of deaths in prison and rate of death in prison declined between 1995 and 2000 (3,311 in 1995, a rate of 3.2 per 1,000 inmates; 3,175 in 2000, a rate of 2.4 in 2000), which was likely due to a reduction in AIDS-related fatalities (Stephan and Karberg, 2003). To some, these death statistics are problematic, especially the homicide, suicide, and "other" violence totals ($n = 421$ in 2000); to others, they are a demonstration that despite the recent prison buildup, our prisons do a good job protecting prisoners from themselves and each other (Useem and Piehl, 2006).

In any event, these are the numbers: 3,175 of the nearly 1.3 million offenders incarcerated in federal and state prisons died between July 1, 1999 and June 30, 2000. Of these deaths, only 56 were officially labeled homicides, leading some to argue that based on these official statistics, an individual's probability of being a homicide victim is actually several times higher in the community (where the inmate lived prior to incarceration) than in prison. However, we should point out that an unknown number of those deaths classified as suicides ($n = 198$) and deaths by other causes, such as public executions, unspecified accidents, and drug overdoses ($n = 217$), may actually have been *misclassified* homicides. And there are those who would argue that at least some of the 302 AIDS-related deaths in 2000 were actually homicides as well. If the official homicide statistics underreport homicide by an unknown amount, which could vary from year to year, studies using prison homicide trend data as a primary outcome measure (see e.g., Useem and Piehl, 2006) are likely to be inaccurate. Although the problem of underreporting in official prison records is not homicide-specific, we suspect that with greater independent external review, the number of deaths officially classified as homicides (or suicides) will increase dramatically. As we note in the conclusion of this review, the limitations found in existing prison records offer a compelling rationale for external oversight and review, a national prison database, and greater transparency in institutional corrections.

Our focus, so far, has been on completed acts of violence in prison. It is somewhat more difficult to estimate the number of attempted murders and suicides in prison during this same period. A recent review of the information systems used in our state and federal prison system documented the extent of this problem and offered recommendations on how to develop a nationwide performance measurement system to monitor our prisons (Wright, Brisbee, and Hardyman, 2003). In the interim, we must rely on data from selected state and federal institutions to estimate attempted murders and suicides (see Table 1.1). *Corrections Compendium* recently completed a survey of "Riots, Disturbances, Violence, Assaults, and Escapes" that does include information from 40 state correctional systems (May 2002) on suicides; 25 of these states also included information about attempted suicides in 2000, with 27 states also reporting attempted suicides in 2001. In these states, the ratio of attempted to completed suicides was 16:1 with a total of 2,474 attempted suicides (and 147 deaths from suicide) in 2000 and 1,830 attempts (and 124 deaths) in 2001. It is likely that the number of attempted suicides in prison during this period was even higher, but state-specific variations in what actually constitutes an "attempt" (e.g., verbal threat, suicide gestures, serious attempts) preclude a more precise estimate at this time. Unfortunately, no data on attempted murder is available, which forces us to rely on a review of existing assault data to estimate the severity of this form of prison violence.

Assault in Prison

Both physical and sexual assaults occur in prison settings, but there is much debate over the nature, extent, and severity of the problem (Krienert and Fleisher, 2005; Welch, 2004; Struckman–Johnson and Struckman–Johnson, 2000; Dumond, 2000; Mair, Frattaroli, and Teret, 2003). Official statistics appear to underreport the problem, due—at least in part—to variations in the way corrections departments define assault, and whether they consider such factors as verbal threats, attempts, and extent of injury when

TABLE 1.1   *Inmate Deaths in Correctional Facilities under State or Federal Authority (July 1, 1999–June 30, 2000)*

Inmate Deaths	*Total[a]*	*Federal*	*State*	*Private*
Total	3,175	253	2,855	67
Illness/natural causes (excluding AIDS)[b]	2,402	216	2,142	44
Acquired Immune Deficiency Syndrome (AIDS)	302	18	275	9
Suicide	198	13	179	6
Homicide by other inmate(s)	56	3	51	2
Other causes[c]	217	3	208	6

[a]Including death of inmates confined in regular and special facilities (hospitals, medical/treatment/release centers, halfway houses, and work farms)

[b]Includes AIDS-related mortalities resulting from Pneumocystis carinii pneumonia Karposi's sarcoma, or other AIDS-related diseases.

[c]Other causes of death include executions, unspecified accidents, and drug overdoses.

Source: Stephan, J. and J. Karberg (2003). *The Census of State and Federal Correctional Facilities.* Washington, D.C.: U.S Department of Justice.

reporting the level of assault in their institutions. Because data collected by BJS for *The Census of State and Federal Correctional Facilities* (Stephan and Karberg, 2003) do not allow us to distinguish between physical and sexual assault, it is not possible to provide an "official" portrait of specific forms of assault. However, the recent passage of the "Prison Rape Elimination Act of 2003" suggests the following: (1) there is a general consensus that we currently have a significant prison sexual assault problem in both male and female prisons in this country; and (2) there is a need to collect—through BJS—reliable data (using standardized definitions) on the incidence of prison sexual assault (Mair, Frattaroli, and Teret, 2003). Until this new wave of incidence studies is completed, we must rely on overall assault estimates provided by BJS to gauge the extent of the assault problem in our federal and state prisons. It is with these caveats in mind that we present the following description of assault in federal and state prisons.

Examination of the "official" picture of prison assault reveals several interesting differences in the reporting of assault on inmates and staff by both institution-type (federal, state, private); and for inmate assault on staff, level of security (e.g., maximum, medium, minimum). Stephan and Karberg (2003) compared data collected from the 2000 *Census of State and Federal Correctional Facilities* to similar data collected in 1995 and found that

> ....Facilities reported more than 34,000 inmate-on-inmate assaults and nearly 18,000 inmate-on-staff assaults in the 12-month period preceding the 2000 census. The number of assaults, including both physical and sexual assaults, was [32%] higher than in a similar period preceding the 1995 census. (2003:VI)

The number of assaults (inmate-on-inmate and inmate-on-staff) increased between 1995 and 2000 for each facility type, although the size of the increase was greatest for privately operated correctional facilities. These increases are not surprising, given the corresponding increases in the number of inmates in each facility type during this period (from 1,023,572 in 1995 to 1,305,253 in 2000 overall). When the actual "population at risk" is factored in, Stephan and Karberg (2003) report that the rate of inmate-on-inmate assaults increased slightly, from 27.0 per thousand inmates in 1995 to 28.0 inmate-on-inmate assaults in 2000. However, even if the *rate* of assault has remained relatively stable despite the recent prison population buildup, we should point out that the increased *number* of known assault victims (and offenders for that matter) has consequences for the communities these offenders will return to someday, because unfortunately we now know that "what happens in prison, doesn't stay in prison" (Byrne, 2006). Inmates involved in assault situations in prisons—as victims, offenders, and even as bystanders—may upon return to the community, view assault as an appropriate—and effective—problem-solving strategy. When viewed in this context, assault rates are largely beside the point; what really matters is the proportion of the 600,000 inmates released from prison who now view assault as an effective problem-solving strategy.

A similar argument can be made when reviewing the official statistics on inmate assaults on corrections officers. During this same period the overall number of inmate assaults on staff increased 27 percent, "from about 14,200 in 1995 to 18,000 in 2000" (Stephan and Karberg, 2003:9), while the *rate* of assault on staff per 1,000 inmates decreased from 14.8 (1995) to 14.6 (2000). However, the use of this overall rate statistic is somewhat misleading, because the rate of inmate assault on staff actually increased at both state and privately operated facilities (14.9–15.0 state; 6.2–13.5 private), while decreasing in federal facilities (14.3–11.9), which suggests that differences in management practices across different facility types (federal vs. state) and administration (public vs. private) need to be explored further using both levels and rates of inmate assaults on staff. In the interim, it is worth noting that approximately 90 percent of the 18,000 inmates officially classified as assaultive on guards in 2000 have returned to the community (or will soon). Once again, if inmates view assault on guards as an appropriate—and effective—conflict resolution strategy *in prison,* then we suspect that they will follow the same pattern in resolving the inevitable conflicts they face *in the community.*

Examination of inmate assault on staff by facility security level (see Table 1.2) reveals that the risk of assault on staff increases by security level (4.9 min, 10.7 med., 24.5 max in 2000 overall). However, it is interesting to note that while the rate of inmate assault on staff dropped significantly in *federal* maximum security facilities between 1995 and 2000 (52.5 per 1,000 inmates in 1995; 27.8 per 1000 inmates in 2000), the rate of inmate assault on staff actually increased in privately operated facilities during this same period (14.5 per 1,000 inmates in 1995; 33.7 per 1000 inmates in 2000). One possible explanation for variations across facility type but within security levels is that inmate assault on staff is affected not only by the background and type of inmates held (i.e., violent drug, property, public order) but also the organization, management and prevailing "culture" of these institutions. It is important to consider such conflicting trends in the broader context of correctional costs and privatization, because it may be that what we gain in cost savings (via privatization), we lose in terms of offender and staff protection.

It would seem logical to suggest that staff assault on inmates would *also* vary by both security level and facility type. Unfortunately, we do not collect these data in the current census of state and federal correctional facilities (see, e.g., Stephan and Karberg, 2003). The *Corrections Compendium* (2002) survey did collect information on inmates injured and killed by staff, but it was plagued by both a low response rate and a large number of "unavailable/unknown" responses to specific questions by those states that participated in the survey. In 2000, 40 states responded to the survey, but data on inmates injured by staff were only available/known for 18 states and the District of Columbia. In 2001, the same 40 states responded and data were again available/known for 18 states. The Federal Bureau of Prisons did not respond to the survey in either 2000 or 2001. For the states that did report, the official numbers are quite small: 115 inmates were injured by staff (and one inmate was killed by staff) in 2000, and 107 inmates were injured by staff (with no inmates killed by staff) in 2001. Obviously, a piece of the official picture of assault in prison is currently missing, which leads commentators and researchers on prison conditions to rely on other sources of information, including both surveys and interviews with prison management/staff and the prisoners themselves.

TABLE 1.2   *The Number and Rate of Assaults in Federal, State, and Private Prisons*

Inmate Characteristics	Total 1995	Total 2000	Federal 1995	Federal 2000	State 1995	State 2000	Private 1995	Private 2000
Number of Inmates								
Total	1,023,572	1,305,253	80,960	110,974	925,949	1,101,202	16,663	93,077
Under age 18	5,309	4,095	0	0	5,303	3,927	6	168
Non–U.S. citizen inmates[a]	51,500	95,043	16,556	27,318	33,971	56,741	973	10,984
Number of Assaults[b]								
On other inmates	25,208	34,355	989	1,706	23,715	30,344	504	2,305
On staff	13,938	17,952	1,121	1,295	12,739	15,664	78	993
Rate of assault on staff per 1000 inmates								
All confinement facilities	14.8	14.6	14.3	11.9	14.9	15	6.2	13.5
Maximum Security	25.2	24.5	52.5	27.8	24.5	24.2	14.5	33.7
Medium Security	10.2	10.7	18.3	12.1	9.7	10.1	6.2	15.1
Minimum Security	4	4.9	3.8	7.1	4.2	0.4	2.1	4.1

[a]Data from 1995 were based on reporting from 81% of facilities, and on 93% of facilities in 2000.

[b]In confinement facilities during the 12 months preceding the census.

Source: Stephen, J. and J. Karberg (2003). *The Census of State and Federal Correctional Facilities, 2000.* Washington, D.C.: U.S. Department of Justice.

Riots/Major Disturbances

As part of their census of state and federal correctional facilities, the Bureau of Justice Statistics collects data on major disturbances, fires, and other disruptions in prisons, such as hunger strikes and work slowdowns (Stephan and Karberg, 2003). Table 1.3 highlights the results of this review. BJS has defined "major" disturbances as "incidents involving five or more inmates resulting in serious injury or significant property damage" (Stephan and Karberg, 2003:10). The BJS census revealed that there were twice as many major incidents in 2000 (606) than in 1995 (317). It should be noted that such increases in the number of major incidents are likely a direct function of increases in the size of prison population during this review period. The actual rate (per 1,000 inmates) of major disturbances was quite low in 2000 (0.5), although it is higher than the reported major disturbance rate in 1995 (0.3). While it is important to consider both numbers and rates when describing major disturbances in prison, these data certainly suggest that the recent increases in major disturbances represent a significant and serious offender/prison management problem that needs to be addressed.

In addition to collecting information about major disturbances, BJS includes questions in their census about the number of suspicious fires (that resulted in damage over $200) and a variety of other disturbances, such as hunger strikes and prisoner work slowdowns (Stephan and Karberg, 2003). Surprisingly, there were significant reductions

TABLE 1.3 *Inmate Violations in Confinement Facilities under Federal or State Authority between July 2, 1994 and June 30, 1995, and between July 1, 1999 and June 30, 2000*

Inmate Violation	Number of Violations		Violations per 1,000 Inmates[a]	
	1995	2000	1995	2000
Assaults on inmates	25,948	34,355	27.0	28.0
Resulting inmate deaths	82	51	0.1	≠
Assaults on staff	14,165	17,952	14.1	14.6
Resulting staff deaths	14	5	0.1	≠
Major disturbances[b]	317	606	0.3	0.5
Fires[c]	816	343	0.8	0.3
Other disruptions[d]	1,808	639	1.8	0.5

Less than 0.1 per 1,000

[a]Based on average daily population.

[b]Includes major incidents involving five or more inmates which resulted in serious injury to anyone or significant property damage. Excludes federal facilities.

[c]Deliberately set or suspicious fires that resulted in damage exceeding $200.

[d]Includes hunger strikes and work slowdowns.

Source: Table 16 in Stephan, J. and J. Karberg (2003). *The Census of State and Federal Correctional Facilities.* Washington, D.C.: U.S Department of Justice.

in both categories of disturbances between 1995 and 2000. The number of reported fires dropped from 816 (1995) to 343 (2000), while the number of "other" reported disturbances dropped from 1,808 (1995) to 639 (2000). These declines occurred despite significant increases in the prison population during this period; consequently, both the rate of fires per 1,000 inmates (0.8 in 1995 vs. 0.3 in 2000) and the rate of other disturbances (1.8 in 1995 vs. 0.5 in 2000) declined noticeably during the review period.

Although the BJS census does not attempt to distinguish "riots" from "disturbances," this distinction is made in *The Corrections Compendium* survey of state and federal prisons (2002). According to the authors of the report, "the survey definition used to determine riots as opposed to disturbances was *any action by a group of inmates that constitutes a forcible attempt to gain control of a facility or area within a facility*" (*Correction Compendium,* 2002: 6). Using this definition, "there were only two riots indicated for 2000 and 19 for 2001, with 750 inmates involved" (2002:6). When considering these riot reports, it should be recognized that twelve states, plus the Federal Bureau of Prisons, refused to respond to this section of the survey. Without these data, we can only speculate that the problem is likely to be getting worse in these states as well. How much worse? At this time, we simply don't know. Until we collect accurate data on the extent of both riots and disturbances in prison using standard definitions of these terms, any assessment of trends is likely to be misleading (see e.g., Useem and Piehl, 2006).

The Warden/DOC Director's View of Prison Problems

Based on our review of official reports of violence and disorder in prison, it can certainly be argued that although the *rate* of violence and disorder in prison has remained fairly stable between 1995 and 2000, the increased *number* of new incidents—in conjunction with increases in the prison population—has taxed the resources and skills of today's prison managers, who must respond to these incidents at both an individual level (e.g., sanctions, reclassification, segregation, transfer) and an organizational level (changes in size of segregation units, changes in access to common areas within prisons, changes in staffing levels, changes in technology, etc.). But how much of a priority are the current levels of prison violence and disorder to today's prison managers, who are faced each day with a wide range of prison, staff, management, and resource issues?

To answer this question, we have examined the types of prison problems identified by wardens and DOC directors participating in the Institutional Culture Initiative during 2004 (Byrne, Taxman, and Hummer, 2005). While we caution the reader not to generalize from this small number of prison managers to *all* prison managers, we do suspect that the perceptions of these wardens are illustrative of the kinds of management problems that exist in prisons today.

Twelve wardens (or in some jurisdictions, state DOC directors) formally requested assistance from NIC and were selected to participate in one (or more) of NIC's Institutional Culture Initiatives during our initial evaluation review period (2003–2004). Table 1.4 highlights the types of problems these managers identified in

TABLE 1.4 *Types of Prison Problems Identified by Wardens, and DOC Directors Participating in the Institutional Culture Change Initiative**

Area 1: Offender-Specific Problems (n=6)	
Offender-on-offender violence	1
Escapes	1
Prisoner drug use	2
Numerous conduct violations	1
Racial tension among inmates	1

Area 2: Staff-Related Problems (n=32)	
Staff sexual misconduct	4
Staff sexual harassment of prisoners	1
Discrimination	1
Staff morale	4
Limited experience of staff/supervisors	2
Staff turnover	2
Excessive use of sick leave by staff	1
Staff assault on inmates/high level of use of force incidents	2
Poor staff attendance	1
Confrontational episodes/staff vs. inmates	2
Difficulty recruiting/retaining quality staff	2
Staff overfamiliarity with inmates	2
High utilization of overtime by security staff	1
CO's exert too much influence	1
Minimal staff ethnic diversity	4
"Good-old-boys" system	1
Staff dismissals and suspensions	1

Area 3: Management/Leadership Problems (n=21)	
Transition from a psych hospital to prison; max. to mod.	1
Leadership changes	3
Lack of consistent institutional leadership	2
Reductions in staff	3
Ineffective/poor communication	1
Convoluted mission/multiple missions	3
Poor relationships with the central office	3
Lack of supervisory staff	3
Lack of ownership/pride in institution	1
Noxious odor from diary farm	1

Total Number of Problems Identified	*59*

*Note: The requests for assistance from NIC come either directly from the warden of a specific facility or from the central office of that state's DOC. The above totals include eleven state and one federal correctional facilities. Adapted from Byrne, Taxman, and Hummer (2005).

their requests for assistance. Overall, 59 different problems were identified, which can be classified into one of three categories: (1) offender-specific problems, (2) staff-related problems, and (3) management and leadership problems. By far the most frequently cited problems were staff related (32/59), followed by management/leadership problems (21/59). Surprisingly, only a small number of offender-specific problems (6/59) were specifically identified in the request for NIC assistance, which certainly suggests that for these managers, staff- and management-related problems were a more immediate concern than the types of offender-specific problems (e.g., offender-on-offender violence, drug use, conduct violations, escapes, racial tension) described in the previous section of this review. However, this interpretation of the warden/DOC director's requests for assistance may be too simplistic; offender, staff, and management problems are often interrelated.

For example, further examination of Table 1.4 reveals that in a number of instances (12), staff problems focus on the nature/content of staff-offender interactions: staff sexual misconduct and/or sexual harassment of prisoners, staff assault on inmates, excessive use of force, confrontations between staff and inmates, staff overfamiliarity with inmates, and discrimination. These problems are also likely to be related not only to *other* staff-related problems (e.g., staff morale, staff turnover, the "good old boys" system), but also to the various types of management problems identified in the requests for assistance to NIC, such as leadership change, lack of consistent leadership, transitions in the security level at the institution, ineffective/poor communication, and lack of ownership and/or pride in the institution. Given the obvious interrelation between/among offenders, staff, and prison management, an intervention targeting any *one* of these problem areas is likely to be less successful than a strategy recognizing the need for system-wide change. In this regard, if the types of problems identified by wardens and DOC directors in Table 1.4 are, in fact, "caused" by a negative prison culture, then a system-wide response to the problem of culture change is needed, rather than a strategy limited to addressing any one of these problems (e.g., sexual harassment).

Unofficial Estimates of Prison Violence and Disorder

Even a cursory examination of the available research on interpersonal violence in prison reveals a simple truth: *"Official data often substantially understate the extent of violent victimization among inmates"* (Bottoms, 1999:222). There are two primary sources of underreporting: (1) inmates refuse to report victimization; and/or (2) staff refuses to report victimization. While a detailed review of why inmates and staff tend to significantly underreport violent victimization is beyond the scope of this review, it should come as no surprise that (1) the base rate for prison violence is quite low based on official facility records and (2) the results of self-report, anonymous surveys—although yielding significantly higher estimates—vary widely from study to study, based on such factors as how questions are asked, survey administration strategies, and survey completion rates. In a recent review of the prison rape problem, for example, researchers from the Bureau of Justice Statistics (Beck, Hughes, and Harrison,

2004) concluded: "At present, there is no reliable collection methodology for measuring prison rape" (2004:1). To underscore this conclusion, they compared the percentage of prisoners who revealed a rape victimization in a personal interview to the percentage reporting such victimizations when a self-administered questionnaire was used:

> Personal interviews of inmates generally yielded low response rates (below 1%). These low rates of reporting make it impossible to perform further analyses of victim, perpetrator, and facility characteristics. More recent studies utilized self-administered questionnaires, which yielded higher prevalence rates (around 20% with a broad definition of sexual assault). However, questions about the credibility of such studies remain due to low questionnaire completion rates (e.g., 25% response rate) and loss of control over who completes the forms and under what settings in the facility. (Beck, Hughes, and Harrison, 2004:1)

Based on the BJS review, it appears that current estimates of the extent of prison rape problem—regardless of data collection method—are unreliable. To address this problem, BJS is pilot testing several different self-report survey methodologies, and they plan to collect "facility-level measures of sexual assault using victim self-reports... for the 12-month period ending June 30, 2006" (Beck, Hughes, and Harrison, 2004:7). Until these reviews are completed, the debate will continue on the prison rape problem and we should anticipate that strikingly different estimates of the size of the problem will be offered for public consumption (see, e.g., Krienert, and Fleisher, 2005; Dumond, 2000, 2002; Bottoms, 1999; Struckman–Johnson and Struckman–Johnson, 2000; LIS, 2000; Gilligan, 1996; Welch, 2004; Beck and Harrison, 2006).

Similar problems arise when reviewing the available research on other forms of violence in prison. It seems certain that official records only represent a (small) percentage of the interpersonal, intrapersonal, institutional, and collective violence that occurs in prison (Bottoms, 1999; O'Donnell and Edgar, 1998; Gilligan, 1996), but it is difficult to give a precise estimate on the extent of the underreporting problem, due to the limited quality of the existing survey research on various forms of prison violence.

For example, it is certainly possible that official records on the number of murders in prison are lower than the actual levels, due to the misclassification of murders as suicides, as deaths from "other" causes (e.g., drug overdoses), or as disease-related deaths (e.g., AIDS). Similarly, the level of suicide in prison will be affected by the classification criteria used by the medical staff at each facility to distinguish/determine cause of death (Liebling, 1999). While it is certainly possible to offer a low/high range by combing various death categories (e.g., murder, suicide, unknown, disease), or by combining suicides with death from unknown causes, such efforts simply mask the real problem: We currently use unreliable data to estimate these two forms of prison violence (Mumola, 2005).

When we examine other forms of prison violence, the same pattern emerges. We base our assessment of collective violence in prison on official records of riots and disturbances that likely underreport this form of violence. However, facility-specific and state-specific variations in the operational definition of riots and disturbances make it impossible to estimate the extent of the underreporting for collective violence. Somewhat better data are available on the level of underreporting for assault (and threats), based on personal interviews with offenders in prison (see, e.g., O'Donnell and Edgar, 1998; and Bottoms, 1999 for a review). If these estimates are accurate, then official records of assault only capture between 10 and 20 percent of all assaults that occur in prison.

Finally, studies that examine the overall level of disorder in prison typically rely on data from facilities on incidents (usually prepared monthly) and on inmate grievances. However, Bottoms (1999: 223) argues that "institutional culture" results in significant underreporting of incidents by both inmates (who may fear retaliation, transfer, or some other sanction) and staff (who may respond differently to rule-breaking based on an inmate's race, conviction offense/criminal history, and/or classification level). If Bottoms is correct, improvements in the institutional culture of a prison may actually result in *increases* in the number and types of incidents reported, due to changes in the reporting practices of inmates and/or staff. Once again, we need to recognize that without accurate baseline data, tracking incident trends relying solely on official statistics are bound to be futile. As we have learned through decades of community research, our best strategy will be to use a combination of victimization, self-report, and official data sources.

Conclusion

Overall, it appears that the unofficial estimates of various forms of prison violence are likely to be closer to the actual level of prison violence in federal and state prisons, given the reporting problems we have highlighted. However, until a nationwide, standardized data collection system is fully operational, we will continue to argue about the nature and extent of the prison violence problem (Wright et al., 2003). The reason such disagreements "matter" in the context of "what works" reviews of the existing research on prison violence is simple to articulate but much harder to address: We will draw different conclusions about the effectiveness of particular violence reduction strategies using official versus unofficial sources of information on the level of various forms of violence and disorder in prison.

References

Beck, A. and Harrison (2006). *Sexual Violence Reported by Correctional Authorities, 2005* (July) Bureau of Justice Statistics Special Report. Washington, DC: US Department of Justice, Office of Justice Programs.

Beck, A., Hughes, and Harrison (2004). "Data Collections for the Prison Rape Elimination Act of 2003." *Bureau of Justice Statistics Status Report* (June 30, 2004). Washington, D.C:U.S. Department of Justice, Office of Justice Programs.

Bottoms, A. E. (1999). "Interpersonal Violence and Social Order in Prisons." In M. Tonry and J. Petersilia, eds., *Prisons.* Chicago, IL: The University of Chicago Press.

Bureau of Justice Statistics (BJS) (2000). *Correctional Populations in the United States, 1997.* Washington, D.C.: U.S. Department of Justice, Office of Justice Programs, Bureau of Justice Statistics.

Byrne, J. M. (2006). Testimony before the Commission on Safety and Abuse in America's Prisons. Public Hearing #4: Oversight, Accountability, and Other Issues. Los Angeles, CA, February 8–9.

——— (2005). *An Evaluation of the Implementation and Impact of NIC's Institutional Culture Initiative: Year 2 Update.* Prepared for the National Institute of Corrections, Federal Bureau of Prisons, U.S. Department of Justice. Project #S10002750000006.

Byrne, J. M., F. S. Taxman and D. Hummer. "The National Institute of Corrections' Institutional Culture (Change) Initiative: A Multisite Evaluation" *(this volume).*

Carroll, L. (2003). "Institutional Culture." Unpublished paper.

Center for Civic Innovation (2000). *Transforming Probation through Leadership: The 'Broken Windows' Model.* New York, NY: Center for Civic Innovation at the Manhattan Institute and the Robert A. Fox Leadership Program at the University of Pennsylvania.

Commission on Safety and Abuse in America's Prisons (2006). *Confronting Confinement.* Washington D.C.: Vera Institute of Justice.

Corrections Compendium (2002). "Riots, Disturbances, Violence, Assaults, and Escapes." *Corrections Compendium, 27,* 6–19.

Dumond, R. (2000). "Inmate Sexual Assault: The Plague that Persists." *The Prison Journal, 80,* 407–414.

Edgar, K. "A Culture of Violence in England's Prison System: An Assessment of Causes and Solutions." *Journal of Offender Rehabilitation (this issue).*

——— (2005). "Bullying, Victimization and Safer Prisons." *Probation Journal, 52,* 390–400.

Edgar, K., I. O'Donnell and C. Martin (2003). *Prison Violence: The Dynamics of Conflict, Fear and Power.* Devon, UK: Willan Publishing.

Gilligan, J. (1996). *Violence: Reflections on A National Epidemic.* New York: Random House.

Hensley, C., R. Tewksbury and T. Castle (2003). "Characteristics of Prison Sexual Assault Targets in Male Oklahoma Correctional Facilities" *Journal of Interpersonal Violence, 18,* 595–606.

Krienert J. and M. Fleisher (2005). "It ain't happening here: Working to understand prison rape" *The Criminologist* 30(6): 1, 3–5.

Liebling, A. (1999). "Prison Suicide and Prisoner Coping." In M. Tonry and J. Petersilia, editors, *Prisons.* Chicago, IL: The University of Chicago Press pp. 283–359.

Mair J. S., S. Frattaroli, and S. P. Teret (2003). "New Hope for Victims of Prison Sexual Assault." *The Journal of Law, Medicine & Ethics, 31,* 602–606.

Mumola, C. J. (2005) *Suicide and Homicide in State Prisons and Local Jails:* Special Report. Washington, D.C. Bureau of Justice Statistics, Office of Justice Programs.

National Center for State Courts (2003). *Health Insurance Portability and Accountability Act of 1996; Standards for Privacy of Individually Identifiable Health Information. Applicability to the Courts: An Initial Assessment.* Denver, CO: National Center for State Courts in conjunction with the National Governors Association Center for Best Practices.

National Institute of Corrections (NIC) (2003). Institutional Culture Initiative, Program Meeting, Washington, D.C.

National Research Council (2004). *Fairness and Effectiveness in Policing.* Washington, D.C.: National Academy Press.

O'Donnell, I. and K. Edgar (1998). "Routine Victimization in Prisons" *Howard Journal of Criminal Justice, 37,* 266–279.

Pattavina, A., J. M. Byrne and L. Garcia (2006). "An Examination of Citizen Involvement in Crime Prevention in High-Risk versus Low-to-Moderate Risk Neighborhoods." *Crime and Delinquency, 52,* 203–231.

Riveland, C. (1999) "Prison Management Trends, 1975–2025." In M. Tonry and J. Petersilia, eds., *Prisons.* Chicago, IL: The University of Chicago Press, pp.163–203.

Sampson, R. J., H. MacIndoe, D. McAdam, and S. Weffer-Elizondo (2005). "Civil Society Reconsidered: The Durable Nature and Community Structure of Collective Civic Action." *American Journal of Sociology, 111,* 673–714.

Stephan, J. and J. Karberg (2003). *The Census of State and Federal Correctional Facilities.* Washington, D.C.: U.S. Department of Justice.

Struckman–Johnson, C. J. and D. L. Struckman–Johnson (2000). "Sexual Coercion Rates in Seven Midwestern Prison Facilities for Men." *Prison Journal, 80,* 279–390.

The Lifers Public Safety Steering Committee of the State Correctional Institution (2004). "Ending the Culture of Street Crime." *The Prison Journal, 84* (supp.), 48s–68s.

Useem, B. and A. M. Piehl (2006). "Prison Buildup and Disorder." *Punishment and Society, 8,* 87–115.

Welch, M. (2004). *Corrections: A Critical Approach* (Second Edition). New York: McGraw-Hill.

Wortley, R. (2002). *Situational Prison Control: Crime Prevention in Correctional Institutions.* Cambridge, UK: Cambridge University Press.

Wright, K.N., with J. Brisbee and P. Hardyman (2003). *Defining and Measuring Corrections Performance: Final Report.* Washington, D.C.: U.S. Department of Justice.

2

Does What Happens in Prison Stay in Prison? Examining the Reciprocal Relationship between Community and Prison Culture

Jacob I. Stowell

University of Massachusetts Lowell

James M. Byrne

University of Massachusetts Lowell

Introduction

The lives and experiences of those held in American institutions of correction have long been of interest to academics and social thinkers. According to Michel Foucault (1977) in his book *Discipline and Punish,* the objectives of the modern American penal system, with the primary goal of reforming individuals, can be traced to philosophies embraced during the enlightenment. By removing transgressors from society and actively seeking to correct criminal propensities through psychological, rather than physical (i.e., torture), means, advocates argued that American prisons represented the "most immediate and civilized form of all penalties" (see Foucault, 1977, p. 233). This sentiment is echoed by Alexis de Tocqueville in his seminal work *Democracy in America*. After touring American correctional facilities in the nineteenth century, Tocqueville concluded that due to their emphasis on redeeming

So America was new and first [handwritten annotation]

individuals, U.S. prisons represented "durable monument[s] to the gentleness . . . of our age" (Tocqueville 1969, p. 250).

Human Rights [handwritten annotation]

Despite the lofty ambitions and positive reviews historically, it is difficult to imagine that the same evaluation could be used to characterize the current state of American prisons. It is certainly true that constitutional provisions place limits on the types of punishments to which inmates can be subjected while incarcerated. However, exposure to violence remains a mainstay of life behind bars, as indicated in a recent study conducted by the Commission on Safety and Abuse in America's Prisons. In that report, authors contend that inmates in state and local correctional facilities are exposed, as observers and victims, to high levels of interpersonal violence (i.e., gang violence, rape, assaults on inmates) (Gibbons and Katzenbach, 2006). Culture, or more precisely, *prison culture,* has often been cited as an important factor contributing to observed levels of violence and disorder within prisons.

Culture reform, they conform. [handwritten annotation]

It appears that the institutions that were created to reduce violence and disorder in the community may actually be having the opposite effect on inmates both within institutions and in the "communities" to which inmates return. This view stands in stark contrast to those advanced by advocates of the modern institutions of correction. The image of prisons as institutions of reform has been supplanted by the reality of the prison system whose stated purpose is undermined by a culture of fear, violence, and control.

Researchers and corrections officials have cited culture as one of the sources of prison violence, although the concept has proven difficult to quantify (see Byrne et al., *this volume*). In their recent review of prison culture and violence, Byrne and colleagues recognize that part of the challenge in measuring prison culture stems from the fact that it is "defined and operationalized in different ways by different researchers." Nevertheless, the authors argue that the different measures of culture share a common conceptual definition. Generally, prior research on culture agrees that the behavior of prisoners is affected by a normative order that exists within correctional institutions. What is less clear, however, is the manner in which this value system was established and how it is maintained.

Interestingly, although researchers have recognized that prison culture may be influenced by exogenous factors, such as the values inmates carry with them into prison from their respective communities, few describe the formation of culture as an evolving or mutually reinforcing process. For example, the prison importation model asserts that "negative culture is simply a reflection—albeit in a new setting—of values, assumptions, and beliefs found in the home communities of inmates" (Byrne et al., 2006, p. 8; see also Irwin, 1981; Irwin and Cressey, 1962). Despite the insightful contributions of this perspective, however, we believe that it is unable to capture the dynamic connection between communities and correctional institutions. There is a scarcity in the research literature of studies that are sensitive to the countervailing process, or that the values imprinted while in prison can also be exported back into communities as inmates are released from custody.

This chapter will present a model of understanding, and researching culture that is based on the notion that value systems in institutions and neighborhoods influence one another. The goal of this chapter, then, is to draw from existing research on prisons and communities to highlight how prison culture is tied to communities, and vice versa. We contend that incorporating an expansive view of culture may have implications for criminal justice policy decisions and efforts to reduce levels of criminal violence on both sides of the prison walls.

Changing Perceptions of Prison Culture

Evaluations of the environmental conditions within prisons have generally been consistent over time. Indeed, it has been observed that being held in captivity has a discernible impact on behavior patterns, as prisoners are less trusting of other inmates and more likely to resort to violence to settle disputes (Sykes, 1958; Toch, 1992). Yet researchers have offered somewhat differing explanations as to the origins of this cultural orientation. Traditionally, examinations of prison culture were focused narrowly on the prisons themselves. From this perspective, the formation of prison culture was presented as a geographically circumscribed process, or that prison culture was the result of the experiences and demands unique to the prison experience.

There is little disputing the fact that the conditions of incarceration, and particularly the deprivation of personal liberties, are those under which a subcultural value system will flourish. Still, this perspective emphasizes the fact that prison conditions are the leading cause of prison culture. This point is clearly evident in Sykes's (1958) classic, *A Society of Captives*. In this work, Sykes (1958:22) asserts that because prisoners are "subjected to prolonged material deprivation . . . and rubbed raw by the irritants of life under compression . . . [they are] . . . pushed in the direction of deviation from, rather than adherence to, the legal norms." In the above passage, Sykes is clearly recognizing that prison life is characterized by deviant behavior, including violence. Further, in this description it is also clear that Sykes believes that this culture is a byproduct of the various interactions inmates have while in prison. According to Sykes (1958:6), to understand prison culture requires observing the exchanges between inmates and correctional staff because "in this interaction we can see the realities of the prison social system emerge."

It is important to mention that the "society" Sykes describes is one with limited ties to the broader community. In other words, upon entering prison, the lives of inmates are resocialized and are evaluated according to the social mandates of the institution. Thus, through incarceration, prisons isolate and insulate individuals from the larger society, effectively minimizing external influences on inmate conduct. The origins of established set of normative expectations and regulations that guide inmate behavior, then, are thought to have been sown on prison grounds. Not surprisingly, traditional perspectives on prison culture also paid little attention to the influence of prison culture on the communities into which inmates return, again owing to their primary concentration on the internal conditions of prisons.

In light of more recent criminological research, there is reason to question the narrow view of prison culture presented in the traditional model. Similar to other theoretical perspectives, a limitation of the initial descriptions of prison culture is their portrayal of prisons as socially isolated institutions. For example, Heitgard and Bursik (1987) contend that a shortcoming of the community-based theories of crime is that they rely on rigid, and somewhat arbitrary, definitions of "community." In other words, Heitgard and Bursik (1987:776) argue that the "overriding emphasis on the internal dynamics" of single geographical units is problematic because community dynamics often extend beyond administratively derived boundaries. Indeed, this argument has been substantiated by empirical research, which has clearly documented the importance of not perceiving social institutions as isolates, but rather recognizing that they influence and are influenced by factors beyond their borders (see Baller et al., 2001; Anselin et al., 2000).

In accepting the logic underpinning this argument, it stands to reason that prison culture is, in part, a product of the community characteristics inmates experienced before they were incarcerated (see Byrne et al., 2005). Specifically, Gibbons and Katzenbach (2006:66) describe prison culture as a normative order in which inmates are distrustful of authority and that interpersonal exchanges are often "antagonistic." Further, it is argued that inmates are concerned with establishing a reputation and minimizing their risk of victimization by settling disputes using "overt hostility, aggression, and physical violence" (Gibbons and Katzenbach, 2006:66). Indeed, ethnographic research indicates that elements of this value structure can be traced to the disadvantaged inner-city neighborhoods in which many inmates lived (and will return to) prior to incarceration (see Anderson, 1990, 1999; Suttles, 1968; LeBlanc, 2003; Bourgois, 1995). For example, in *Code of the Street,* Elijah Anderson (1999:92) describes community culture as follows:

> Central to this issue of [community culture] is the widespread belief that one of the most effective ways of gaining respect is to manifest nerve. A man shows nerve by taking another man's possessions, messing with someone's woman, throwing the first punch, "getting in someone's face," or pulling a trigger. Its proper display helps check others who would violate one's person, and it also helps build a reputation that works to prevent future challenges.

In this passage the characteristics of what have been described as community culture bear a striking resemblance to those observed in prison. In both cases, the presentation of self is used as both a protective mechanism and as a way to curry the respect of peers, and violence is described as the primary response to being slighted. Although ethnographers do discuss how involvement with the criminal justice system is perceived as a "right of passage" in some communities, the community-level influences on prison culture are not mentioned directly. Nevertheless, the logic of their descriptions does suggest a process by which culture is imported into prisons (see also Irwin, 1981; Irwin and Cressey, 1962).

It is worth noting that the normative expectations described above are those frequently attributed to gang-related behavior. As some scholars contend, it is reasonable to assume that gangs emerge in prisons and communities for similar reasons. In his testimony before the Commission on Safety and Abuse in America's Prisons,

James Byrne (2006) argued that there are likely to be psychological benefits (i.e., identity, sense of pride) to joining gangs in both settings (see also Riedel and Welsh, 2002). More pragmatically, it is also true that gangs will offer a certain degree of protection against victimization (see Anderson, 1999). Recognizing the ecological commonalities in environmental conditions does cast some light on how the gang tradition may become rooted in communities and correctional institutions. Still, we submit that this explanation alone cannot fully explain the similarities between the cultural adaptations observed in prisons and communities because it presents an overly simplified view of the manner in which prison culture is affected by external community factors.

The discussion of their similarities is in no way meant to suggest that there is no meaningful difference between community and prison cultures; or that prison culture is merely a reflection of neighborhood "codes." Such a conclusion would, in our estimation, be incorrect because it deemphasizes the institutional influence on culture. We recognize that, as Krienert and Fleisher (2005:5) argue, culture in prison operates according to "its own logic that creates its own reality." However, it is also inaccurate to presume that many of the properties of prison culture are impervious to outside influence. Because the inmate population is comprised of individuals with unique socialization histories and experiences, it is unrealistic to assume that deeply seeded behavior patterns will be completely subsumed while in prison. Moreover, it is also true that through incarceration social or peer groups may be reestablished, which would likely reinforce existing cultural beliefs and practices (see Krienert and Fleisher, 2005). For these reasons, we believe that it is important for researchers to move beyond the importation model, which suggests that prison culture is the result of the transference of external norms and values into prisons. More accurately, we believe that prison culture is the outcome of the *interaction* between imported community culture and existing institutional behavioral expectations (see also Pattavina et al., 2006). Stated simply, the experiences unique to incarceration can "exacerbate the inmates' pre-existing potential for violence" (Gilligan 1996, p. 163).

At the same time, there are also reasons to expect that influence also runs in the opposite direction, or that some influences on community culture emanate from correctional institutions. The community link to prisons is maintained due to that fact that a large majority of inmates are released from prisons (some estimate over 90%) after serving relatively short sentences (see Clear and Cole, 1997). The prevalence of prisoner reentry, coupled with what Rose and Clear (1998: 450) term the "stronger deviant orientation" of prison culture, is likely to increase levels of neighborhood disorganization by reinforcing existing cultural value systems. Due to the high levels of inmate release, it stands to reason that prison culture is likely to be "exported" back into communities. More generally, the processes described above suggest that a reciprocal, or mutually reinforcing, association exists between prison and community cultures.

The awareness of bidirectional causality, or "feedback loops," is a concept that has received empirical support in prior research. Specifically, one criticism of many criminological perspectives is that they assume a recursive (i.e., one-directional) causal relationship between crime and community characteristics (Liska and Bellair,

1995; Liska, et al. 1998; Morenoff and Sampson, 1997). Stated in causal terms, for example, criminological theories focus on the causes of criminal behavior, treating crime as a *dependent* variable. Moreover, theoretical explanations focus on linear causal processes, overlooking the possibility of bidirectional causality, or that crime may also operate as an *independent* variable. However, current research has quantified that while social structure certainly has an impact on crime, it is also important to recognize the influence that crime rates may have on the structural composition of communities. By raising the issue of reciprocal causation, contemporary research attempts to account for a degree of complexity that is traditionally not observed by criminological theories.

Research conducted by Todd Clear and colleagues has documented that levels of incarceration do have deleterious effects on the social structure of the communities from which prisoners are removed (see Clear et al., 2001; Rose and Clear, 1998). Rather than perceiving that inmates are solely a "liability" to their communities, Clear contends that many offenders also provide some "assets" to their neighborhoods. For example, Rose and Clear (1998:451–453) indicate that incarceration can lead to increased levels of economic disadvantage and crime by disrupting informal networks of social control, to which offenders belong. Further, the authors argue that offenders often "contribute to the welfare of their families and intimates in the same way that noncriminal males do." The negative consequences of incarceration are exacerbated by the fact that high-incarceration communities also tend to have relatively low levels of social and human capital, meaning they have more difficulty overcoming the removal of financial and other resources (see Clear et al., 2001).

It should be noted that while research has revealed that there are some negative consequences of incarceration for communities, the authors also point out that communities also benefit from the removal of some individuals. In fact, Rose and Clear (1998:469) indicate that the "imprisonment of individuals who threaten the personal safety of residents" is a necessary response, and one that is likely to enhance community strengths (i.e., cohesion, involvement). Indeed, there is little disputing the fact that residents may become more active in their communities if their fear of victimization is reduced through the removal of dangerous or violent offenders.[1] A valuable contribution of this research generally is that it is able to document an array of outcomes, both anticipated and unanticipated, which are associated with increased incarceration. More central to this discussion is the fact that prison culture is exported back into communities.

The explanations for the negative impacts of incarceration on communities typically concentrate on the structural factors, drawing from social disorganization theory. In other words, they are primarily concerned with the mechanisms through which incarceration compromises a community's capacity for social organization by undermining networks of social control. For example, Rose and Clear, (1998:450) perceive imprisonment as a disorganizing social process, as "it affects the three

has to impact cltmeth work.

[1] According to Clear et al. (2001:337), previous studies have found evidence of an imprisonment "tipping point," meaning that once levels of incarceration exceed a given level (approximately 1.5% of the total population), the community costs associated with the removal outweigh the benefits.

disorganizing factors originally identified by Shaw and McKay."[2] However, it is important for researchers to recognize that incarceration may also impact communities through its impact on culture. This is not to say that previous researchers were unaware of the potential cultural influences associated with incarceration. Indeed, scholars have mentioned the fact that high rates of imprisonment are likely to increase opportunities for community residents "to be socialized into prison subcultures" (Rose and Clear, 1998, p. 450). Despite the broad awareness of this process, however, we believe that additional research on this issue is warranted because culture does not factor prominently into existing explanatory models.

doesn't explain all problems

The New Cultural Paradigm

New explanations of cultural processes are sought, in part, because existing hypotheses are at odds with a new wave of contemporary empirical findings. Namely, a growing body of scholarship calls into question the "racial invariance" hypothesis proposed by Sampson and Wilson (1995) (see Martinez, 2002; Lee et al., 2001; Lee, 2003). In this theory, Sampson and Wilson (1995) propose that racial differences in involvement in criminal deviance are caused by differential exposure to community-level causes of crime. In other words, the racial invariance hypothesis argues that if members of different racial groups resided in structurally equivalent communities, no meaningful racial differences in offending would emerge. However, Ramiro Martinez and colleagues find little support for the racial invariance hypothesis, particularly as it applies to Latinos. Martinez and Lee (2000:486) argue that "in many cases, compared with native groups, [Latino] immigrants seem better able to withstand crime-facilitating [neighborhood] conditions than native groups."[3] Based on these findings, it stands to reason that culture, in addition to structure, may be a property of communities that helps to explain racial/ethnic involvement in crime.

racial impact on crime & socio-economic

Recent scholarship appears to hold much promise for the study of the link between institutional and community culture (see Table 2.1). Sampson and Bean (2006) present a model of community-level processes that focuses primarily on the formation of culture. Applying Swindler's (1986) notion of "culture in action," Sampson and Bean (2006:24) dispense with the traditional perspective that culture is "something that is embedded *within* us." Rather, they argue that culture is "created *between* us in everyday social interaction" (Sampson and Bean, 2006:24). At its core, the multidimensional model they describe, though abstract, conceives of culture as a socially constructed and ever-changing reality. Moreover, this perspective is explicit in its presentation of culture's dynamic nature, or that culture helps to shape and is shaped by both macrolevel (i.e., structural) and microlevel (i.e., interpersonal) community processes. Unlike traditional definitions of culture, Sampson and Bean (2006:29) assert that it is important to

---

[2]Specifically, Shaw and McKay (1969 [1942]) highlighted three factors as the causes of social disorganization: socioeconomic disadvantage, racial/ethnic heterogeneity, and residential instability.

[3]See Sampson and Bean (2006:20–21) for a discussion of the "Latino Paradox."

TABLE 2.1 *A Comparison of Two Distinct Typologies of Culture (Adapted from Sampson and Bean (2006)).*

"Culture as Values"[*]	*"Culture in Action"*[**]
1. Culture is personal: Our cultural values are "embedded deep within us."	**1. Culture is Intersubjective:** Our cultural values are "created between us in everyday social interaction."
2. Culture is Authentic: "People behave morally because they are essentially moral;" moral choices are a reflection of our "true self" and our culture.	**2. Culture is Performative:** "Identity is performed and is more than a post-hoc rationalization of one's behavior." When this performance of "identity is threatened, violence may erupt, suggesting that the performance of identity can play a role in precipitating a contentious encounter."
3. Culture Demonstrates Value-Rationality: "When people attempt rationality, culture guides the construction of both means and ends by providing heuristics, metaphors, and models for action."	**3. Culture Demonstrates Affective Cognition:** "When behavior is driven by impulse or habit rather than calculation, people often construct legitimate post-hoc accounts of their behavior." People "adopt the course of action that uses the practical skills and cognitive tools that they have at hand, *without* thinking of their preferred ends."
4. Culture is Consensual: People in a community "agree on a set of shared values," which helps achieve collective goals. While culture may be personal, "it is directed toward the common good," and it is a basic of "social solidarity."	**4. Culture is Relational:** "People use culture to define themselves and their friends as uniquely worthy, and to draw symbolic boundaries between worthy selves and unworthy others." The culture wars in the United States serve as a prime example.
5. Culture Reflects a Distinct Worldview: "Culture guides our understanding of 'what is' as well as what 'should be.' People 'recognized a difference between their values and hopes and their mundane pursuits and expectations.'"	**5. Culture is World-Making:** "The hard facts of social structure—the economy, the state, violence—are themselves continually produced and enacted by our skillful and purposeful social action," and by our accumulation of both cultural and symbolic capital. *Cultural capital* consists of the mastery of performances, styles, language, and familiarity that can be used to gain access to status or resources. *Symbolic capital* consists of accumulated honor or prestige that resides in a person, analogous to charisma in positive forms and stigma in negative forms."

[*]Wolfgang and Feracuti (1967); Shaw and McKay (1942); Merton (1938).

[**]Swindler (1986); Sampson and Bean (2006).

understand culture not as "a simple adaptation to structure in a one-way causal flow, but as an intersubjective *organizing mechanism* that shapes unfolding social processes and that is constitutive of social structure" (emphasis in original).

Key to the idea of intersubjectivity, which emphasizes the perpetual creation and redefinition of culture, is the notion of individual agency. In other words, although cultural expectations may be prevalent within disadvantaged communities, observed behavior should not be seen as merely the adaptation to violent or disadvantaged social conditions. Rather, Sampson and Bean (2006:29) argue that culture is actively (and consciously) created, or that broader community contexts are influenced by the "cultural agency of neighborhood residents." Following the logic of this perspective, then, it is when residents in communities cease to engage in the cultivation/perpetuation of the violent community culture that these communities will cease to be violent. A similar argument could be offered about the effect of changes in prison culture on the level of violence in prison.

However, we currently know remarkably little about how and why either community or prison culture might change in this manner, independent of changes in structural conditions or the demographic profile of either neighborhood residents or prison inmates. When viewed in this context, much of the recent discussion of the "Latino paradox" that has linked the lower levels of violence among Latino immigrants to the values held by individual immigrants (e.g. hard work, the importance of family) are ignoring a critical dimension: the intersubjectivity of person–environment interactions. As Sampson and Bean emphasize, "People use frames to reach a shared definition of the situation, account for their behavior, or interpret others' intentions. People activate symbolic boundaries, or highlight intergroup distinctions, to mobilize people for collective action" (2006:24).Nonetheless, it is certainly worth noting that as the proportion of Hispanics generally, and Hispanic immigrants, in particular, in federal and state prisons has increased during the past decade, the official levels of prison violence and disorder have declined (Harrisson and Beck, 2006).

In addition to the contention that culture is "intersubjective, not personal," Sampson and Bean (2006) also argue that culture should be viewed as "performative, not authentic." Borrowing from Goffman (1974), they include the concept of Goffman's "facework" as the second dimension of the "culture in action" paradigm. They suggest that we present ourselves differently to different audiences (to quote Eminem, "I am whatever you say I am; if I wasn't then why would I say I am?); and that "People do not behave morally because they are essentially moral. Rather, they stick to the straight-and-narrow to impress others and save face" (Sampson and Bean, 2006:25).The authors go on to note that, "If we adopt such a performative notion of culture, then it makes no sense to ask if "decent" people are truly decent, and "street" people are truly street. It makes more sense to ask which audience people are performing for, and in what venues" (2006:25). Whether in prison or in the community, it is certainly possible that violence—both individual and collective—is more likely in situations or encounters where the "performance of identity" is challenged in some way.

A third dimension of the "culture in action" paradigm emphasizes that "affective-cognition, not value-rationality drives individual actions (Sampson and

Bean, 2006). In a departure from the ends–means typology of adaptations at the core of Merton's theory of anomie (conformists, innovators, ritualists, rebels, and retreatists), Sampson and Bean challenge the notion that behavior is rational and goal-driven: "People often adopt the course of action that uses the practical skills and cognitive tools they have at hand, without thinking of their preferred ends. For example, if students lack the cultural capital that they need to navigate the academic world, they may direct their efforts into the social games that they know how to play, (e.g. street fighting and popularity contests). Ultimate ends are invented in retrospect, to justify their course of action after it has been completed" (2006:25–26).

It is difficult to argue against the notion that we sometimes act out of "impulse or habit" and/or fall back on the problem-solving strategies that have worked for us in the past (Sampson and Bean, 2006:26). In this regard, inmates in prison may find it easier to rely on activities, behaviors, and problem-solving strategies (e.g. gang involvement, drug dealing/use, and violence) that have actually worked well for them in community settings. Despite the risks involved and the adverse consequences for prison classification (higher security level) and time in prison (increased time served, segregation), such activities as gang involvement, drug dealing, and the situational use/threat of violence in prison may represent the primary "skill sets" of many of today's inmates. Once released from prison, inmates return to the same high risk, poverty pocket neighborhoods they left behind (Byrne and Taxman, 2006). Faced with the same (or worsening) opportunity structure, it is not surprising that they continue to make what you or I might consider "bad" choices and decisions, given their immersion in both institutional and community culture. From the perspective of the actor, however, the choices they made were good choices, not in terms of potential outcomes, but rather because they were justified based on their perception of appropriate behavior and their view of self. In both community and prison settings, their behavior was less a function of rational choice based on an assessment of goals and means, and more an emotional, experience-driven cultural adaptation.

The fourth dimension of the "culture in action" paradigm focuses on the premise that culture is "relational, not consensual" as most observers—including Sampson—had traditionally argued in their discussions of such concepts as social disorganization, collective efficacy, social capital, and informal social control (Pattavina, Byrne, and Garcia, 2006). When viewed from a relational foundation, "Culture is not the glue that holds society together; it is a weapon for reproducing social hierarchies and excluding social challengers. People use culture to define themselves and their friends as uniquely worthy, and to draw symbolic boundaries between worthy selves and unworthy others. . . . Culture is not *consensual* (a basis of social solidarity) but instead *relational* (the map that people use to position themselves in social space). The "culture wars" in the United States serve as a prime example" (Sampson and Bean, 2006:26). Sampson and Bean contend that "culture does not *constrain* conflict so much as *structure* it" (2006:27) in both public and private. When viewed from a relational context, it appears that many recent attempts to change inmate, staff, and management culture in prison may have placed an inordinate emphasis on developing and maintaining a consensual culture that was impossible to achieve (Byrne, Taxman, and Hummer, *this text*; Liebling, *this text*;

Edgar, *this text*). Obviously, we need to know much more about how the symbolic violence used by individuals to carve out a "worthy" identity (compared to some unworthy other) results in higher rates of *physical* violence in certain social contexts (e.g. poverty pockets/areas of extreme poverty, prisons); but it might be that in both contexts, violence and/or the threat of violence offers a viable means to an end.

The final dimension of the "culture in action" paradigm emphasizes the dynamic quality of cultural mechanisms (where culture is described as world-making, not a reflection of a particular world view). Sampson and Bean point out that "Cultural sociologists conceive of culture as world-*making*. The hard facts of social structure—the economy, the state, violence—are themselves continually produced and enacted by our skillful and purposive social action. Culture plays a structural role in the making of this world" (2006:28). The notion of culture as world making offers a mechanism to consider the dynamic interaction between culture and social structure. To paraphrase actor Jack Nicholson's opening monologue in the film, *The Departed*, "I do not want to be a product of my environment; I want my environment to be a product of me." As Sampson and Bean demonstrate, individuals—like the character played by Nicholson—affect their environment in a variety of ways through the acquisition of both cultural and symbolic capital. At the core of any discussion of person-environment interactions is the assumption that the level of violence and disorder in a particular community is a product of the characteristics of both people (demographic composition, culture) and places (economic, physical, and political structure). A similar statement can be offered about the causes of prison violence and disorder (Byrne and Hummer, 2007). The challenge for researchers studying the link between culture and violence in both institutional and community settings is to establish a definitive link between changes in demographic composition (e.g. the higher proportion of Hispanic immigrants in high-risk communities and in our federal and state prisons), changes in community and prison culture, and changes in the levels of violence and disorder in both settings.

Conclusion

It appears that prison culture and community culture are linked in ways that are important to understand, in particular if we are serious about addressing the "churning" of offenders in and out of our prisons. According to a recent Bureau of Justice Statistics Bulletin, we incarcerated 2,320,359 persons at year-end 2005 (Harrison and Beck, 2006). During the same year, we had roughly the same number of individuals leaving prisons as we had enter as new admissions (600,000). The individuals we send to prison are disproportionately male, minority (40% black; 20% Hispanic), and living in a relatively small number of high-risk, poverty pocket neighborhoods before admission to prison and upon reentry. The proportion of violent offenders in prison increased from 47% (1995) to 52% (2003), which suggests that despite the downward trend in violence nationally, prison administrators are faced with an increasingly violence-prone inmate population to manage, while a small number of communities must absorb the impact of violence, not only in terms of the destabilizing effect of incarceration on community social control, but also in terms of the negative effect of living in a high-risk community on the reentry prospects of individual offenders.

We agree with Sampson and Bean's conclusion that, "There is little research to date that directly tests the way social and cultural mechanisms at the community level explain the race gap in violence, especially in conjunction with concentrated disadvantage" (2006:16). In our view, Sampson and Bean's analysis of Swidler's "culture in action" paradigm offers a fresh perspective from which to examine the influence of culture in both institutional and community settings. Offering examples from recent research on prison culture, we considered the key dimensions of this new cultural paradigm, which described culture as " intersubjective, performative, cognitive, relational, and world-making" (Sampson and Bean, 2006:33). Further examination of the reciprocal relationship between institutional and community culture is needed before we can begin to consider the policy implications of Swidler's "culture in action" paradigm.

References

Anderson, Elijah (1990). *Streetwise: Race, Class, and Change in an Urban Community.* Chicago: University of Chicago Press.

Anderson, Elijah (1999). *Code of the Street: Decency, Violence, and the Moral Life of the Inner City.* New York: W.W. Norton and Company.

Anselin, Luc, Jacqueline Cohen, David Cook, Wilpen Gorr, and George Tita (2000). "Spatial analyses of crime." In *Measurement and Analysis of Crime and Justice, Volume 4,* edited by D. Duffee. Criminal Justice 2000, National Institute of Justice, pp. 213–262.

Baller, Robert D., Luc Anselin, Steven F. Messner, Glenn Deane, and Darnell F. Hawkins (2001). "Structural Covariates of U.S. County Homicide Rates: Incorporating Spatial Effects." *Criminology, 39,* 561–588.

Bourgois, Philippe (1995). *In Search of Respect: Selling Crack in El Barrio.* Cambridge: Cambridge University Press.

Byrne, James M. (2006). "Gang Affiliation and Drug Trafficking in Prison." Presented to the Commission on Safety and Abuse in America's Prisons, February 8, Los Angeles, CA.

Byrne, James M. and Don Hummer (2007). "Myths and Realities of Prison Violence: A Review of the Evidence." *Victims and offenders* 2(1): 77–90.

Byrne, James M. and Faye Taxman (2006). "Crime Control Strategies and Community Change" *Federal Probation* 70(2): 3–12.

Byrne, James M., Faye S. Taxman, and Don Hummer (2005). "Examining the Impact of Institutional Culture (and Culture Change) on Prison Violence and Disorder: A Review of the Evidence on Both Causes and Solutions." Paper presented at the 14th World Congress of Criminology, Philadelphia, August 11, 2005.

Clear, Todd R. and George F. Cole (1997). *American Corrections* (Fourth Edition). Belmont, CA: Wadsworth.

Clear, Todd R., Dina R. Rose, and Judith A. Ryder (2001). "Incarceration and Community: The Problem of Removing Offenders." *Crime and Delinquency, 47,* 335–351.

Foucault, Michel. 1977. *Discipline and Punish: The Birth of the Prison.* New York: Vintage Books.

Gibbons, John J. and Nicholas de B. Katzenbach (2006). "Confronting Confinement: A Report of the Commission on Safety and Abuse in America's Prisons." Vera Institute of Justice, New York. http://www.prisoncommission.org/pdfs/Confronting_Confinement.pdf.

Gilligan, James (1996). *Violence: Reflections on a National Epidemic.* New York: Random House.

Goffman, Erving. 1974. *Frame Analysis: An Essay on the Organization of Experience.* Cambridge, MA: Harvard University Press.

Harrisson, Paige M. and Allen J. Beck (2006). "Prisoners in 2005." U.S. Department of Justice, Bureau of Justice Statistics, Washington, D.C (NCJ215092). http://www.ojp.usdoj.gov/bjs/pub/pdf/p05.pdf.

Heitgard, Janet L. and Robert J. Bursik (1987). "Extracommunity Dynamics and the Ecology of Delinquency." *American Journal of Sociology, 92,* 775–87.

Irwin, John K. (1981). "Sociological Studies of the Impact of Long-term Confinement." In D. A. Ward and K. P. Schoen (Eds.), *Confinement in maximum custody: New Last-Resort Prisons in the United States and Western Europe.* Lexington, MA: D.C. Heath pp. 49–60.

Irwin, John K. and Donald Cressey (1962). "Thieves, Convicts, and the Inmate Culture." *Social Problems, 10,* 142–155.

Krienert, Jessie L. and Mark S. Fleisher (2005). "'It Ain't Happening Here': Working to Understand Prison Rape." *The Criminologist, 30,* 1–6.

LeBlanc, Nicole Adrian (2003). *Random Family: Love, Drugs, Trouble, and Coming of Age in the Bronx.* New York: Scribner.

Lee, Matthew T (2003). *Crime on the Border: Immigration and Homicide in Urban Communities.* New York: LFB Scholarly Publishing.

Lee, Matthew T., Ramiro Martinez, Jr., and Richard Rosenfeld (2001). "Does Immigration Increase Homicide? Negative Evidence From Three Border Cities." *The Sociological Quarterly, 42,* 559–580.

Liska, Allen E. and Paul E. Bellair (1995). "Violent-Crime Rates and Racial Composition: Convergence over Time." *American Journal of Sociology, 101,* 578–610.

Liska, Allen E., John R. Logan, and Paul E. Bellair. 1998. "Race and Violent Crime in the Suburbs." *American Sociological Review, 63,* 27–38.

Martinez, Ramiro, Jr (2002). *Latino Homicide: Immigration, Violence, and Community.* New York: Routledge Press.

Martinez, Ramiro, Jr. and Matthew T. Lee (2000a). "On Immigration and Crime." In *Criminal Justice 2000: The Changing Nature of Crime, Volume I,* G. LaFree and R. Bursik (Eds.), Washington, D.C.: National Institute of Justice.

Merton, Robert K. (1938). "Social Structure and Anomie." *American Sociological Review* 3:672–682.

Morenoff, Jeffrey D. and Robert J. Sampson (1997). "Violent Crime and The Spatial Dynamics of Neighborhood Transition: Chicago, 1970–1990." *Social Forces, 76,* 31–64.

Pattavina, April, James M. Byrne, and Luis Garcia (2006). "An Examination of Citizen Involvement in Crime Prevention in High-Risk versus Low-to-Moderate-Risk Neighborhoods." *Crime and Delinquency, 52,* 203–231.

Riedel, Marc and Wayne Welsh (2002). *Criminal Violence: Patterns, Causes, and Prevention.* Los Angeles: Roxbury Publishing.

Rose, Dina R. and Todd R. Clear (1998). "Incarceration, Social Capital, and Crime: Implications for Social Disorganization Theory." *Criminology, 36,* 441–480.

Sampson, Robert J. and Lydia Bean (2006). "Cultural Mechanisms and Killings Fields: A Revised Theory of Community-Level Racial Inequality." In *The Many Colors of Crime: Inequalities of Race, Ethnicity, and Crime in America,* Ruth Peterson, Laurie Krivo and John Hagan (Eds.), New York: New York University Press, pp. 8–36.

Sampson, Robert J. and William Julius Wilson (1995). Toward a Theory of Race, Crime, and Urban Inequality. In *Crime and Inequality,* John Hagan and Ruth Peterson (Eds.), Stanford, CA: Stanford University Press, pp. 37–56.

Shaw and McKay (1969 [1942]). *Juvenile Delinquency and Urban Areas.* Chicago: University of Chicago Press.

Suttles, Gerald D. (1968). *The Social Order of the Slum: Ethnicity and Territory in the Inner City.* Chicago: University of Chicago Press.

Swindler, Ann (1986). "Culture in Action." *American Sociological Review, 51,* 273–286.

Toch, Hans (1992). *Living in Prison: The Ecology of Survival.* Washington, D.C.: The American Psychological Association.

Tocqueville, Alexis de (1969). *Democracy in America.* George Lawrence (Trans.), Garden City, NY: Anchor Books.

3

Examining the Impact of Institutional Culture on Prison Violence and Disorder: An Evidence-Based Review*

James M. Byrne, PhD
Department of Criminal Justice and Criminology
University of Massachusetts Lowell

Don Hummer, PhD
Department of Criminal Justice
Penn State Harrisburg

Introduction: Assessing the Culture of Violence in Prison

In the following article, we provide an overview of potential solutions to the prison violence problem, based on a comprehensive evidenced-based review of the research conducted over the past two decades (1984–2006). Of particular interest was the notion that prison "culture," whether defined in terms of inmate culture, staff culture, or even management culture, was linked—directly or indirectly—to levels of prison violence and disorder. We were surprised by how little research had been conducted on this basic research question over the past two decades. To examine the recent research on prison culture in the broader context of *all* research conducted on prison

*Case cited: *Johnson v. California* (03-636) 543 U.S. 499 (*2005*).

40

violence and disorder, we decided to complete a comprehensive evidence-based review of the empirical research conducted in this area during the past two decades (1984–2006).

We identified three broad categories of responses to the prison violence and disorder problem: (1) inmate-focused strategies (e.g., classification, offender profiling, and conflict resolution strategies); (2) staff-focused strategies (including the National Institute of Corrections Culture Change Initiative); and (3) management-focused strategies (such as increased access to treatment programs, crowding reduction, and changes in situational context). Overall, our review revealed that the research supporting both inmate and staff-focused violence reduction strategies is either weak or nonexistent; management-focused strategies appear to be on firmer ground, particularly in the area of treatment program availability and quality. The implications of these findings are discussed, focusing on the need for a dramatic change in our approach to the problem of prison violence and disorder in this country, based on an emerging recognition of the link between prison violence and disorder and community violence and disorder.

The Prevention and Control of Prison Violence and Disorder—A Review of the Empirical Evidence

Throughout the country, legislators and policymakers are incorporating evidence-based research reviews in new legislation and program initiatives for a broad range of criminal justice initiatives, including both institutional and community corrections. In at least five states, legislation has been passed that *prohibits* the development of new initiatives unless they are based on a detailed "evidence-based" review. Although there is currently a debate over the standards to be established for such a review (e.g., gold vs. bronze standards), there is an emerging consensus on the need for more—and better designed—evaluations of criminal justice interventions generally, and corrections strategies in particular.

There are a number of recent comprehensive reviews of the effectiveness of various *prison-based* treatment (and control) programs on the behavior of inmates post-release (see, e.g., Farrington and Welsh, 2005; Latessa, 2004; and Cullen, 2005, for an overview). A much smaller number of research reviews examined the impact of various interventions on the institutional behavior of offenders (see, e.g., Liebling and Maruna, 2005; Edgar et al., 2003; Wortley, 2002; and Bottoms, 1999). In the following section, we present our own review of the recent empirical research (1984–2006), which certainly underscores the need for more (and better designed) evaluations of specific factors often discussed as the likely cause (or causes) of prison violence or disorder. (*See Appendix A for a summary of the empirical literature on the correlates of prison violence and disorder from the past 20 years.*)

Most discussions of the problem of prison violence and disorder first identify likely "causes" of prison violence and disorder in U.S. prisons as jumping off points for recommendations for changes in the U.S. prison system's policies and practices. We highlight the research on several of these factors, using the established criteria for review offered by the Campbell Collaborative for evidence-based reviews of this kind, along with the specific study identification and classification protocol developed by researchers at the University of Maryland. We decided to focus our review on all studies completed between 1984 and 2006, because we are most interested in assessing the impact of recent prison policies and practices during a period of unprecedented prison buildup. To identify this group of research studies, we searched all published research articles, reports, and reviews included in *Criminal Justice Abstracts* that met our minimum review criteria, supplementing the list with studies identified from a variety of other sources (e.g., meta-analyses, government documents). For our current review, we examined all studies which included prison violence and disorder (intra-personal, inter-personal, institutional, and collective violence and disorder) as a dependent variable and one or more of our review measures (see above listing) as independent variables in their analyses. A total of 57 studies was identified and included in our final review, including 35 level 1, 10 level 2, 6 level 3, 1 level 4, and 5 level 5 studies. While the overall quality of the studies we reviewed was quite low, our review certainly revealed a number of promising strategies, while also providing the framework for an aggressive research agenda for policy-makers to consider as they debate the inevitable call for a new wave of prison reform in this country.

Typically, the completion of an evidence-based review includes an assessment of what works, what doesn't work, what is promising, and what is unknown (see Appendix B for specific details on review criteria, the scope of our research review, and scoring procedures for individual studies). We use this terminology to summarize the results of our research review in eight separate areas of inquiry. Given the focus of this text on prison culture, we begin by examining the empirical research on the link between prison culture—however defined—and prison violence and disorder.

Culture, Violence, and Disorder in Prison

The research on the link between prison culture and prison violence and disorder can be divided into three categories: (1) research on the impact of prison management practices (or *management culture*), which we cover in more detail later in this review (e.g., DiIullio, 1987); (2) research on the impact of *staff culture*, which we review in this section; and (3) research on the link between *inmate culture* and prison violence and disorder, which we also review in this section. While the term *culture* is defined and operationalized in different ways by different researchers, the research studies we reviewed shared a common theme: Values affect behavior. For prisoners, inmate culture may take the form of a unique "inmate code" that defines how prisoners should act and react in prison settings (Sykes, 1958); some have argued that inmate culture is both a reflection and continuation of a culture of street crime that exists in a small number of urban communities in this country, described by some as "poverty pockets" (Lifers Public Safety Steering Committee, 2004; Sampson and Bean, 2006). For prison staff—including corrections officers, supervisors, treatment providers, and program/administrative personnel, a unique staff culture can be identified that takes the form of a "staff code" defining how staff should act in their assigned positions, regardless of formal rules and regulations; and how they should respond to the inevitable conflicts that arise in prison, including inmate–inmate, staff–inmate, and staff–management conflicts. And for prison management, a prison's unique management culture is perhaps most clearly represented in the balance between care and custody (also described by some as the balance between offender change and offender control) that exists in a particular prison.

Perhaps the best recent example of research on the impact of prison management "culture" on incidents of misconduct was a study conducted by Sparks, Bottoms, and Hay a decade ago, which is described in *Prisons and the Problem of Order*. In this study, Sparks, Bottoms, and Hay (1996) compared two British prisons with differing management approaches to maintaining order and concluded that tight security controls in facilities reduced incidents of individual-level violence such as inmate on inmate assaults, but resulted in more self-injury and propensity for collective violent actions by inmates. A more lenient approach had a diametrically opposite effect, in that assaults on inmates and staff increased, but collective violence by inmates was less likely due to the legitimacy afforded the prison population. Therefore, the authors conclude that the key to maintaining order and control in prisons is for administrators to strike the appropriate balance between facility security and inmate autonomy.

Similar research findings were reported in a recent study of four Belgian prisons by Snacken (2005), who concluded that management culture can be linked directly to the level of violence and disorder in prison. According to Snacken (2005: 335),

> *Prisons are like balloons or waterbeds. The deprivation of liberty and its consequences will lead to frustrations, tensions, and conflicts. Prisons where this reality is accepted succeed in channeling these tensions into manageable forms while repression of a particular form of violence seems to foster the emergence of a different form. More liberal, active and nonauthoritarian regimes [were found in prisons where] relations between prisoners and between prisoners and staff, are less strained [and] that have many activities, work or education, and more autonomy for prisoners. This results in lower levels of institutional violence, less collective resistance, less violence between prisoners and staff, and less self harm.*

While the two studies we have just described are certainly worthy of consideration and review (see our separate discussion of management practices later in this chapter), we need to emphasize a critical point: There is no body of empirical research (level 3 quasi-experiments or above) that can be identified directly linking "institutional culture" (however defined and operationalized) to prison violence and disorder.

Perhaps more importantly, much of the research on the general subject of institutional culture conducted over the past 50 years [from Sykes (1958) to Toch (1977) to Bottoms (1987) and Liebling (2005)] has examined *inmate* culture; staff/management culture has been the subject of much speculation (see, e.g., DiIulio, 1987, 1991; Riveland, 1999; Useem and Piehl, 2006) but almost no empirical research. When viewed in this context, the need for external, independent (level 3 or above) research and evaluation on various aspects of prison culture—inmate-, staff-, and management-based—is certainly underscored.

At present, there is little empirical research, beyond a few case studies of prison reform initiatives (see, e.g., Maruna and Toch, 2005; or The Lifers Public Safety Steering Committee, 2004), that links negative institutional culture to prison violence and disorder. However, a number of recent reports and reviews on the problem of prison violence have posited a direct relationship between negative prison culture and various forms of violence and disorder in prison (see, e.g., Commission on Safety and Abuse in America's Prisons, 2006). Typically, the authors of these reviews suggest that changes (from negative to positive) in inmate culture, staff culture, and/or management culture will have a direct effect on all forms of prison violence and disorder. Unfortunately, the research base for these claims is—at best—sketchy.

Until we clearly define what we mean by prison culture (e.g., are we referring to inmate culture, staff culture, or management culture?) and then conduct rigorous research on culture change initiatives, the relationship between negative prison culture and prison violence and disorder will continue to be the subject of much speculation and debate. Without such clear definitions of terms and the necessary objective and quality research (i.e., a systematic, evidence-based review of level 3, 4, and 5 research studies), discussions of institutional culture will continue to be based largely on the subjective experience of inmates, staff, and management.

Our search for empirical research studies conducted since 1984 identified only two (both multi-site) research studies that met our minimum review criteria: one level 2 study (Liebling, 2006) focusing on intra-personal violence; and one level 3 study (Byrne, Taxman, and Hummer, 2005) examining the impact of NICs Institutional Culture Change Initiative on reported levels (pre/post comparisons) of prison violence and disorder. The few researchers studying prison culture during this review period conducted qualitative case study research, utilizing both direct observations and interviews with staff, management, and/or inmates (see, e.g., Useem and Piehl , 2006, for a brief overview; or Maruna and Toch, 2005). As a result of this research shortfall, we must conclude that the relationship between inmate culture, staff culture, and/or management culture and prison violence and disorder must be classified as "unknown."

The two studies we highlight in Table 3A.1 (in this chapter's appendix) certainly support the notion that changes in prison environment/social climate generally—and prison culture in particular—will result in less disorder in prison. Liebling's (2005) research, for example, demonstrates that improvements in what she refers to as the "moral performance" of prisons will reduce the level of intra-personal violence (i.e., self-injury) in these facilities. Another recent study that focuses directly on the culture–violence connection using a pre-post quasi-experimental design is the recently completed evaluation of the National Institute of Corrections' Institutional Culture Change Initiative (Byrne, Taxman, and Hummer, 2005). The results of the evaluation (see Table 3A.1 in the appendix) provide new information on the importance of staff culture (and culture change) as a prison violence control mechanism. Based on this evaluation, it appears that initiatives designed to address long-standing issues related to "negative" staff culture—through a combination of culture assessment, short-term workshops on how to "promote" a positive corrections culture, and the use of short-term change "consultants" by prison management—do have at least a short-term impact (on average, about a hundred fewer reported incidents (per month) over a two-year review period) on the overall number of incidents reported to prison officials. However, it is important to emphasize that these NIC-sponsored initiatives did *not* reduce the level of reported violence at these institutions.

We describe the NIC initiative in much more detail in a separate chapter (*this text*), but we should emphasize that from a problem-oriented perspective, institutional culture is perhaps best described as an explanation for why inmates, staff, and management within prisons resist our best efforts to reform these institutions, rather than an underlying cause of the problem. Unless culture-related resistance to change by inmates, staff, and management can be overcome, even the best-designed problem-solving strategies—focusing on the seven major causes of violence and disorder identified below—will not be fully implemented (see also Liebling this text).

Although we should emphasize that we simply do not have the necessary empirical evidence to support this claim, we nonetheless suspect that changes in negative inmate, staff, and/or management culture may be the necessary before other, problem-oriented reforms can be introduced to a prison system. It can be argued that culture change initiatives may have an indirect—rather than direct—effect on prison violence and disorder. However, we emphasize that there is currently no strong empirical evidence to support this view. Donald Spence, director of the Prison Law Office, offered a much stronger assessment—based on experience, not research—in the following testimony to the Commission on Safety and Abuse in America's Prisons: *"The culture of our prisons virtually dictates the level of violence you will have in them. And if you change that culture, you will reduce the violence"* (2006: iv). Is Spence correct in suggesting that culture change will have a direct effect? We simply do not have sufficient research evidence available to assess the direct and/or indirect effect of culture change initiatives on violence and disorder in prison.

The Impact of Prison Crowding on Prison Violence and Disorder

It is difficult to imagine that anyone would argue that we don't have a prison crowding problem in this country. According to a recent review of this issue by the Commission on Safety and Abuse in America's Prisons (2006: 23):

Crowding, and the tremendous increase in the prisoner population that underlies it fuels violence. Crowding severely limits or eliminates the ability of prisoners to be productive, which can leave them feeling hopeless; pushes officers to rely on forceful means of control rather than communication, and makes it harder to classify and assign prisoners safely and identify the dangerously mentally ill. Services ranging from nutrition to dental and medical care are affected by crowding. Every vital service is diluted or made operationally impossible. And then there is simply the excessive noise, heat, and tension. This is fertile ground for violence.

While we agree with the assessment of likely effects of prison crowding identified by the Commission, we would caution the reader to distinguish between the "likely" and the *known* effects of crowding on prison violence and disorder (Useem and Piehl, 2006).

There is currently some debate over the nature and extent of the prison crowding problem; it appears that much of this debate can be largely attributed to the use of design versus operational capacity to determine whether a particular facility is "crowded" (Commission on Safety and Abuse in America's Prisons, 2006: 104). Prison crowding researchers have typically defined crowding at the facility level in terms of a particular prison's design (rated) and/or operational capacity. In addition, some researchers prefer to examine density rather than crowding, focusing on the actual living space available to inmates, which shrinks when cells are double- or even triple-bunked due to crowding. In each instance, however, the same general assumption applies: Crowded prisons are more dangerous places than uncrowded prisons, regardless of *who* is living in prison.

Using *design* capacity as the operational definition of crowding, U.S. prisons were operating at 115 percent of capacity in 2004; using *operational* capacity, these same prisons were at 99 percent of capacity (Harrison and Beck, 2005). We could not find a single study that included a nationwide assessment of density, but it certainly seems likely that in many states, prison administrators increased their operational capacity by either increasing the density of offenders at the facility or by transferring the "overflow" to other states and/or county jails. In any event, we need to know much more about offender density at the facility level before we can offer a definitive statement about the level of crowding and density in the U.S. prison system.

Our review of the empirical research on the impact of crowding on the level of prison violence and disorder between 1984 and 2006 identified eight research studies (and one nonempirical essay on the subject). Unfortunately, these eight studies are all level 1 nonexperimental research studies, which unequivocally leads to the conclusion that the relationship between crowding/density and prison violence must be categorized as *unknown*, using the standard Campbell Collaborative review criteria (see Appendix A, Table 3A.2 for a summary of key study findings).

The studies we have included in our review present an inconsistent view of the effect of crowding levels (and density) on the institutional behavior of prisoners, although it should be noted that in six of the eight research studies, prison crowding had negative consequences for inmates in these facilities. Evidence supporting the crowding–violence connection can be found in a study of three state correctional systems—in New York, Washington, and Vermont—by Wooldrege,

Griffin, and Pratt (2001), who found that crowding had a significant, independent effect on the level of misconduct reported in these systems. The authors suggested that crowding levels affected offender density, increasing the physical proximity of inmates to one another, but they do not attempt to measure density directly. Similarly, Ruback and Carr (1993) examined data from 65 facilities (prisons, jails, and adult and juvenile facilities) and found that measures of "institutional density" and the "rate of change in facility population" had significant, but small, effects on both violent and nonviolent infractions reported at these facilities. In addition, Gaes and McGuire (1985) present correlational research linking crowding to the level of violence and disorder in prison, while two recent research studies linked crowding to higher levels of drug abuse (Gillespie, 2005) and inmate stress, apparently tied to personal space infringement at one crowded facility (Lawrence and Andrews, 2004).

A different view of the relationship between crowding and violence/disorder in prison is reported in a study of one federal prison by Walters (1998). Using data on reported assaults, selected inmate and staff characteristics, and crowding in this facility over a nine-year period, Walters found an *inverse* relationship between crowding, staff experience, and reported assaults, perhaps linked to heightened security measures taken at this prison to address both overcrowding and staff inexperience. Unfortunately, since changes in security measures were not documented, there is no way of verifying whether this occurred. Finally, Pelissier (1991) found that there was no difference in rule infraction rates after a sudden increase in the population of inmates at one federal prison, using standard pre/post increase comparisons (with no control sites identified).

Overall, six out of eight level 1 nonexperimental research studies identified a link between crowding (and by inference, density) and a variety of adverse inmate outcomes, including increased inmate self-injury, heightened stress levels/perceptions of aggressive behavior in other inmates, increased drug use in prison, and higher levels of inmate-on-inmate violence and disorder. Clearly, we need to conduct much more—and much higher quality—research on this topic before we can offer a definitive statement of the relationship between crowding/density and the level of violence and disorder in our prisons today. Absent this research, we will be forced to rely on anecdotal information and observational data; these are important, but incomplete, knowledge-building strategies.

Staffing Levels, Staff Characteristics, Staff Quality, and Prison Violence

To some observers of corrections policy and practice, staffing levels and inmate–staff ratios are key indicators of U.S. corrections management culture, which is firmly grounded in the notion that offender control—and not offender change—represents the primary mission of the prison system in this country. Utilizing a combination of hard and soft control technology, a small number of line staff are asked to control a very large number of inmates. In U.S. prisons today, staffing ratios of 100 (inmates) to 1 (line officer) are not unusual; in contrast, 10:1 inmate to officer staffing ratios are found in the British prison system. With high staffing ratios and a large inmate population, controlling inmates becomes a difficult task, at least in part due to the need to emphasize formal over informal control mechanisms. Not surprisingly, officers rely on sanctions to induce compliance in these situations, resulting in high utilization rates for segregation/disciplinary units, as well as the reclassification of inmates from lower to higher security levels. Because of their focus on inmate control strategies, efforts to *change* inmates (through education and treatment) are—at best—a secondary concern. Moreover, high staffing ratios make interaction between line staff and inmates less frequent and more formalized, undermining the informal social control mechanisms that would be a natural outgrowth of the relationship developed between line staff and inmates in less control-centered settings.

In addition to staffing levels, management culture is also reflected in decisions on who we hire to work in prisons (staff characteristics) and the quality of workforce (e.g., education, training, experience). The adage "you get what you pay for" can easily be applied to both publicly and privately operated prisons in this country. According to a recent review:

> The corrections profession is an integral part of the American criminal justice system. The 400,000 corrections officers working in U.S. prisons and jails play a large role in determining how incarceration affects the roughly 13.5 million people who are locked up over the course of a year. Yet the officer corps is an extraordinarily unstable workforce. (Commission on Safety and Abuse in America's Prisons, 2006: 70)

It can be argued that a greater proportion of the 60 billion dollars we currently spend each year on corrections should be allocated to staff salaries and retention, because corrections officers are among the lowest paid personnel working in the criminal justice system, with annual turnover rates averaging 16 percent nationwide (American Correctional Association, 2004). If we want to attract—and retain—more educated line staff, then we have to find ways (salary increases are only one) to make a career in corrections more attractive.

The argument in favor of lower staffing ratios and higher quality (and more culturally diverse) staff is straightforward: Staffing levels, staff characteristics, and staff quality are all directly related to the level of violence and disorder in prison. But is this argument based on conjecture or sound empirical research? Table 3A.3 presents our review of the empirical research on this issue (1984–2006). Seven studies have been conducted during our review period focusing on the purported link between staffing levels, staff characteristics (age, gender, diversity), and staff quality (education, experience, training, competence), and institutional violence and disorder. In each instance, the authors of the studies employed a nonexperimental research design, which leads us to conclude that the relation between staffing and prison violence and/or disorder is currently unknown. Given the importance of this issue to prison resource allocation decisions, it is remarkable that not one quality research study (level 3 or above) has been conducted on this topic in the past 20 years.

A review of the current staffing research included in Table 3A.3 does offer very preliminary support for a link between staffing levels, staffing quality, staff diversity, and prison violence and disorder. In a recent study by Camp, Gaes, Langan, and Saylor (2003), inmate institutional misconduct rates were significantly higher in facilities with a higher percentage of white staff, female staff, and staff with less than one year's experience. Similarly, McCorkle, Miethe, and Drass (1995) found that assaults on both inmates and on staff were significantly higher in prisons with higher white–black guard ratios. In addition to staff diversity, researchers also looked at staffing levels in two studies. Eckland–Olson (1986) found that lower inmate-to-staff ratios were associated with lower inmate on staff assaults, while Hensley, Koscheski, and Tewksbury (2003) found that inmate–staff ratio was *not* associated with the rate of sexual assault in prison (but size of inmate population was associated with sexual assault).

As we mentioned in our earlier discussion of crowding effects, it is certainly possible that prison management will respond proactively to certain "risk" factors, thereby reducing their potential impact. For example, Walters (1998) suggests that the Bureau of Prisons responded to the dual problems of staff inexperience and overcrowding by increasing security measures in these facilities, which resulted in lower reported assaults despite the presence of inexperienced staff and prison crowding. Of course, Sparks (1995) and others have found that while utilization of new control strategies and technology may reduce one type of violence (e.g., inter-personal violence), it may actually increase other forms of violence (intra-personal, collective, and/or institutional violence) at the same time.

Finally, two studies were included in Table 3A.3 that did not measure prison violence and disorder directly, relying instead on the perceptions of prison executives (Useem and Resig, 1999) and inmates (Patrick, 1998). According to prison executives, both poor staff morale and inmate perceptions of procedural justice were related to collective inmate disturbances; according to inmates, abuse of authority by staff was associated with higher levels of assault on staff.

It is difficult to argue with the conclusions of the Commission on Safety and Abuse in America's Prisons: "America's correctional facilities cannot operate safely and effectively without a qualified, stable, and diverse corps of officers" (2006: 72). However, we need to conduct a series of quality research studies on the staffing issues we have identified here before *research* can accurately inform *practice* in this critical policy area.

The Impact of Programming (Availability and Quality) on Prison Violence and Disorder

As we noted at the outset, there is now a fairly sizable research base from which to evaluate the evidence on the link between in-prison programming and post-release offender behavior (see, e.g., Wilson, Bouffard, and MacKenzie, 2005; and Welsh and Farrington, 2001 for detailed evidence-based reviews). Based on recent research reviews, it has been estimated that provision of various forms of treatment in prison settings (for mental health, drug/alcohol problems, educational deficits, etc.) will have a significant, but modest (10% reduction), impact on subsequent offender criminal behavior (Welsh and Farrington, 2001). Given the movement of offenders back and forth between institutional and community control, even modest reductions in return to prison rates can—over time—have a major impact on the size of our corrections population (Jacobsen, 2005). Clearly, a strong argument can be made that based on an evidence-based review of the research, the provision of treatment—in both institutional and community settings—is the most effective crime control strategy currently available in this country (Byrne and Taxman, 2006). It appears that while many legislators, governors, and corrections administrators have been preoccupied with the latest innovations in the technology of control, the real cost savings and crime reduction effects are to be found in the technology of change, both at the individual and community levels.

An argument can also be made that the provision of treatment—and programming generally—will reduce the level of violence and disorder *in prison*. While this makes sense intuitively, some have argued that expensive, high-quality, in-prison treatment programs are too costly and too difficult to implement in prison settings; and, that you will yield the same prison violence and disorder reduction effects by putting offenders in recreation programs (Farabee, 2005). While our research review identified only one study comparing the relative effects of various types of programming (including recreation) on prison violence and disorder (Wormith,1984), we did identify 17 separate research studies conducted during our review period (1984–2006) that evaluated the impact of specific types of programming on institutional behavior. Included among the 17 studies (summarized in Table 3A.4) were three randomized field experiments, three quasi-experiments, and 11 level 1 or 2 studies using non-experimental research designs. Using the Campbell Collaborative (and University of Maryland) review criteria (at least two level 3 or above quality research studies are needed), we can offer an assessment of "what works" in the area of offender programming as a prison violence and disorder reduction strategy.

Two of the three randomized field experiments we reviewed found that program participation resulted in significant improvement in institutional behavior (experimental vs. control group comparisons of disciplinary infraction rates). All three quasi-experiments reported similar, statistically significant reductions in confrontations and disciplinary infractions for program participants (treatment vs. comparison group). These positive findings were supported by the findings from the 11 additional non-experimental research studies conducted on the same topic area, i.e., the link between program participation and institutional behavior. Overall, we find that the provision of treatment in prison is an effective, evidence-based, prison violence and disorder reduction strategy. Because the type of treatment varied across the 18 studies we reviewed, it appears that there are a wide range of treatment programs that may be applicable to a particular prison setting; the key finding is that inmate involvement in some aspect of the change process (e.g., through cognitive behavioral programs focusing on drug treatment, group discussions on self-control, and lifestyle change, therapeutic communities) improves their institutional behavior.

Our research review revealed that one proven strategy for reducing prison violence and disorder is to expand and improve our in-prison programming. However, we recognize that given the system's current emphasis on the technology of control, this recommendation is "easier said than done." The current management culture that exists does not value individual offender change, because many corrections leaders simply do not believe that offender change is possible, given the educational, economic, and social deficits these individuals must overcome. The research we summarize here suggests a different approach to the correctional control of offenders, one that emphasizes the importance of prison-based programming for education, vocational training, mental health, substance abuse, and a variety of other problems (including health) as an offender control mechanism.

In developing new *change*-based initiatives, we need to recognize that program availability and/or program participation should not be confused with program quality. Unfortunately, there is no empirical research testing the proposition that higher quality in-prison treatment programs will result in lower levels of various forms of institutional violence and disorder. However, we do know that such a link exists between in-prison treatment quality and post-prison behavior (see, e.g., Wilson, Bouffard, and MacKenzie, 2005). Assuming for the moment that subsequent research does demonstrate that such a link can be established, the implications for treatment program funding/staffing are straightforward: Before we can improve the custody and treatment provided in prison we will first need to upgrade the education and training of line corrections officers *and* treatment personnel.

The Impact of Prison Classification Practices on Institutional Violence and Disorder

One of the underlying assumptions of the U.S. prison system is that prison violence and disorder is affected by decisions we make each day, not only about *who* should be in prison and for *how long*, but also *where* offenders will be housed within the prison system and *when* they should be moved from one level of security to the next. The United States currently has over 5,000 adult prison and jails, each with its own unique design features, staffing ratios, design and operational capacity, offender population, and resource level. In each of these facilities, classification decisions are made that directly affect the level of violence and disorder in that prison. According to the Commission on Safety and Abuse in America's Prisons:

> Reducing violence among prisoners depends on the decisions corrections administrators make about where to house prisoners and how to supervise them. Perhaps most important are the classification decisions managers make to ensure that housing units do not contain incompatible individuals or groups of people: informants and those they informed about, repeat and violent offenders and vulnerable potential victims, and others who might clash with violent consequences. And these classifications should not be made on the basis of race or ethnicity, or their proxies. (*Johnson v. California*, 2005) (2006: 29)

In a recent nationwide review of prison classification systems, Austin (2003) high-lighted the difference between external and internal classification systems:

> External classification places a prisoner at a custody level that will determine where the prisoner will be housed. Once the prisoner arrives at a facility, internal classification determines which cell or housing unit, as well as which facility programs (e.g. education, vocational, counseling, and work assignments) the prisoner will be assigned. (2)

Austin (2003) points out that we currently are farther along in the development of external than internal classification systems, but a review of the research on the effectiveness of current classification schemes reveals limitations for both external and internal classification systems.

Table 3A.5 presents the results of our review of the research on the impact of classification decisions on the level of violence and disorder in prison. Only seven research studies were completed on the relationship between classification decisions and inmate behavior in prison during our study review period (1984–2006), including three randomized field experiments and four nonexperimental, level 1 and level 2 studies. Focusing first on external classification, we looked at two randomized field experiments that asked deceptively simple questions: What would happen if we placed a high-risk, maximum-security inmate in a medium-security housing unit? And similarly, what would happen if we placed a medium-risk inmate in a low-risk environment? If *where* we place inmates affects their behavior—and more specifically, if such placement has a mediating effect on their behavior—we would expect higher rates of inmate misbehavior in lower risk settings.

Camp and Gaes (2005) randomly assigned medium-security inmates to minimum-security facilities, while Bench and Allen (2003) randomly assigned maximum-security inmates (based on the external risk classification) to medium-security facilities; both studies found no significant differences in either overall misconduct or serious misconduct violations across experimental and control groups. The implications of these findings for external classification systems are straightforward: (1) contrary to expectations, placement of higher risk offenders in more restrictive prison settings does not lower their rate of institutional misconduct, while placement of higher risk offenders in lower risk settings does not raise their rate of misconduct; and (2) alternatives to control-based placements should be field-tested to determine their effect on inmate misconduct. Unfortunately, we currently know very little about the link between inmate classification level and prison classification level (minimum, medium, maximum, supermax) outside these two well-designed, but narrowly focused, studies.

Once the results of external classification determine where an offender should be located within a federal or state system, an internal classification system is employed to determine where in that prison each new offender should be housed and, equally important, which programs they will have access to while in that prison. Essentially, these internal classification systems focus on three separate, but related, issues: (1) risk (of escape); (2) treatment (for mental health, physical health, educational/vocational deficits, substance abuse, multiple problems, etc.); and (3) control (of intra-personal, intra-personal, and collective violence and disorder).

A review of Table 3A.5 reveals that very little quality research has been conducted over the past two decades on (1) how to identify the potential high-risk (or high-rate) offenders (i.e., high risk for institutional violence and/or disorder) at the internal classification stage (Berk, Krieger, and Baek, 2006); and (2) how to respond proactively (and programmatically) to offenders with identified risk factors associated with institutional misconduct. For example, age (younger), gender (male), history of violence (known), history of mental illness (known), gang membership (known), program participation (low), and recent disciplinary action (known) have been identified by Austin (2003) as variables included in risk classification systems because of their known correlation with inmate misconduct. The question is: Once these risk factors have been identified, how should prison managers respond programmatically?

Berk, et al. (2006) offer one possible model for predicting "dangerous" inmate misconduct (defined as assault, drug trafficking, and robbery) based on data from 9,662 inmates assigned and classified (between November 1,1998 and April 30, 1999) by the California Department of Corrections and Rehabilitation, with prison misconduct monitored during a 24-month follow-up (from intake). While they caution that predicting a rare event (only 3% of inmates had one serious misconduct during the review period) such as serious prison misconduct will necessarily involve selecting 10 false positives for every one true positive, this is a cost they are willing to pay, because "false positives have a configuration of background characteristics that make them almost sure bets to engage in one of the less-serious forms of misconduct" (2006: ii). According to Berk and his colleagues, "The high risk inmates tend to be young individuals with long criminal records, active participants in street and prison gangs, and sentenced to long prison terms" (2006: 9). Given the researchers' questionable decision regarding the "acceptable" level of false positives (10:1), the very low base rate for serious misconduct (3%), and the 50 percent accuracy rate for the forecasting model, it appears that discussion of the application of this technique to inmate classification levels is premature.

Finally, it is disappointing that few quality research studies have been conducted that focused on how effective current internal classification systems have been at classifying offenders for appropriate treatment while in prison. Are we getting drug-dependent inmates into appropriate drug treatment programs? Are we getting mentally ill inmates the mental health care they need? What about the offender with deficits in education/vocational skills and the multiple-problem inmate? Research linking classification, prison program placement, and inmate in-prison behavior has simply not been conducted. Although a few high-quality research studies on *external* prison classification systems have been conducted on the link between classification and control (it appears tenuous at best), we have to conclude that we "don't know" whether classification, treatment/programming, and control decisions made in conjunction with *internal* classification systems are effective. —Lots of don't Knows—

Given recent reviews highlighting the overclassification of female inmates (Austin, 2003) and the expansion of protective custody, administrative and disciplinary segregation (Commission on Safety and Abuse in America's Prisons, 2006), it appears that the primary purpose of current external and internal classification systems is the short-term control of our inmate population. There is no evidence that our current emphasis on control-based classification systems makes prisons any safer; but there is a mounting body of evidence that we can reduce violence and disorder in prison by increasing inmate program participation rates (see Table 3A.4).

Prison Management Practices and Institutional Violence and Disorder

One of the enduring "myths" in the field of corrections is that leadership and management style can have a direct effect on the level of violence and disorder in prison. Importantly, these effects are often described as independent of specific problem-solving strategies; "it's not *what* you do but *how* you do it that matters" appears to be the prevailing sentiment. This view of the charismatic leader as the key to success in a difficult field needs to be juxtaposed against the backdrop of ongoing, disruptive, but predictable change in correctional leadership in this country. On average, Commissioners of state corrections systems hold their positions for about three and a half years, while Wardens of individual facilities last only slightly longer—about four years. Crisis is inevitable in any state prison system; and Governors have made commissioners and wardens accountable for those crises that occur under their watch and threaten the public's view of the competence level of an administration. As a consequence of this constant turnover in correctional leadership, resistance to change in these correctional organizations is inevitable. And because corrections leaders come and go but midlevel managers and most line staff remain much longer, it is not surprising that an "us vs. them" mentality emerges in many corrections institutions today.

It is within this context that research on management styles and management practice needs to be considered. Wortley (2002: 47–54) provides a concise summary of currently thinking in this area, which appears to be based largely on qualitative research on (1) the deprivation model's impact on inmate subcultural development (Goffman, 1961; Sykes, 1958); (2) the assessment of prison institutional "personality" (involvement, support, autonomy) and its effect on inmate "social climate" (e.g., Moos, 1968; Wright, 1986); and more recently, (3) case studies of management practices in selected state prison systems and the subsequent depiction of three distinct management styles (the control model, the responsibility model, and the consensual model (DiIulio,1987). Remarkably little empirical research has been conducted in each of these areas over the past two decades. However, the small number of studies available for review focus on the impact of specific management practices and prison "regimes" on prison violence and disorder (see, e.g., Snacken, 2005; or Sparks, et al., 1996).

Because at least some empirical research has been conducted (1984–2006) testing the impact of each of the three distinct management models identified by DiIulio (1987) on prison violence and disorder, we will highlight the key dimensions across which management practices are likely to vary. According to a recent summary by Reisig (1998), control, responsibility, and consensual models vary across eight distinct dimensions:

1. organizational communication
2. personal relations
3. inmate/staff communication
4. discretion
5. regimentation of inmate lives
6. response to inmate rule violations
7. response to inmate disruptiveness
8. inmate participation in decision making

Each of the three management models varies across the eight dimensions just identified. For example, the *control* model is consistent with an earlier generation of prison management, where a military/hierarchical style of management was popular, based on the premise that "strict and predictable control was the best guarantee of a humane, safe and productive environment for prisoners and staff (Wortley, 2002: 50). In contrast, as Wortley recently observed, "the *responsibility* model is broadly consistent with third generation thinking on prisoner control. Control of behavior in the responsibility model is based on psychological principles such as conveying appropriate expectancies, reducing frustrations and inhibiting neutralizing cognitions" (2002: 51). The *consensual* model took a middle ground between these two models' approaches to responsibility and control, based on the notion that "prison management is a balancing act" (Wortley, 2002: 50) between these two orientations. Observational research by DiIulio (1987) suggests that the "control" model was found in the Texas prison system in the 1960s and 1970s, while the "responsibility" model was found in the Michigan system he visited in the 1980s, and the "consensual" model existed during the same period in California (Reisig, 1998 as summarized in Wortley, 2002).

Assuming for the moment that DiIulio's classification scheme accurately depicts the possible range of management styles currently being used, both statewide and in individual prisons within states, it should be possible to examine the link between management style (consistent with the control, responsibility, or the consensual model) and the level of prison violence and disorder. Table 3A.6 includes the results of our review of the research in this area: Of the three research studies identified, two were level 1 nonexperimental research studies and one was a level two research study. Clearly, the lack of quality research in this area leads us to conclude that despite popular conceptions of the need for leadership and new styles of management, the actual relationship between management style and prison performance—as measured by the level of violence and disorder—is unknown.

In fact, even the research summarized in Table 3A.6 skirts the issue of prison performance measurement; in three of four studies (Reiseg, 1998; Gordon, Moriarty, and Grant, 2003; and Gendreau and Keyes, 2001), staff *perceptions* of violence and disorder were measured, rather than the actual levels of violence and disorder. In the one study using a measure of institutional violence, Reiseg (2002) found that management/staff conflict, along with prison gang activity, was correlated with in-facility homicides in 300 state prisons across the United States.

In terms of the research we have included on staff perceptions, perhaps the most interesting research study was again conducted by Reiseg (1998). This study examined the impact of managerial practices on subjective levels of prison disorder. Data were collected from mail surveys administered to superintendents and wardens ($N = 306$) from 11 higher custody state prisons for males in the United States. As we noted earlier, DiIulio has outlined three managerial approaches: the "control model," which applies rigid formal restraints to nearly every aspect of prison life; the "responsibility model," which relies on minimizing official control mechanisms and providing inmates with self-governance opportunities; and the "consensual model," which incorporates features from both of the others. At the aggregate level, respondents from the responsibility model and consensual model facilities reported lower levels of disorder than did respondents from control model facilities. However, the characteristics of the specific institutions under observation must also be taken into account. Overall, while the results call into question DiIulio's hypothesis (1987) that the control model is the most effective way to manage higher custody-level state prisons, both the quality level of the research study conducted and the focus on *perceptions* rather than actual levels of violence and disorder, once again lead to the conclusion that more—and higher quality—research needs to be conducted in this important area of inquiry.

The Situational Context of Institutional Violence and Disorder

Since the release of Richard Wortley's *Situational Prison Control*, there has been much discussion of how the situational context of prisons can be altered in ways that reduce prison violence and disorder (Wortley, 2002). While Wortley's application of both *precipitation-control* strategies (e.g., controlling prompts, controlling pressures, reducing permissibility, and reducing provocations) and *opportunity-reduction* strategies (e.g., increasing perceived effort, increasing perceived risks, reducing anticipated rewards, and increasing anticipated punishments) in prison settings appear to hold considerable promise, we agree with Wortley's assessment of the research testing the impact of various elements of his situational control model on prisoner-on-prisoner violence: "Generally, the available research is methodologically weak, and contradictory findings are common. Moreover, little of the research comes explicitly from a situational perspective, with most researchers focusing on broad, institution-wide measures" (Wortly, 2002: 98).

Our research review identified only five empirical research studies that examined the link between situational context and various measures of prison violence and disorder during our review period (1984–2006) (see Table 3A.7). Since only one of these studies was a level 3 (time series with comparison) study, we must—once again—conclude that the relationship between situational context and prison violence and disorder is currently unknown. In terms of the prison environment, the one level 3 study we reviewed (Briggs, Sundt, and Castellano, 2003) examined the effect of placement in a supermax facility on prison violence and the authors of the study found no support for the argument that supermax prisons reduce levels of inmate-on-inmate violence, and mixed, conflicting findings on staff safety effects. While we hesitate to draw any firm conclusions from a single research study, it does appear that the cost effectiveness of this strategy can be challenged (not only in terms of economic costs but also personal/social costs to inmates).

Discussion of the situational context of prison violence and disorder can take a variety of forms. In addition to the question of whether use of supermax prisons (or *any* security level or segregation strategy for that matter) can be justified based on its violence reduction effects, the examination of the situational context of prison violence and disorder necessarily includes an examination of features of inmate housing (e.g., single cell vs. dormitory housing) staff monitoring of inmates (e.g., utilizing new video monitoring technologies vs. direct supervision strategies) and inmate routines and movements (e.g., utilizing new inmate monitoring and location strategies, new programming for inmates, and the identification of hot spots for violence and disorder within a particular prison). Unfortunately, the link between each of these situational factors and prison violence must be classified as unknown, because the necessary quality research (level 3 and above) has simply not been conducted.

According to the recently released report from the Commission on Safety and Abuse in America's Prisons, "Prison and jail architecture, management, and models of supervision combine to create either safe and humane conditions or disruptive and dangerous ones" (2006: 29). Unfortunately, the Commission could only identify case study research (see, e.g., NIC's 1989 study of direct supervision facilities) and anecdotal evidence to support this assessment of the importance of situational context. However, a recent review of the research on the direct supervision system of correctional design and management by Wener (2006), while emphasizing the serious limitations of almost all the available research on this topic, does offer tentative support for the Commission's recommendation regarding the need to expand our use of direct supervision. According to Wener (2006: 403), "DS (direct supervision) facilities are consistently perceived by staff and inmates to have safer environments and, in fact, experience fewer violent or security-related incidents. The emerging pattern indicates that serious and major infractions are much lower in DS facilities, whereas minor infractions and property theft may be the same or higher." The problem with Wener's assessment is that it is based entirely on level 1 and 2 studies. Once again, the field needs better research that addresses this critical prison policy area before any *evidence-based* recommendations for reform can be offered.

Inmate Profiles, Gang Membership, and Prison Violence and Disorder

A variety of inmate characteristics have been linked to higher levels of prison violence and disorder. Based on this purported link, prison classification systems are designed to identify those inmate characteristics (age, race, prior incarceration, prior record, instant offense, mental health history, etc.) that are likely to be associated with an inmate's risk level while incarcerated—risk to self, risk to other inmates, risk to the community (due to escape), and risk to prison staff. The one factor most often discussed as a possible "cause" of prison violence and disorder is gang involvement (Byrne, 2006; Fleisher, 2006). Advocates of importation theory would argue that gangs are responsible for a disproportionate amount of both community *and* prison violence and disorder. If this view is correct, then the determination of gang membership is a critical step in the initial inmate classification process. Once gang membership is determined, it will likely affect both external (i.e., security level) and internal (i.e., location and movement within a particular prison) classification decisions. Of course, if gang membership is *not* associated with prison violence and disorder, we would be wasting valuable time and resources on a problem we don't need to solve. This general caveat about gang affiliation can be applied to other inmate characteristics as well. The question is what—if anything—do we actually know about the link between or among various inmate characteristics and institutional violence and disorder?

Table 3A.8 highlights the results of our review of the research on the link between inmate profiles, gang membership, and prison violence and disorder. Only six level 1 research studies were conducted during our review period (1984–2006), which leads us to conclude that contrary to public perception, the relation between inmate characteristics generally, and gang affiliation in particular, and prison violence and disorder, is unknown.

Although we recognize that the quality of the research is poor, we would be remiss if we didn't briefly summarize the results included in these studies. A review of the six studies included in Table 3A.8 suggests that there may be inmate characteristics associated with various forms of institutional violence and disorder, which is not surprising given our earlier discussion of inmate classification systems generally and attempts to predict the "violent" inmate in particular. Cunningham, Sorenson, and Reidy (2005), for example, found that younger inmates, inmates with less education, a prior prison term, and those inmates serving a term sentence had a higher probability of violent misconduct, while inmates who were either lifers or sentenced to death actually had lower risks of violent misconduct.

In addition, one study touched directly on the gang–violence connection. Gaes, Wallace, Klein-Saffron, and Suppa (2002) examined the relationship between gang affiliation and prison misconduct in a sample of 7,445 male federal prison inmates and found that "active" gang membership was associated with significant increases in the likelihood of various forms of institutional violence and disorder, including violent misconduct, serious violent misconduct, drug violations, and total misconduct.

This heightened risk level remained even after the researchers controlled for such individual level factors as inmate classification level and the inmate's previous history of violence. Similar results were reported by Fischer (2001) in a study examining gang affiliation and interpersonal violence and disorder in Arizona's prison system. According to Fischer (2001), prison gang members are significantly more likely to be involved in a serious incident (74% more likely) than nongang members. Finally, Porporino, Doherty, and Sawatsky (1987) reported that homicides in Canadian prisons were more likely to involve multiple assailants in the early eighties than in the 1970s, which may indicate increased gang involvement during this period. Taken together, these studies offer an agenda for future research—using better designs—on the link between inmate characteristics and prison violence and disorder.

How Can We Reduce Prison Violence and Disorder? Key Findings from Our Evidence-Based Review

Our review of the research on a wide range of possible correlates of various forms of prison violence and disorder underscored the need for systematic evidence-based reviews of correctional policy and practice. Not surprisingly, much of the research conducted in institutional settings during the past two decades is of such poor quality to be useless for policy and program development. However, we were able to offer our assessment of "what works" in two of the nine areas of inquiry we designated at the outset: (1) inmate program availability and quality, and (2) external inmate classification systems. *Only 2 of 9 - less than stellar*

First, inmate programming designed to focus on a number of dimensions of individual change (education, vocational training, treatment for mental health problems and/or drug/alcohol addiction, lifestyle/life course decisions, and physical health problems come immediately to mind) has been directly linked to lower levels of violence and disorder in prison. The policy implications of this evidence-based assessment are easy to articulate: *increase the quantity and quality of inmate programming and you will reduce the level of violence and disorder in our prisons.* Secondly, contrary to the general perception, there is no evidence that current prison classification schemes result in safer prisons, primarily because placement in a particular custody level—by itself—does not appear to reduce the "risk" of inmate misconduct (overall, and violent) while in prison. Since placement in a particular custody level does not appear to either decrease or increase an individual inmate's probability of misconduct—but it is linked to that inmate's probability of victimization and/or self-injury—a persuasive argument can be made that we are currently over-classifying our inmate population, which is not a cost-effective offender control strategy. This finding suggests a second policy recommendation: We need to field test a new generation of prison classification systems, which link an inmate's risk level to specific in-prison treatment programming; these new classification systems would be designed to focus on offender change, rather than offender control, as the outcome of classification decisions.

When considering the two policy recommendations that emerge from our evidence-based review, it is useful to reflect on Snacken's recent depiction of the two major policy choices currently available for those interested in addressing the problems associated with prison violence and disorder:

1. **[Option One]**: "Policies based on the assumption that problematic behavior in prison is linked to individuals with certain problematic characteristics. This approach leads to the elaboration of more or less sophisticated prediction and classification methods, categorization of prisoners, and specific control techniques for "high risk," dangerous or disruptive prisoners (segregation, special security units, specific programs, etc." (Snacken, 2005: 307).

2. **[Option Two]**: "Policies based primarily on the prevention of the emergence of problems in the general prison population through the provision of the same programs and activities to all prisoners and the tackling of individual problems on an individual basis" (Snacken, 2005: 307).

The policy recommendations we offer here are consistent with Snacken's option 2, and they underscore the importance of a proactive, problem-oriented approach to the problem of prison violence and disorder.

Concluding Comments on Prison Culture and Offender Change

As we noted at the outset, a number of recent, comprehensive reviews of the research on the causes of various forms of prison violence (e.g., Edgar et al., 2003; Bottoms, 1999; Liebling, 1999; Braswell, Montgomery, and Lombardo, 1994; Adams, 1992) have discussed the impact of "culture" on the level of order and control within the prison. However, much of the research identified in these reviews examined inmate (not staff) culture; and with few exceptions, no attempt was made to link changes in inmate (or staff) culture to changes in prison violence and disorder. Our evidence-based research review revealed that the link between institutional culture and prison violence and disorder has not been established. We know much more about the effects of prison programming and prison classification systems on prison violence and disorder than we do about the effects of prison culture, prison crowding, staffing levels, and a variety of other factors that have been linked to prison violence and disorder. Without a new emphasis on the importance of conducting independent, quality research in federal and state prisons, prison policy-makers will be forced to rely on inadequate information, not only about the nature and extent of the problem, but also about what constitutes "best practices" in this 60 billion dollar per year business.

The challenge for prison policy makers, administrators, and practitioners interested in culture change (whether inmate, staff, or management culture) is to develop an array of *evidence-based*, problem-solving strategies and then integrate these strategies into current inmate, staff, and management-based culture change initiatives (e.g., NIC's current Culture Change Initiatives). Our review has identified two strategies that have demonstrated effects on prison violence and disorder: (1) increase programming for inmates, and (2) improve the link between classification and treatment in existing prison classification systems. Ultimately, we suspect that specific problem-solving interventions designed to reduce the levels of violence and disorder in prison will need to address issues related to staff and inmate culture, as well as the prevailing management culture in the state or federal system at the time the strategy is introduced.

References

Adams, K. (1992). "Adjusting to Prison Life." in *Crime and Justice: A Review of Research*, Vol. 16. Chicago, University of Chicago Press.

American Correctional Association (ACA) (2004). *A 21st Century Workforce for America's Correctional Profession: Part One of a Three-Part Study Commissioned by the American Correctional Association.* Baltimore, MD: American Correctional Association.

Armstrong, T. A. (2002). "The Effect of Environment on the Behavior of Youthful Offenders: A Randomized Experiment." *Journal of Criminal Justice*, 30:19–28.

Austin, J. (2003). *Findings in Prison Classification and Risk Assessment.* Washington D.C.: U.S. Department of Justice, National Institute of Corrections.

Baro, A. (1999). "Effects of a Cognitive Restructuring Program on Inmate Institutional Behavior." *Criminal Justice and Behavior*, 26:466–484.

Beck, A., T. Hughes and Harrison (2004). "Data Collections for the Prison Rape Elimination Act of 2003." *Bureau of Justice Statistics Status Report* (June 30, 2004) Washington, D.C.: U.S. Department of Justice, Office of Justice Programs.

Bench, L. L. and T. D. Allen (2003). "Investigating the Stigma of Prison Classification: An Experimental Design." *Prison Violence* 83 (4): 367–382.

Berk, R. A., B. Kriegler, and J. Baek (2006). *Forecasting Dangerous Inmate Misconduct.* Berkeley: University of California, California Policy Research Center.

Borrill, J., A. Maden, A. Martin, T. Weaver, G. Stimson, M. Farrell, T. Barnes, R. Burnett, S. Miller, and D. Briggs (2003). "Substance Misuse among White and Black/Mixed Race Female Prisoners." *Prisoners' Drug Use and Treatment: Seven Research Studies (Home Office Research Study 267).* London: Home Office Research, Development and Statistics Directorate.

Bottoms, A. E. (1999). "Interpersonal Violence and Social Order in Prisons." In M. Tonry and J. Petersilia, Editors, *Prisons.* Chicago: The University of Chicago Press.

Braswell, M. C., R. H. Montgomery, Jr., and L. X. Lombardo, Editors (1994). *Prison Violence in America*, 2nd ed. Cincinnati: Anderson.

Briggs, C. S., J. L. Sundt, and T. C. Castellano (2003). "The Effect of Supermaximum Security Prisons on Aggregate Levels of Institutional Violence." *Criminology*, 41:1341–1376.

Bullock, T. (2003). "Changing Levels of Drug Use Before, During and After Imprisonment." *Prisoners' Drug Use and Treatment: Seven Research Studies (Home Office Research Study 267).* London: Home Office Research, Development and Statistics Directorate.

Bureau of Justice Statistics (BJS) (2000). *Correctional Populations in the United States, 1997.* Washington, D.C.: U.S. Department of Justice, Office of Justice Programs, Bureau of Justice Statistics.

Byrne, J. M. (2006). Testimony before the Commission on Safety and Abuse in America's Prisons. Public Hearing #4: Oversight, Accountability, and Other Issues. Los Angeles, CA, February 8–9.

Byrne, J. M. and F. S. Taxman (2006). "Crime Control Strategies and Community Change: Reframing the Surveillance vs. Treatment Debate." *Federal Probation*, 70(2): 3–12.

Byrne, J. M., F. S. Taxman, and D. Hummer (2005). *An Evaluation of the Implementation and Impact of NIC's Institutional Culture Initiative: Year 2 Update.* Prepared for the National Institute of Corrections, Federal Bureau of Prisons, U.S. Department of Justice. Project #S10002750000006.

Camp, S. D. and G. G. Gaes (2005). "Criminogenic Effects of the Prison Environment on Inmate Behavior: Some Experimental Evidence." *Crime and Delinquency*, 51: 425–442.

Camp, S. D., G. G. Gaes, N. P. Langan, and W. G. Saylor (2003). "The Influence of Prisons on Inmate Misconduct: A Multilevel Investigation." *Justice Quarterly* 20(3): 501–533.

Carroll, L. (2003). "Institutional Culture." Unpublished Paper.

Center for Civic Innovation (2000). *Transforming Probation Through Leadership: The 'Broken Windows Model'.* New York: Center for Civic Innovation at the Manhattan Institute and the Robert A. Fox Leadership Program at the University of Pennsylvania.

Commission on Safety and Abuse in America's Prisons (2006). *Confronting Confinement.* Washington D.C.: Vera Institute of Justice.

Cooke, D. J. (1989). "Containing Violent Prisoners: An Analysis of the Barlinnie Special Unit." *British Journal of Criminology*, 29:129–143.

Corrections Compendium (2002). "Riots, Disturbances, Violence, Assaults, and Escapes." *Corrections Compendium*, 27: 6–19.

Cullen, F. T. (2005). "The Twelve People Who Saved Rehabilitation: How the Science of Criminology Made a Difference." *Criminology*, 43:1–42.

Cunningham, M. D., J. R. Sorensen, and T. J. Reidy (2005). "An Actuarial Model for Assessment of Prison Violence Risk among Maximum Security Inmates." *Assessment*, 12: 40–49.

Dietz, E. F., D. J. O'Donnell, and F. R. Scarpitti (2003). "Therapeutic Communities and Prison Management: An Examination of the Effects of Operating an In-Prison Therapeutic Community on Levels of Institutional Disorder." *International Journal of Offender Therapy and Comparative Criminology*, 47: 210–223.

DiIulio, J. J. (1991). *No Escape: The Future of American Corrections.* New York: BasicBooks.

DiIulio, J. J. (1987). *Governing Prisons: A Comparative Study of Correctional Management.* New York: Free Press.

Duguid, S. (1997). "Confronting Worst Case Scenarios: Education and High Risk Offenders." *Journal of Correctional Education*, 48:153–159.

Dumond, R. (2000). "Inmate Sexual Assault: The Plague that Persists." *The Prison Journal*, 80: 407–414.

Edgar, K. "A Culture of Violence in England's Prison System: An Assessment of Causes and Solutions." *Journal of Offender Rehabilitation, this issue.*

Edgar, K. A. (2005). "Bullying, Victimization and Safer Prisons." *Probation Journal*, 52: 390–400.

Edgar, K., I. O'Donnell, and C. Martin (2003). *Prison Violence: The Dynamics of Conflict, Fear and Power.* Devon, UK: Willan Publishing.

Ekland-Olson, S. (1986). "Crowding, Social Control, and Prison Violence: Evidence from the Post-*Ruiz* Years in Texas." *Law and Society Review*, 20: 389–422.

Farabee, D. (2005). *Rethinking Rehabilitation: Why Can't We Reform Our Criminals?* Washington, D.C.: AEI Press, American Enterprise Institute.

Farrington, D. P. and B. C. Welsh (2005). "Randomized Experiments in Criminology: What Have We Learned in the Last Two Decades?" *Journal of Experimental Criminology*, 1: 9–38.

Ferrell, S. W., R. D. Morgan, and C. L. Winterowd (2000). "Job Satisfaction of Mental Health Professionals Providing Group Therapy in State Correctional Facilities." *International Journal of Offender Therapy and Comparative Criminology*, 44: 232–241.

Fischer, D. R. (2001). *Arizona Department of Corrections Security Threat Group Program Evaluation: Final Report.* Washington, DC: Department of Justice, Office of Justice Programs, National Institute of Justice.

Fleisher, M. (2006). "The Culture of Prison Sexuality and Rape." Unpublished Paper.

French, S. A. and P. Gendreau (2006). "Reducing Prison Misconducts: What Works!" *Criminal Justice and Behavior*, 33: 185–218.

Gaes, G. G. and A. Goldberg (2004). *Prison Rape: A Critical Review of Literature*. Working Paper, National Institute of Justice, Office at Justice Programs, Washington, D.C.

Gaes, G. G. and W. J. McGuire (1985). "Prison Violence: The Contribution of Crowding versus Other Determinants of Prison Assault Rates." *Journal of Research in Crime and Delinquency*, 22: 41–65.

Gaes, G. G., S. Wallace, E. Gilman, J. Klein-Saffran, and S. Suppa (2002). "The Influence of Prison Gang Affiliation on Violence and Other Prison Misconduct." *The Prison Journal*, 82: 359–385.

Gendreau, P., C. E. Goggin, and M. Law (1997). "Predicting Prison Misconducts." *Criminal Justice and Behavior*, 24: 414–431.

Gendreau, P. and D. Keyes (2001). "Making Prisons Safer and More Humane Environments." *Canadian Journal of Criminology*, 43: 123–130.

Gesch, C. B., S. M. Hammond, S. E. Hampson, A. Eves and M. J. Crowder (2002). "Influence of Supplementary Vitamins, Minerals and Essential Fatty Acids on the Antisocial Behaviour of Young Adult Prisoners." *British Journal of Psychiatry*, 181: 22–28.

Gillespie, W. (2005). "A Multilevel Model of Drug Abuse Inside Prison." *The Prison Journal*, 85: 223–246.

Gilligan, J. (1996). *Violence: Reflections on A National Epidemic*. New York: Random House.

Goffman, E. (1961). *Asylums: Essays on the Social Situations of Mental Patients and Other Inmates*. Oxford, UK: Doubleday (Anchor).

Gordon, J. A., L. J. Moriarty, and P.H. Grant (2003). "Juvenile Correctional Officers' Perceived Fear and Risk of Victimization: Examining Individual and Collective Levels of Victimization in Two Juvenile Correctional Centers in Virginia." *Criminal Justice and Behavior*, 30: 62–84.

Hardyman, P. L., J. Austin, and O. C. Tulloch (2002). *Revalidating External Prison Classification Systems: The Experience of Ten States and Model for Classification Reform*. Washington, D.C.: U.S. Department of Justice, National Institute of Corrections.

Harer, M. D. and N. P. Langan (2001). "Gender Differences in Predictors of Prison Violence: Assessing the Predictive Validity of a Risk Classification System." *Crime and Delinquency*, 47: 513–536.

Harrison, P. M. and A. J. Beck (2006). "Prison and Jail Inmates at Midyear 2005." *Bureau of Justice Statistics Bulletin, May 2006*. Washington, D.C.: U.S. Department of Justice, Office of Justice Programs.

Hensley, C., M. Koscheski, and R. Tewksbury (2003). "The Impact of Institutional Factors on Officially Reported Sexual Assaults in Prisons." *Sexuality and Culture*, 7: 16–26.

Hensley, C., R. Tewksbury, and T. Castle (2003). "Characteristics of Prison Sexual Assault Targets in Male Oklahoma Correctional Facilities." *Journal of Interpersonal Violence*, 18: 595–606.

Jacobson, M. (2005). *Downsizing Prisons*. New York: New York University Press.

Jiang, S. and M. Fisher-Giorlando (2002). "Inmate Misconduct: A Test of the Deprivation, Importation, and Structural Models." *The Prison Journal*, 82: 335–358.

Johnson, B. R. (1987). "Religiosity and Institutional Deviance: The Impact of Religious Variables upon Inmate Adjustment." *Criminal Justice Review*, 12: 21–30.

Kinlock, T. W., K. E. O'Grady, and T. E. Hanlon (2003). "The Effects of Drug Treatment on Institutional Behavior." *The Prison Journal*, 83: 257–276.

Langan, N. P. and B. M. M. Pelissier (2001). "The Effect of Drug Treatment on Inmate Misconduct in Federal Prisons." *Journal of Offender Rehabilitation*, 34:21–30.

Latessa, E. J. (2004). "The Challenge of Change: Correctional Programs and Evidence-Based Practices." *Criminology and Public Policy*, 3:547–559.

Lawrence, C. and K. Andrews (2004). "The Influence of Perceived Prison Crowding on Male Inmates' Perception of Aggressive Events." *Aggressive Behavior*, 30:273–283.

Liebling, A. (2005). *Prisons and Their Moral Performance: A Study of Values, Quality, and Prison Life*. New York: Oxford University Press.

Liebling, A. (1999). "Prison Suicide and Prisoner Coping." In M. Tonry and J. Petersilia, Editors, *Prisons.* Chicago, IL: The University of Chicago Press, pp. 283–359.

Liebling, A. and S. Maruna (2005). "Introduction: The Effects of Imprisonment Revisited" pp. 1–29 in A. Liebling and S. Maruna, editors, *The Effects of Imprisonment* Devon, UK: Willan Publishing.

LIS, Inc. (2000). *Sexual Misconduct in Prison: Law, Agency Response, and Prevention.* Washington, D.C.: U.S. Department of Justice.

MacKenzie, D. L. and J. W. Shaw (1990). "Inmate Adjustment and Change During Shock Incarceration: The Impact of Correctional Boot Camp Programs." *Justice Quarterly,* 7:125–150.

Mair J. S., S. Frattaroli, and S. P. Teret (2003). "New Hope for Victims of Prison Sexual Assault." *The Journal of Law, Medicine & Ethics,* 31:602–606.

Maruna, S. and H. Toch (2005). "The Impact of Incarceration on the Desistance Process." In J. Travis and C. Visher, Editors, *Prisoner Reentry and Public Safety in America.* New York: Cambridge University Press.

McCorkle, R. C., T. D. Miethe, and K. A. Drass (1995). "The Roots of Prison Violence: A Test of the Deprivation, Management, and 'Not-So-Total' Institution Models." *Crime and Delinquency* 41(3): 317–331.

McShane, M. D. and F. P. Williams III (1990). "Old and Ornery: The Disciplinary Experiences of Elderly Prisoners." *International Journal of Offender Therapy and Comparative Criminology,* 34:197–212.

Moos, R. (1968). "The Assessment of the Social Climates of Correctional Institutions." *Journal of Research in Crime and Delinquency,* 5:174–188.

Morgan, R. D., C. L. Winterowd, and D. R. Fuqua (1999). "The Efficacy of an Integrated Theoretical Approach to Group Psychotherapy for Male Inmates." *Journal of Contemporary Psychotherapy,* 29:203–222.

National Center for State Courts (2003). *Health Insurance Portability and Accountability Act of 1996; Standards for Privacy of Individually Identifiable Health Information. Applicability to the Courts: An Initial Assessment.* Denver, CO: National Center for State Courts in conjunction with the National Governors Association Center for Best Practices.

National Institute of Corrections (NIC) (2003). Institutional Culture Initiative, program meeting, Washington, D.C.

National Research Council (2004). *Fairness and Effectiveness in Policing.* Washington, D.C.: National Academy Press.

National Research Council (2001). *What's Changing in Prosecution?: Report of a Workshop.* Washington, D.C.: National Academy Press.

O'Donnell, I. and K. Edgar (1998). "Routine Victimization in Prisons." *Howard Journal of Criminal Justice* 37: 266–279.

Patrick, S. (1998). "Differences in Inmate-Inmate and Inmate-Staff Altercations: Examples from a Medium Security Prison." *Social Science Journal,* 35:253–263.

Pattavina, A., J. M. Byrne, and L. Garcia (2006). "An Examination of Citizen Involvement in Crime Prevention in High-Risk versus Low-to-Moderate Risk Neighborhoods." *Crime and Delinquency,* 52:203–231.

Pelissier, B. (1991) "The Effects of a Rapid Increase in a Prison Population: A Pre- and Posttest Study." *Criminal Justice and Behavior,* 18:427–447.

Pelissier, B., S. D. Camp, and M. Motivans (2003) "Staying in Treatment: How Much Difference Is There from Prison to Prison?" *Psychology of Addictive Behaviors,* 17:134–141.

Porporino, F. J. (1986) "Managing Violent Individuals in Correctional Settings." *Journal of Interpersonal Violence,* 1:213–237.

Porporino, F. J., P. D. Doherty, and T. Sawatsky (1987) "Characteristics of Homicide Victims and Victimizations in Prisons: A Canadian Historical Perspective." *International Journal of Offender Therapy and Comparative Criminology,* 31:125–135.

Prendergast, M. L., D. Farabee, J. Cartier, and S. Henkin (2002) "Involuntary Treatment within a Prison Setting: Impact on Psychological Change during Treatment." *Criminal Justice and Behavior,* 29:5–26.

Reisig, M. D. (2002) "Administrative Control and Inmate Homicide." *Homicide Studies*, 6:84–103.

Reisig, M. D (1998) "Rates of Disorder in Higher-Custody State Prisons: A Comparative Analysis of Managerial Practices." *Crime and Delinquency*, 41(2): 229–244.

Riveland, C. (1999) "Prison Management Trends, 1975–2025." In M. Tonry and J. Petersilia, Editors, *Prisons*. Chicago: The University of Chicago Press, pp.163–203.

Ruback, R. B. and T. S. Carr (1993) "Prison Crowding over Time: The Relationship of Density and Changes in Density to Infraction Rates." *Criminal Justice and Behavior*, 20:130–148.

Ryan, T. A. and K. A. McCabe (1994). "Mandatory versus Voluntary Prison Education and Academic Achievement." *The Prison Journal*, 74:450–461.

Sampson, R. and Bean, L. (2006). "Cultural Mechanisms and Killing Fields: A Revised Theory of Community-level Racial Inequality." In Peterson, Krivo, and Hagan, Editors, *The Many Colors of Crime: Inequalities of Race, Ethnicity, and Crime in America*. New York: New York University Press. (Retrieved from Robert Sampson's website).

Sampson, R. J., H. MacIndoe, D. McAdam, and S. Weffer-Elizondo (2005). "Civil Society Reconsidered: The Durable Nature and Community Structure of Collective Civic Action." *American Journal of Sociology*, 111:673–714.

Sherman, L.W., D. Gottfredson, D. MacKenzie, J. Eck, P. Reuter, and S. Bushway (1997). *Preventing Crime: What Works, What Doesn't, What's Promising: A Report to the United States Congress*. Washington, D.C.: U.S. Department of Justice, Office of Justice Programs, National Institute of Justice.

Snacken, S. (2005) "Forms of Violence and Regimes in Prison: Report of Research in Belgian Prisons." In A. Liebling and S. Maruna, Editors, *The Effects of Imprisonment*. Portland, Oregon: Willan Publishing, pp. 306–339.

Sparks, R. (1995). "Situational and Social Approaches to the Prevention of Disorder in Long-Term Prisons." In T. Flanagan, Editor, *Long Term Imprisonment: Policy, Science and Correctional Practice*. Thousand Oaks, CA: Sage.

Sparks, R., A. Bottoms, and W. Hay (1996). *Prisons and the Problem of Order*. Oxford: Clarendon Press.

Stephan, J. and J. Karberg (2003). *The Census of State and Federal Correctional Facilities*. Washington, D.C.: U.S Department of Justice.

Struckman-Johnson, C. J., and D. L. Struckman-Johnson (2000). "Sexual Coercion Rates in Seven Midwestern Prison Facilities for Men." *Prison Journal*, 80: 279–390.

Sykes, G.M. (1958). *The Society of Captives: A Study of Maximum Security Prison*. Princeton, NJ: Princeton University Press.

Tartaro, C. (2002). "The Impact of Density on Prison Violence." *Journal of Criminal Justice*, 30:499–510.

The Lifers Public Safety Steering Committee of the State Correctional Institution. (2004). "Ending the Culture of Street Crime." *The Prison Journal*, 84 (supp.):48s–68s.

Toch, H. (1977). *Living in Prison: The Ecology of Survival*. New York: Free Press.

Useem, B. and A. M. Piehl (2006). "Prison Buildup and Disorder." *Punishment and Society*, 8:87–115.

Useem, B. and M. D. Reisig (1999). "Collective Action in Prisons: Protests, Disturbances, and Riots." *Criminology*, 37:735–759.

Walrath, C. (2001). "Evaluation of an Inmate-Run Alternatives to Violence Project." *Journal of Interpersonal Violence*, 16:697–711.

Walters, G. D. (2003). "Changes in Criminal Thinking and Identity in Novice and Experienced Inmates: Prisonization Revisited." *Criminal Justice and Behavior*, 30:399–421.

Walters, G. D (1999). "Short-Term Outcome of Inmates Participating in the Lifestyle Change Program." *Criminal Justice and Behavior*, 26:322–337.

Walters, G. D (1998). "Time Series and Correlational Analyses of Inmate-Initiated Assaultive Incidents in a Large Correctional System." *International Journal of Offender Therapy and Comparative Criminology*, 42(2): 124–132.

Warren, J. I., S. Hurt, A. B. Loper, and P. Chauhan (2004). "Exploring Prison Adjustment among Female Inmates: Issues of Measurement and Prediction." *Criminal Justice and Behavior*, 31:624–645.

Welch, M. (2004). *Corrections: A Critical Approach* (2nd ed.). New York: McGraw-Hill.

Welsh, B. C., and D. P. Farrington (2001). Toward an Evidence-Based Approach to Preventing Crime. *Annals of the American Academy of Political and Social Science*, 578:158–173.

Welsh, B. C., and D. P. Farrington (2000). "Monetary Costs and Benefits of Crime Prevention Programs." In M. Tonry, Editor, *Crime and Justice: A Review of Research, Vol.27*. Chicago: University of Chicago Press.

Wener, R. (2006). "Effectiveness of the Direct Supervision System of Correctional Design and Management." *Criminal Justice and Behavior*, 33:392–410.

Williams, J. L., D. G. Rodeheaver, and D. W. Huggins (1999). "A Comparative Evaluation of a New Generation Jail." *American Journal of Criminal Justice*, 23:223–246.

Wilson, D. B., L. A. Bouffard, and D. L. MacKenzie (2005). "A Quantitative Review of Structured, Group-Oriented, Cognitive-Behavioral Programs for Offenders." *Criminal Justice and Behavior*, 32:172–204.

Wooldredge, J. D. (1998). "Inmate Lifestyles and Opportunities for Victimization." *Journal of Research in Crime and Delinquency*, 35:480–502.

Wooldredge, J., T. Griffin, and T. Pratt (2001). "Considering Hierarchical Models for Research on Inmate Behavior: Predicting Misconduct with Multilevel Data." *Justice Quarterly*, 18:203–231.

Wormith, J. S. (1984). "Attitude and Behavior Change of Correctional Clientele." *Criminology*, 22:595–618.

Wortley, R. (2002). *Situational Prison Control: Crime Prevention in Correctional Institutions*. Cambridge, UK: Cambridge University Press.

Wright, K. N. (2005). "Designing a National Performance Measurement System." *The Prison Journal*, 85:368–393.

Wright, K. N. (1986). *Improving Correctional Classification Through a Study of the Placement of Inmates in Environmental Settings*. Binghamton, NY: Center for Social Analysis, State University of New York at Binghamton.

Wright, K. N., with J. Brisbee and P. Hardyman (2003). *Defining and Measuring Corrections Performance: Final Report*. Washington, D.C.: U.S. Department of Justice.

Appendix A

Empirical Research on 'Causes' of Prison Violence & Disorder, 1984–2006

TABLE 3A.1 *Highlights of Recent Research on Prison Culture and Institutional Violence and Disorder*

Author (year)	Scientific Method Score	Key Findings	Quantitative Evidence
Byrne, Taxman & Hummer (2005)	3	• Total incidents at study facilities in the National Institute of Corrections' Institutional Culture Initiative decreased by an average of more than 100 incidents in a 2-year period during which culture change initiatives were implemented. Disorder violations were most affected—violent incidents less so.	Time series analysis of total incidents (May 2003–March 2005) $t = -5.804$ ($p = .000$)
Liebling (2006)	2	• Results indicate that facilities successfully implementing culture change strategies show more positive perceptions among staff and correspondingly lower levels of anxiety, distress, and self-injury among inmates.	• Composite Prisoner Dimensions (2002) (scoring = 1–5): *Care dimension* 'good' implementers = 2.87 'bad' implementers = 2.78 difference ns *Distress dimension* 'good' implementers = 2.81 'bad' implementers = 3.00 difference significant $p < .01$ • Composite prisoner dimensions (2004) (scoring = 1–5): *Care dimension:* 'good' implementers = 3.10 'bad' implementers = 2.78 difference significant $p < .001$ *Distress dimension:* 'good' implementers = 3.05 'bad' implementers = 2.90 difference significant $p < .05$

TABLE 3A.2 Highlights of Recent Research on Prison Crowding and Institutional Violence and Disorder

Author (year)	Scientific Method Score	Key Findings	Quantitative Evidence
Gillespie (2005)	1	• Survey of over 1,000 inmates in 30 correctional institutions in three Southern states. Aggregate measures of crowding and history of prior street drug use were positively associated with drug abuse inside prisons.	• Significant HLM coefficients for select independent variables and mean drug use: Previous use of illegal drugs = 0.481 Aggregate inmate perceptions of overcrowding = 0.692 Inmate age = −0.053 Inmate race = −0.722 Years incarcerated = 0.041
Lawrence & Andrews (2004)	1	• British study of perceptions of aggressive behavior among a sample ($n = 79$) of inmates from one institution. Results show that crowding is significantly correlated with feelings of arousal, stress, and a reduction in psychological well-being. Inmates experiencing crowding were also more likely to perceive behavior as aggressive and violent. • Inmates from crowded facilities also were most sensitive to personal space infringement as scored on a four-item scale.	• Significant correlations with crowding: Perceived aggression − .27 Personal space preferences − .43 Stress − .45 Fatigue − .26
Tartaro (2002)	1	• Spatial density (inmate count divided by rated capacity) was examined as a correlate of inmate-on-inmate and inmate-on-staff assault. Spatial density and assaults on inmates were *negatively* associated, while transiency was positively and	• Significant multiple regression coefficients for inmate-on-inmate assaults: −Spatial density = −.144 • Significant multiple regression coefficients for inmate-on-staff assaults:

(continued)

TABLE 3A.2 *(Continued)*

Author (year)	Scientific Method Score	Key Findings	Quantitative Evidence
		significantly associated with assaults on staff.	–spatial density = –.128 –number of bookings (transiency) – .109
Wooldredge, Griffin, & Pratt (2001)	1	• Data from three state correctional systems were analyzed to disentangle the associations of individual and situational factors influencing prison violence and misconduct. Results show crowding to be a consistent predictor of individual level misconduct and support the notion that prison crowding may exacerbate violence problems by increasing the physical proximity of inmates to one another.	• Significant HLM coefficients between crowding and misconduct: New York–.65 Washington–2.47 Vermont–1.62
Ruback & Carr (1993)	1	• Data from 65 facilities (state prisons, county jails, adult and juvenile) examined by month over a 10-year period. Institutional density and rate of change in the population both had significant effects on violent and nonviolent infractions. • Effect sizes for the crowding measures were small; multivariate analysis indicated that prison administration and management issues were far stronger predictors of inmate misconduct.	• Significant F statistics related to violent infractions: System factors–4.04 Institution factors–55.07 Size of prison–51.86 Crowding factors–4.57 • Significant F statistics related to nonviolent infractions: System factors–25.27 Institution factors–50.40 Size of prison–74.01 Crowding factors–11.10
Pelissier (1991)	1	• Pre- and post-test analysis (no control or comparison group) of the impact on rule infractions after an increase in population density at one federal prison.	• Rule Infraction rates for 6-month periods before, during, and after population increase: *Before* 1/85–6/85 = .07 7/85–12/85 = .10

		• Overall, results indicate no difference in rule infraction rates after population density increased at the facility.	*During* 1/86–6/86 = .08 *After* 7/86–12/86 = .08 1/87–6/87 = .09 7/87–12/87 = .08

Porporino (1986) 1

• Data from Canadian correctional facilities from 1980 to 1984 show that prison crowding is negatively associated with violence and disorder. Author hypothesizes that necessary security controls at crowded institutions eliminate many opportunities for assaults to take place.

• These data also indicate that transiency within institutions is significantly correlated with assaults, demonstrating that a stable population is a necessary prerequisite to stemming institutional violence.

• Significant correlations pertaining to crowding:
Assaults on inmates = .61
Assaults on staff = .59
Self-directed violence = .64
Other security incidents = .52

• Significant correlations pertaining to transience:
Assaults on inmates = .58
Assaults on staff = .48
Other security incidents = .44

Gaes & McGuire (1985) 1

• Examines the impact of crowding, age, and prisonization on assaults incarcerated in 19 Federal prisons over a nearly 3-year period ($n = 627$).

• Controlling for numerous situational variables, crowding was by far the most influential variable in the predictor models.

• While significant predictors, inmate-on-staff assaults level out at 60–65% overcrowded, while inmate–inmate assaults continue to rise in proportion to percent of overcrowding at a facility.

• Significant TOBIT coefficients for crowding variables and type of assault by inmates:
–other inmate, no weapon = .05
–other; inmate, weapon = .02
–staff, no weapon = .05
–staff, weapon = .07

TABLE 3A.3 Highlights of Recent Research on Prison Staffing and Institutional Violence and Disorder

Author (year)	Scientific Method Score	Key Findings	Quantitative Evidence
Camp, Gaes, Langan, & Saylor (2003)	1	• Study of a large sample of inmates across facilities in the United States demonstrate that situational variables pertaining to staff and prison environment affect levels of misconduct in addition to, and separate from, individual-level characteristics of inmates.	• Significant odds-ratio coefficients (95% l.c.) between institutional level variables and all forms of misconduct include % white staff (1.01), % female staff (1.02) Percent of staff on the job less than 1 year was significant (1.03) for security-related incidents or misconducts
Hensley, Koscheski, & Tewksbury (2003)	1	• Sexual assault in prison significantly associated with size of the inmate population and security level. More prisoners in higher security facilities equates to more reports of sexual assaults. • Overcrowding, Inmate-Staff Ratio, and Conjugal Visitation Programs were not associated with in-facility sexual assault.	• Significant odds-ratios: inmates–1.00; Security Level–3.60
Useem & Reisig (1999)	1	• Cross-sectional survey of prison executives assessing factors related to inappropriate collective action by inmates. In terms of riot occurrence, poor morale among staff was significantly associated with rioting. In terms of lower-level inmate disturbances, as the percentage of upheld administrative sanctions decreased, the likelihood of inmate disturbance increased. • Participation in prohibited groups (e.g., prison gangs) was positively associated with disturbances.	• Significant logistic regression coefficients for riot occurrences: Poor staff morale–0.37 • Significant logistic regression coefficients for inmate disturbances: Percent administrative sanctions upheld–3.30 Prohibited group activity–0.09
Patrick (1998)	1	• Inmates surveyed attributed inmate-on-inmate assault to a violent subculture of offenders within the population. Minor incidents were perceived as a means of establishing an inmate's position in the subcultural hierarchy. • Assaults on staff were perceived to have occurred when a staff member abuses their authority and inmates are	• Inmate perceptions of violence and assault: Frequency of inmate–inmate altercations: Monthly–43.8% Weekly–37.5% Daily–9.4%

Walters (1998)	1	'forced' to strike back with the limited means at their disposal. • Nine years of BOP data analyzed within one large correctional system showed an inverse relationship between crowding, staff experience, and total assaults. Author attributes these findings to heightened security measures taken in prisons to combat overcrowding issues and staff inexperience.	How often corrections staff threatens use of force: Always–6.3% Usually–12.5% Sometimes–21.9% Seldom–21.9% Never–37.5% • Significant linear regression coefficients on predictors and total assaults: Percent young inmates–3.60 Staff inexperience–.76 Population density–3.14
McCorkle, Miethe, & Drass (1995)	1	• Data from the 1984 and 1990 census of adult prisons found that poor prison management (as indicated by guard–inmate ratio, guard turnover rate, white–black correctional staff ratio, program involvement, and institutional size) is positively correlated with assaults against both inmates and staff. • Poor management was not associated significantly with large-scale violence such as inmate rioting.	• Significant OLS coefficients of indicators associated with assaults on both inmates and staff: –white–black guard ratio = .11 & .19 (respectively); program involvement = –.11 & –.12; security level = .41 & .25
Ekland-Olson (1986)	1	• Analysis of variants of prison violence (inmate-on-inmate, inmate-on-staff, homicide) controlling for crowding and the social control/ordering of prison life. Results indicate social control factors are more closely associated with inmate-on-inmate violence, while crowding is only marginally correlated with inmate-on-staff assaults.	• Significant correlations, inmate-on-staff assaults: –& inmate to staff ratio–.66 • Significant correlations, inmate-on-inmate assaults: –& percent of inmates classified as habitual offenders–.45 –& median sentence–.61 –& percent of inmates in segregation class II (high repeat offenders or higher–.55)

TABLE 3A.4 Highlights of Recent Research on Prison Program Quality and Levels and Institutional Violence and Disorder

Author (year)	Scientific Method Score	Key Findings	Quantitative Evidence
Armstrong (2002)	5	• Randomized experimental design evaluating the effectiveness of a therapeutic-based treatment paradigm for youthful offenders that provided opportunities for personal development and advancement. • Increasing amounts of time in the program were significantly associated with decreases in disciplinary violations.	• Significant posttest beta coefficients for program participants: Total disciplinary violations: $-.0041$ Serious aggressive violations: $-.0058$ Serious rule violations: $-.0099$
Wormith (1984)	5	• Randomized experimental design evaluating the impact of group discussions led by a trained or volunteer moderator and other concurrent activities (either a self-control program or recreational activity), representing four experimental groups total as well as a nonparticipant control group. Results indicate those participants in the trained-moderator group discussions plus self-control program improves their institutional behavior significantly in comparison to the other four groups in the study.	• Significant mean differences of trained-moderator plus self-control program participants vs. other four study groups: Incidence of disciplinary offenses– $F_{(1, 30)} = 4.47, p < .05$ Interpersonal behavior ratings by staff– $F_{(1, 30)} = 6.58, p < .05$
Morgan, Winterowd, & Fuqua (1999)	4	• Experimental design related to the efficacy of an integrated theoretical approach to group psychotherapy for male state prison inmates. Pre- and posttest analysis showed no significant differences in the disciplinary records of treatment vs. control group inmates.	• Pre- and posttest results of disciplinary records for treatment and control groups: *Mean # of disciplinary actions (SD)* Prestest: $T = .80 (1.70), C = .31 (.79)$ Posttest: $T = .75 (1.21), C = .13 (.34)$
Walrath (2001)	3	• Quasi-experiment evaluating an Alternatives to Violence Project (AVP) designed to reduce inmate violence.	• Incident rate ratio between treatment and comparison group at 6 month follow-up:

		Preliminary impact evaluation of the AVP demonstrated a significant reduction in confrontations reported by inmates in the treatment group as well as a positive impact on anger. However, no significant reduction occurred in the actual reduction of confrontations turning violent.	.432 ($p < .0005$); treatment group inmates reported nearly half as many confrontations vs. comparison group self-reports.
Baro (1999)	3	Quasi-experiment followed 41 inmates through Phase I of the cognitive restructuring program 'Strategies for Thinking Productively' (STP). Another 41 were followed for the same time period who had completed Phase II of STP. A comparison group of 41 was also included comprised of inmates who had completed programming other than STP. Results show that Phase I of the STP program is significantly associated with reductions in failures to obey orders while Phase II of STP produced fewer inmate-on-inmate assaults.	• Significant chi-square results: Phase I STP & disobeying a direct order = 7.093; Phase II STP & assault = 6.354; Phase II & number of days in disciplinary detention = 6.037
Walters (1999)	3	Impact evaluation of a 'Lifestyle Change Program' implemented at one federal correctional facility. Those inmates who completed the program ($n = 291$) received significantly fewer disciplinary reports vs. comparison group of inmates who were transferred or released before the program was initiated.	• Correlates of normalized annual rate of disciplinary infraction measure (control = 0, treatment = 1): group membership and infractions–$r = -.25$ ($p = .000$)
Dietz, O'Connell, & Scarpitti (2003)	2	Evaluation of therapeutic community initiative at one medium/high security state prison. When contrasted with a comparison group of inmates from the same institution, treatment group inmates had significantly fewer disciplinary infractions (violent and nonviolent) and a more positive perception of their environment.	• Infraction rates by group: *Total infractions* $T = 28.81$, $C = 109.29$ *Violent infractions* $T = 7.63$, $C = 49.0$ *Nonviolent infractions* $T = 41.53$, $C = 129.42$

(continued)

TABLE 3A.4 *(Continued)*

Author (year)	Scientific Method Score	Key Findings	Quantitative Evidence
Kinlock, O'Grady, & Hanlon (2003)	2	• Examines the effect of drug treatment on the behavior of drug-involved offenders during incarceration and subsequent in-facility misconduct violations (*n* = 170). • Cognitive-behavioral treatment associated with reduced likelihood of reclassification to more secure facility.	• Significant odds ratios associated with reclassification to more secure facility: Treatment group participation–3.10 Passive-aggressive personality–1.04 Self-defeating personality– .05
Pelissier, Camp, & Motivans (2003)	2	• Nationwide sample of federal inmates completing drug treatment programs in-facility found that younger male inmates, those diagnosed with antisocial personality disorder (ASP), and those with a violent background were most likely to get a disciplinary discharge from treatment programs and were more likely to receive misconduct violations overall than were inmates successfully completing the programs or voluntarily withdrawing.	• Significant HLM coefficients for predictors of disciplinary discharge: Age–0.055 Sex–0.845 Past violence–0.596 Diagnosis of ASP–0.470
Prendergast, Farabee, Cartier, & Henkin (2002)	2	• Quasi-experimental design analyzing the impact of in-facility drug treatment programs on inmate psychological and social functioning. Significant changes were observed on most measures of psychological functioning, fewer changes on social functioning (including hostility and social conformity), regardless of whether the inmate volunteered for treatment or treatment was mandated.	• Change in psychological functioning of involuntary treatment group from assessment to prerelease stage: Self-esteem–7.7% Anxiety–7.8% Decision-making–5.4%
Ryan & McCabe (1994)	2	• Regression analysis indicates that educational achievement of inmates does not differ if such programs are voluntary or mandatory. Voluntary programs only average a 9% rate of participation.	• Odds ratios for participation status and achievement: voluntary–1.331 mandatory–1.000

		• Authors argue that mandatory education fulfills the ACA mission of making prisons safer for staff, offenders, and visitors, although evidence is not provided.
MacKenzie & Shaw (1990)	2	• Evaluation of voluntary participation in a shock incarceration program in Louisiana. Program participants had more 'prosocial' attitudes entering the facility when compared with the incarcerated population not participating in the program. However, while attitudes of the comparison group remained static, the attitudes of the treatment group grew more 'prosocial' as time spent in the program increased.	• Significant mean scores on prosocial scales for shock incarceration participants vs. comparison group at time 3: Social maladjustment: $T = 106.4, C = 96.7$ Asocial: $T = 48.2, C = 42.3$ Alienation: $T = 44.4, C = 38.9$
Langan & Pelissier (2001)	1	• Federal prison inmates successfully completing substance abuse program in-facility were 74% less likely to engage in misconduct over a 14-month period vs. comparison group. • Effects were similar for both male and female inmates.	• Significant logistic-regression coefficients for select independent variables and receiving misconduct violations: Received treatment $= -1.362$ Months in prison after completing treatment $= 0.070$ Age in years at completion of treatment $= -0.051$
Ferrell, Morgan, & Winterowd (2000)	1	• Survey assessment of job satisfaction among mental health providers shows that high levels of satisfaction are correlated with institutional culture variables such as adequate support from administration, feeling safe when facilitating groups, and rehabilitation as an overall institutional goal.	• Mean item scores significantly correlating with job satisfaction: Adequate support from prison administration–4.19 Rehabilitation as an overall institution goal–3.64 Feeling safe when facilitating groups–5.73
Duguid (1997)	1	• A study of 654 Canadian inmates demonstrates that inmates completing academic credit while incarcerated recidivated significantly less than their predicted recidivism rates would indicate, regardless of academic 'performance' (i.e., grades they received in courses).	• Predicted and actual percentages of inmate success on parole: –earning A/B in courses: $p = 36\%, a = 53\%$ –earning C/D: $p = 35\%, a = 40\%$

(continued)

TABLE 3A.4 *(Continued)*

Author (year)	Scientific Method Score	Key Findings	Quantitative Evidence
		• Those inmates furthering their education after release improved on predicted recidivism rates by 84%, while those who did not further their education returned to predicted recidivism rates.	• Predicted & actual percentages of inmate success on parole: –furthering education: $p = 36\%$, $a = 66\%$ –not furthering education: $p = 36\%$, $a = 37\%$
Cooke (1989)	1	• Case study and quantitative analysis of the regime of the Barlinnie Special Unit, which houses violent and disruptive prisoners. Although only two dozen prisoners had completed Barlinnie's full program at the time of evaluation, the author concludes that the regime significantly reduced assaults and serious incidents.	• Observed and expected frequency of misconducts within the Barlinnie Special Unit: Assault: Observed = 2 Expected = 105 Serious incidents: Observed = 7 Expected = 49
Johnson (1987)	1	• Study examines the affect of religiosity upon institutional offending using a composite indicator (self-reported religiosity, prison chaplain's perception of inmate's religiosity, and religious service attendance records from the facility) upon time spent in disciplinary confinement. While religiosity has been shown to be inversely related to deviance in general, religiosity was not associated with disciplinary action among inmates in this study.	• Correlations of select measures of inmate religiosity and disciplinary confinement: Inmate's institutional church Attendance = −.024 Chaplain's perception of inmate religiosity = .017 Inmate's self-reported religiosity = .012

TABLE 3A.5 Highlights of Recent Research on Prison Classification/Placement Practices and Institutional Violence and Disorder

Author (year)	Scientific Method Score	Key Findings	Quantitative Evidence
Camp & Gaes (2005)	5	• Percentages of inmates with misconduct violations not significantly different between lower and higher security facilities. • Inmate misconduct not more prevalent in higher security facilities.	• % of inmates receiving any misconduct violations: Level 1 = 64, Level 3 = 60 • % of inmates receiving serious misconduct violations: Level 1 = 33, Level 3 = 36
Bench & Allen (2003)	5	• Randomized experiment in which the 'experimental' group was inmates classified as maximum security and then reclassified to medium-security facilities. Two control groups of medium-security inmates remaining in medium security and maximum-security classifications remaining in maximum security. • Mean differences in number of disciplinary actions for the three groups not statistically significant.	• Mean weighted disciplinaries: Experimental group = 2.30 Control group 1 (medium sec.) = 2.02 Control group 2 (max. sec.) = 2.12
Berk, Kriegler & Baek (2006)	3	• 9,662 inmates from California Department of Corrections randomly assigned to either the traditional CDC classification scheme or a revised classification system to better predict serious misconduct. Inmates records of misconduct were then followed for a 2-year period following intake • Results indicate that only 3% of inmates in the study committed a serious misconduct during the study period and that the new classification scheme had a rate of "false positives" ten times higher than "false negatives." The overall accuracy rate for the predictor model was 50%.	• Model error for predicting serious misconducts: $1 - 0.487 = 51.3\%$ accuracy • Model error for predicting no serious misconducts: $1 - 0.216 = 78.4\%$ accuracy

(continued)

TABLE 3A.5 *(Continued)*

Author (year)	Scientific Method Score	Key Findings	Quantitative Evidence
Bullock (2003)	2	• A small minority of sampled inmates (*n* = 302 pretest, *n* = 227 posttest) who underwent mandatory drug treatment while incarcerated in Great Britain reported that the program deterred them from using drugs while in custody. • Slight decrease in post-release drug use among offenders who served a short term of imprisonment vs. pre-incarceration levels.	• 100% reported drug use prior to entering prison; 59% reported using drugs while incarcerated; 77% reported drug use post-release.
Warren, Hurt, Loper, & Chauhan (2004)	1	• Findings suggest that a two-factor measure bests measures the prison adjustment of female inmates as opposed to the three-factor model forwarded by Wright (1985). Prisoners with close interpersonal ties to the 'outside' (such as a spouse, visits from children, and a supportive family) adjusted more readily to prison life than women without such ties.	• Correlations between those inmates reporting a high degree of 'conflict' (HC) within the institution vs. those reporting low 'conflict' (LC) and various misconduct violations: Violence–HC = .22, LC = .02; Nonviolent–HC = .29, LC = .02; Rule violation–HC = .32, LC = .07;
Hardyman, Austin, & Tulloch (2002)	1	• Study examined classification schemes from ten U.S. state departments of corrections. Results indicate similar risk predictors for both male and female inmates–seven	• Significant multiple regression betas for (risk predictors) male and female inmates: Severity of prior offense–0.47

factors were significant at the 99.9% level of confidence with prison assault irrespective of gender.

Severity of current offense–0.61
Number of prior felony convictions–0.37
Current age–0.30
Stability factors–0.14
Escape history–0.14
History of institutional violence–0.10

Harer & Langan (2001)   1

- Data from federal prison inmate populations between 1991 and 1998 allowed a comparison of classification schemes for male and female inmate. Results indicate that while females are significantly less likely to receive a violence-related misconduct, the same risk classification instrument is equally predictive for both genders.
- Risk predictors at intake include educational attainment and (possibly) substance abuse history, work history, relationship skills, and peer associations.

- Violence-related parameter estimates
  ($n = 202,532$):
  Type of detainer–0.048
  Severity of offense–0.083
  History of escapes–0.051
  History of violence–0.086
  Precommitment status–0.224
  Age at admission–0.417
  Criminal history category–0.165
  Education at Admission–0.090

TABLE 3A.6   Highlights of Recent Research on Prison Management Practices and Institutional Violence and Disorder

Author (year)	Scientific Method Score	Key Findings	Quantitative Evidence
Reisig (1998)	2	• No significant differences in levels of misconduct by managerial style (highly formal vs. less restrictive). • Misconduct measured subjectively as perceptions of institutional staff.	• Mean Serious disorder levels by management style: –Responsibility Model = 4.21 (1.1); –Consensus Model = 3.91 (1.3); –Control Model = 5.20 (1.9)
Gordon, Moriarty, & Grant (2003)	1	• Comparison of juvenile correctional officers' fear of crime and risk of victimization at two detention facilities; one facility categorized as more 'therapeutic' while the other more 'traditional'. Staff fear and perceived risk of victimization were not significantly different.	• Mean fear scores: Therapeutic = 2.31 (1.05), Traditional = 2.28 (1.01) • Mean risk scores: Therapeutic = 2.34 (1.08) Traditional = 2.53 (1.11)
Reisig (2002)	1	• Examination of correlates in-facility homicides in nearly 300 state prisons in the United States. Data indicate prison homicides are strongly correlated with management–staff conflict and prison gang activity.	• Significant binomial regression coefficients associated with homicide: Prohibited groups–0.09 Administrative sanctions upheld by management–1.45
Gendreau & Keyes (2001)	*	• Review of policy recommendations from selected research on prison misconduct. Analysis shows that the most frequent recommendation was 'increased treatment, programming, and/or services' (67% of studies) followed by 'use of segregation' (42%), with improved management style a close third (41%).	

TABLE 3A.7 *Highlights of Recent Research on the Situational Context of Prisons and Institutional Violence and Disorder*

Author (year)	Scientific Method Score	Key Findings	Quantitative Evidence
Briggs, Sundt, & Castellano (2003)	3	• Effects of supermax prisons on levels of institutional violence are examined. Three states with supermax facilities were selected as well as one state as a comparison group. Time-series analyses provide no support for the notion that supermax prisons reduce levels of inmate-on-inmate violence, and mixed support for whether such facilities increase staff safety—one state experienced no changes in staff assaults, one state showed an increase in staff assaults, the other a decrease. The comparison state demonstrated no fluctuations in either type of assault during the study time frame.	• Significant results from the study: Arizona–temporary increase of 6.58 staff injuries, $t = 3.08$ Illinois–permanent decrease equal to 21 fewer staff assaults, $t = 2.57$
Walters (2003)	2	• Study using indicators from Cameron's Social Identity as a Criminal (SIC) questionnaire demonstrated that incarceration produces similar prisonization effects in both novice and experienced inmates. • Scale scores related to in-group ties (e.g., bonding with other inmates) and in-group affect (pride in criminal label) increase during time spent in prison.	• Significant F statistics in ANOVA runs: In-group ties–13.40 In-group affect–8.83
Useem & Piehl (2006)	1	• Analysis of prison incidents over a three-decade period demonstrates that the 'prison buildup' (i.e., more inmates, increase in facilities) has not translated to more interpersonal violence, large-scale disturbances, or rioting	• Inmate homicides per 100,000 population: 1973–62.7 2000–4.6

(continued)

TABLE 3A.7 *(Continued)*

Author (year)	Scientific Method Score	Key Findings	Quantitative Evidence
		• Authors conclude that political and correctional leadership have made prisons more effective, thus negating some of the problems forecasted by critics of incarceration.	• Staff homicides per 1,000,000 inmates: 1979–13.3 1999–1.6 • Assaults on inmates per 1000 inmates: 1984–41.1 2000–29.2 • Assaults on staff per 1000 inmates: 1984–15.7 2000–15.3 • Disturbances and arsons per 1000 inmates: 1984–7.4 2000–1.3
Jiang & Fisher-Giorlando (2002)	1	• Situational and deprivation models significantly with regards to incidents against correctional staff, while situational and importation models contribute to explanations of inmate–inmate violence.	• Significant odds ratios for incidents against correctional staff: Situational model = 1.369 Deprivation model = .700 • Significant odds ratios for incidents against other inmates: Situational model–2.357 Importation model–.840
Williams, Rodeheaver & Huggins (1999)	1	• Evaluation of a 'new generation' jail in a southwestern state. This facility had three distinct housing types: traditional jail setting (linear construction), a nondirect supervision barracks structure, and open space dormitory style units known as 'pods'	• # incidents by housing type, July 1994–August 1995: –Assaults linear = 36 barracks = 13

		pods = 12
		−nonviolent incidents
		linear = 97
		barracks = 90
		pods = 61
		• Significant OLS coefficients of indicators associated with assaults: Education/study hours = −.16 Social distance = .11 Visits per month = .13
		• Disciplinary infractions were lower in the 'pods' units, but not very different from the barracks in terms of assault.
Wooldredge (1998)	1	• Significant results for inmate perceptions of greater social distance (i.e., cannot rely on protection or guardianship) and levels of assault • Correlation between monthly visits ("social ties") and fewer thefts. • No significant difference in risk of victimization for assault or theft between institutions with differing security levels.
French & Gendreau (2006)	*	• A review of the existing research on the effectiveness of correctional treatment for reducing institutional misconduct. "Prison programs producing the greatest reductions in misconducts also were associated with larger reductions in recidivism" (2006:185).
Wener (2006)	*	• Review of the research over the past 30 years on correctional management, design, and staffing issues. Finds support for direct supervision reducing assaults and lowering institutional costs.
Gendreau, Goggin & Law (1997)	*	• Meta-analysis of extant literature on predictors of prison misconduct. Little evidence is demonstrated for crowding effects on misconduct. Authors propose a multidimensional risk assessment protocol emphasizing the interaction effects between individual and situational factors to predict both violent and nonviolent offending.

TABLE 3A.8 *Highlights of Recent Research on Inmate Profiles/Composition of Offenders and Institutional Violence and Disorder*

Author (year)	Scientific Method Score	Key Findings	Quantitative Evidence
Cunnigham, Sorensen, & Reidy (2005)	1	• Study examined records of institutional violent misconduct (retrospectively over an 11-year period) for three different groupings of maximum security inmates ($N = 2,595$) at one state facility. The groupings included: inmates serving parole-eligible terms, life-without-parole-inmates, and death-sentenced inmates mainstreamed into the general prison population. • Results show that younger inmates, inmates with fewer years of formal schooling, prior prison confinement, and serving a term sentence were associated with higher risk of violent misconduct. Being sentenced to a life sentence or death sentence were risk-reducing factors.	• Significant logistic regression coefficients– predictors of violent misconduct: Age less than 21 = 1.131 More than 12 years of education = -0.579 Prior prison term = 0.341 Life sentence = -0.701 Death sentence = -0.577
Borrill, Maden, Martin, Weaver, Stimson, Farrell, Barnes, Burnett, Miller, & Briggs (2003)	1	• Survey of drug and alcohol use among white and non-white female inmates randomly selected from prisons across Great Britain found that a majority of the inmates were drug dependent on entering into custody. • White inmates were more likely to report chemical dependency vs. nonwhites. The 'drug of choice' for white inmates was heroin, crack for the nonwhite subsample.	• Percentage of inmates drug dependent on entering into custody = 66 • Chemical dependency on entering into custody by race: White inmates = 60% Nonwhite = 29%
Gaes, Wallace, Gilman, Klein-Saffran, & Suppa (2002)	1	• Study examines a sample of 7,445 male federal prison inmates with gang affiliation and their subsequent prison misconduct. Using a measure of gang 'embeddedness', results show that 'core' gang members receive the largest	• Discrete changes in probability of misconduct, holding all other variables constant at their mean: Active gang members: Violent misconduct = .207

		• amount of violent misconducts, 'peripheral' gang members committed more violent offenses than nongang members. • Being an active gang member significantly increases the likelihood of all measured forms of misconduct; the increases remain significant after controlling for individual level factors such as classification and previous history of violence.	Serious violent misc. = .079 Drug violations = .059 Total misconduct = .259 Suspected gang members: Violent misconduct = .156 Serious violent misc. = .014 Drug violations = .034 Total misconduct = .129 Gang associates: Violent misconduct = .102 Serious violent misc. = .009 Drug violations = .022 Total misconduct = .114
Fischer (2001)	1	• Survey of correctional managers, staff, and inmates in Arizona details the correlation between gang membership and institutional violence. The effectiveness of Security Threat Group program aimed at reducing institutional violence is also examined. • Key findings include a significant association between gang membership and assault, as well as gang membership and violence in general. Prison gang members are also nearly twice as likely to commit a serious violation than nongang members.	• Concentration of gang members in a housing unit explains: 40% of variation in assault rates 36% of variation in all violent incidents • Prison gang members are 74% more likely to commit a serious violation than nongang members.
McShane & Williams (1990)	1	• Disciplinary records of elderly inmates in one facility were not predicted by a number of individual level variables such as physical health, previous incarcerations, and mental health issues, but associations were found between years in custody, length of sentence, number of visitors, and medical history.	• Significant findings: -Mean years in custody: nondisciplined inmates = 3.02 disciplined inmates = 4.86 -Mean Length of sentence: nondisciplined inmates = 36.78

(continued)

TABLE 3A.8 *(Continued)*

Author (year)	Scientific Method Score	Key Findings	Quantitative Evidence
			disciplined inmates = 52.33 problem inmates = 60.24 –Number of visitors on list: nondisciplined inmates = 5.73 disciplined inmates = 7.30
Porporino, Doherty, & Sawatsky (1987)	1	• Homicides in Canadian prisons between 1979 and 1984 were more likely to be carried out by multiple assailants and for revenge motives as compared to homicides occurring between 1967 and 1978. • Victims of homicides in Canadian prisons during the latter time period more were likely to have a violent criminal record/background.	• Most prevalent reasons given for committing homicide in prison, 1979–1984: Drugs–17.3% Revenge–15.4% Altercation–5.8% Debt–5.8%

Appendix B

Study Inclusion Criteria for Review of the Evaluation Research on 'Causes' of Prison Violence and Disorder

According to the University of Maryland research review protocol, "The scientific methods scale ranks evaluation studies from 1 = weakest to 5 = highest on overall internal validity:

1. Correlational evidence (low offending correlates with the program at a single point in time);
2. No statistical control for selection bias but some kind of comparison (for example, program group compared with nonequivalent control group; program group measured before and after intervention, with no control group);
3. Moderate statistical control (for example, program group compared with comparable control group, including pre-post and experimental-control comparisons);
4. Strong statistical control (for example, program group compared with control group, with control of extraneous influences on the outcome, by matching, prediction scores, or statistical controls); and
5. Randomized experiment: units assigned at random to program and control groups prior to intervention" (as summarized in Welsh and Farrington, 2001: 169).

Definition of Key Terms Used in the Evaluation Review

Welsh and Farrington (2001:169–170) provide the following description of the key terms used in the University of Maryland review of evidence-based crime prevention:

What works. These are programs that the authors (Sherman, Gottfredson, MacKenzie, Eck, Reuter, and Bushway, 1997) were reasonably certain prevent crime or reduce risk factors for crime in the kinds of social contexts in which they have been evaluated and for which the findings can be generalized to similar settings in other places and times. For a program to be classified as working, there must be a minimum of two level 3 studies with significance tests demonstrating effectiveness and the preponderance of evidence in support of the same conclusion.

What does not work. These are programs that the authors were reasonably certain fail to prevent crime or reduce risk factors for crime, using the identical scientific criteria used for deciding what works. For the classification of not working, there must be a minimum of two level 3 studies with significance tests showing ineffectiveness and the preponderance of evidence in the same direction.

What is promising. These are programs for which the level of certainty from available evidence is too low to support generalizable conclusions but for which there is some empirical basis for predicting that further research could support such conclusions. For the classification of promising, at least one level 3 study is required with significance tests showing effectiveness and the preponderance of evidence in support of the same conclusion.

What is unknown. Any program not classified in one of the three above categories is considered to have unknown effects.

Source: Welsh and Farrington (2001:169–170)

4

Legitimacy and Imprisonment Revisited: Some Notes on the Problem of Order Ten Years After

Richard Sparks

University of Edinburgh

Anthony Bottoms

Universities of Cambridge and Sheffield

Introduction

It is almost exactly ten years, at the time of writing, since the publication of our book *Prisons and the Problem of Order* (Sparks et al., 1996). Writing with our friend and colleague Will Hay, we sought in that book both to report on original field research in two English high-security prisons and in some measure to revise and refresh the conceptual terms in which prisons were studied and described. Among the key ideas that we mobilized in our study was that of legitimacy. In this short chapter we seek to restate the main features of our argument concerning legitimacy in prisons; to assess its continuing relevance under contemporary conditions; and to take stock of some of the main criticisms and extensions of our work by others in the intervening decade.

We very much hope that this brief reappraisal will not be viewed as self-indulgent, or merely nostalgic, still less defensive. So much has happened in and around prisons in the United Kingdom and internationally in the last 10 years that revisiting a book published so long ago (and whose earliest preparatory fieldwork dates back almost as long again), which not all that many people have read (and which still fewer are reading now), requires some pretty strong justification. Yet, we suggest, some of the major issues are fairly obdurate; and some of the key conceptual, analytic, and indeed moral and political problems of imprisonment have moved on much less than we might prefer to believe. Moreover, it is at least arguable that in relation to prisons and other criminal justice institutions legitimacy has come to the fore as a more explicit concern and a more focal policy issue in the last few years than ever it was "back then."

We should take care to state certain provisos at the outset. *Prisons and the Problem of Order* (hereafter PPO) was not the first text to address the issue of legitimacy in prisons expressly and in some detail—that distinction probably belongs to Useem and Kimball in *States of Siege* (1989), although the issue dates back very much farther, whether or not it had been named as such. Secondly, PPO was quite clearly and explicitly *not* about riots or other major upheavals. We conceived it as addressing "the *perennial problem* of securing and maintaining order in prisons rather than the *special problem* of the occasional complete or near-complete breakdown of order" (PPO: 2—italics in original). We willingly accept that many applications of the notion of legitimacy (including on occasion by us) have been in the context of discussions of riots and other critical incidents. We merely point out that our own substantive focus was on the "problem of order" as a mundane, chronic issue and not on explaining the most obvious or flagrant disruptions of that admittedly fragile "normality." There is no "theory of riot" in PPO.

Moreover, PPO was never in any case a book *about* legitimacy. In keeping with its focus on the organization of everyday life in prison, the book was at least as much concerned with questions of routinization, and the temporal and spatial ordering of prison environments, influenced in some considerable part by Giddens's theory of structuration (Giddens, 1984), for example. The l-word, as we began to call it, did not really figure among our original inventory of research questions at all. It was, rather, something whose significance became increasingly clear to us as we conducted our work in the prisons and which we attempted to formulate in the course of subsequent reflection. However, to the extent that anything in our work entered the collective psyche of prison researchers, or found echoes elsewhere in the *zeitgeist* of debates about criminal justice, it was clearly this. It has indeed occasionally been a source of puzzlement to us that the book has been discussed, and sometimes criticized, in the literature as if legitimacy were its only topic. Why this should be so, and why legitimacy turns out to be not just any old concept but a protean one that crops up here, there, and everywhere—not just in prisons but in almost every aspect of institutional life—is something we hope to clarify here.

Revisiting Albany and Long Lartin

At the heart of PPO is a quite detailed comparison between two English "dispersal" prisons—which is to say the group of prisons among which prisoners considered as posing the greatest security risks were dispersed—as they were toward the end of the 1980s when our fieldwork took place. With the limited exception of a very small number of places in more specialized units, dispersal prisons then constituted the maximum-security estate of the prison system of England and Wales. The primary focus of our research was on the "problem of order" in dispersal prisons, and the contrasting ways in which order was maintained in our two prisons. In particular, we looked at the implications of the differing histories, populations, and regimes of these prisons for their experience and handling of "control problems," from the vantage points of both staff and prisoners.

The two prisons we studied were Albany on the Isle of Wight, just off the south coast, and Long Lartin in Worcestershire, some 30 miles southwest of Birmingham, close to the well-known beauty spots of the Cotswold Hills. Although formally of the same type (they each held a population of adult men serving long-term sentences, a proportion of whom were in security category A) and of similar age, they differed in many significant ways. Let us sketch a few of these. They had in the first place contrasting histories of control problems. Whereas Albany had experienced significant crises of order in 1973, 1983, and 1985, Long Lartin was (up to the time of our study though less clearly so since) one of only two dispersals to have avoided major collective disorder since the inception of the dispersal system in the early 1970s. They also (and largely because of these differing experiences) differed in terms of their then-current regimes and institutional "climates," roughly in the following ways:

Albany: At the time of our study (1988/9), Albany operated a regime which was stringently controlled relative to other English long-term prisons. This involved, in particular, restrictions on association and movement within the prison which were more pronounced than in the comparison prison. Prisoners in general were well aware of these differences: Indeed prisoners in Albany probably had a slightly exaggerated perception of their relative disadvantage. Accordingly, many felt aggrieved at having been located there, and felt that they had been given no adequate explanation of their differential treatment by comparison with their peers elsewhere. Some went further and interpreted their allocation as deliberately and personally punitive. Throughout the 1980s Albany regularly generated higher recorded levels of minor disciplinary problems (refusals to work, disobedience, fighting) than other "dispersal" prisons, giving rise at least to the suspicion that attending to the risk of disorder on one level might serve to exacerbate it on another level.

The Albany regime was therefore in the main rather unpopular with prisoners, except among older men who often welcomed its restraining effect on the noisiness and bumptiousness of the younger majority. However, with few exceptions (and somewhat against our initial expectations), prisoners drew a rather sharp distinction between the regime as such and the staff who administered it, whom they considered in the main to be reasonable, fair, just doing their job, and so on. Our impression was that, aware that they were administering a disliked system (albeit one which they strongly supported themselves), staff at Albany took some pains to counter their own potential unpopularity by cultivating a rather discreet and amenable interpersonal style. They did this in the hope—realized to some extent—that good relationships would help them retain a degree of legitimate authority. Moreover, the regime at Albany was quite highly procedurally explicit and relatively consistent in its operation, and emphasized good "service delivery" in matters such as food and prerelease programs.

Long Lartin: The regime at Long Lartin was widely regarded by prisoners as having a number of benefits over those of other "dispersal" prisons. Prisoners had significantly more time out of cells than at Albany, more association, more freedom of movement within the prison, and more frequent access to the gymnasium. They also noted and mostly approved the staff's cultivation of a rather relaxed and friendly way of working and a light and unobtrusive style of supervision. The use of first names between prisoners and staff was fairly general, and staff took pride in being able to manage the prison without formally sanctioning every "petty" infraction of the rules. Among the successes claimed for Long Lartin's liberal approach were the avoidance of riots, and hence an unbroken line of continuity with the founding principles of the "dispersal" prison system (Sir Leon Radzinowicz's "liberal regime within a secure perimeter": see Advisory Council on the Penal System, 1968). It was widely accepted that a number of prisoners who had rejected regimes at other long-term prisons and been reckoned unmanageable had settled successfully at Long Lartin. It was also clear that Long Lartin used its rather favored status in the eyes of most inmates as a device for influencing prisoners' behavior. Thus the prison had enjoyed some success in integrating sex offenders and other vulnerable prisoners into the main body of the prison's population, calling on potential predators' fears of being transferred elsewhere. By the same token, vulnerable prisoners were more ready to tolerate the risks involved in mixing with other prisoners for the sake of the perceived benefits of the regime. Yet it was also clear that such people were by no means free from fear. Moreover, the level of *sub rosa* economic activity (especially in the supply of drugs, and gambling) was rather high. There was evidence from hospital records and numbers of alarm bells to suggest that the level of back-stage violence might have been much greater than the official picture of calm would indicate; and when incidents did occur, those within our sample were more likely than at Albany to involve numerous people and the use of weapons. The history of stability (assessed in terms of the absence of large-scale, collective unrest), the favorable regime and the generally approved staff practices lent to Long Lartin an appearance of much greater acceptance in the eyes of the majority of prisoners than was the case at Albany. Yet it also seems probable that the regime gave rise to opportunities for deviance, and predation on fellow inmates, not found to the same degree elsewhere and hence to some risks in day-to-day inmate life. It is certain, from our evidence, that some of the victims of predation felt not only afraid but angry and unsupported. Meanwhile, some of those alleged to have caused trouble, and in consequence transferred from the prison on the governor's authority, felt they had been unfairly treated procedurally. Hence there were two kinds of objection raised by some prisoners against the liberal regime at Long Lartin: one concerning the provision of safe custody, and one concerning its scope for procedural discretion and consequent injustice.

What are we to make of these sorts of institutional differences? What do they imply conceptually for our ways of understanding "the prison"? And what do they entail practically, morally, and politically for the development of prison regimes? What in particular do they have to do with the notion of legitimacy and its application to incarceration?

Revisiting Legitimacy and Order

At the general level the concept of legitimacy refers to the claim by the more powerful party in a social relationship (a decision-maker, a public official, an office-holder of some kind, but also on occasion a parent, for example) to exercise whatever power they hold in a justified manner. It also refers to their success or otherwise in having this claim acknowledged by others, and especially by the people over whom power is deployed. There is, as sociologists have long observed, a crucial difference between the simple *power* of a social actor and his or her *authority*. Authority is, roughly speaking, taken here to mean that the actor and his or her actions enjoy sufficient acceptance in relevant ways among the members of a given population that they feel a normative obligation to comply with her or his laws, instructions, and requests. It is probably safe to say that traditionally the term is most often applied to the actions of states and their agents and employees (soldiers, police officers, judges, tax and customs officers, prison officers, and the like) in their dealings with citizens. However, this is not the only feasible application and the picture is complicated by recent developments such as the privatization of public services.

It should be obvious from this account that a power holder's ability to enforce his or her wishes will be greater if the subject believes his or her power to be held legitimately, for then subjects will have some *moral* reasons to obey. That is to say, their compliance will not simply be the product of coercive force or threat, nor just of an instrumental calculation of costs and benefits, or only a matter of habituation. There will instead (or additionally) be a perception that one *ought* to comply because this distribution of power is sufficiently well grounded in some combination of law, tradition, personal credibility, general utility, democratic deliberation (or whatever) as to command moral assent. It is more or less a matter of definition that legitimate uses of power are more stable and less costly than nonlegitimate ones and that "rulers" (for which read all manner of officials and office-bearers in a multitude of different institutional and cultural settings, and not just kings, generals, or dictators) have a profound interest in sustaining their legitimacy as far as they can. At the same time this constrains their actions in a host of sometimes surprising ways since they need to show that what they do is to some extent consistent with the principles on which they claim legitimacy. Thus, even in situations where power seems formally to lie overwhelmingly on one side, as in a military installation or a prison, arbitrary, contemptuous, or grossly inconsistent uses of power can have drastic consequences for institutional legitimacy. The conditions under which the powerful can safely disregard considerations of legitimacy entirely in the long run will be rare indeed. Those conditions, we argue, do not obtain in the prisons of western liberal democratic countries today, notwithstanding the drift toward a penal "culture of control" (Garland 2001).

In applying this perspective to prisons in PPO, we were, as we saw it, arguing against a weight of received opinion in prison studies, and against the drift of some policy interventions, but *with* the grain of the more successful forms of practice that we observed *in situ*. The conventional wisdom, albeit articulated from very different points on the political compass, consisted in implicitly or explicitly denying the relevance of legitimacy to the practice of imprisonment. Thus, both those whom we termed "conservative pragmatists" (Sparks and Bottoms, 1995:53), of whom DiIulio seemed the most persuasive and scholarly exemplar, and those we styled "radical pessimists" (loc. cit.) appeared to us to be, strangely, in agreement. For example, in an important critical statement Scraton et al. (1991: 63) referred to the "unrelenting imposition" of control on the unwilling as the sole means of keeping the lid on what would otherwise be a ferment of rebellion. Meanwhile, DiIulio had argued in *Governing Prisons* (1987) that *precisely* because prisons are, in the eyes of prisoners, inherently nonlegitimate and hence unruly, they are ungovernable except by the judicious use of compulsion and sanction. DiIulio therefore concluded that the best form of prison management ("the control model") is a benign and efficient authoritarianism, tempered by the scrupulous observance of procedural form and limited individual due-process rights. (For a fuller discussion of these contending positions, and their convergent implications, see Sparks et al., 1996: Chapter 2; Sparks and Bottoms, 1995.) In short, we saw each of these symmetrical ways of minimizing the relevance of legitimacy as generating conceptual errors, which, moreover, also had the unintended effect of limiting the scope, depth, and usefulness of empirical research. Yet our research suggested that there may be good reason to suppose that those prisons which generate fewer major conflicts do so for reasons other than that they are just more completely and perfectly coercive. If so, then this demands both theoretical reflection and empirical inquiry.

We were of course acutely aware in PPO that the many outstanding questions concerning prisons and legitimacy—which we summarized in one question: Can prisons be legitimate?—were unlikely to receive overwhelmingly positive answers. We had no doubt that legitimacy was a vexed issue in relation to prisons. We never for one moment supposed that any actually existing prison—and certainly not the two in which we principally carried out our fieldwork—had somehow cracked this conundrum. It always seemed more plausible to argue that prisons are arrayed on a spectrum of varying degrees of legitimacy deficit. Certainly our analysis was never intended to provide some sort of apologetics on behalf of any current practice or institution. Prisons do not in general bask in the warm approbation of their captives, as everyone agrees. In the empirical cases that we observed key features of the everyday practice of each had developed precisely as responses or adjustments to the limited legitimacy that they each enjoyed and in response to the crises that they had either experienced or feared.

Yet the very fact that prisons might be deficient in point of their legitimacy *in varying degrees* or *in various ways* suggests that legitimacy is indeed usually an issue for them. It is a concern that shapes practice. It emerges in the ways in which members of staff regulate their own and one another's behavior. It is conveyed in the vivid stories that prisoners tell that evaluate their treatment in different prisons or their handling by different officers. Its violation is made manifest in the outrage and indignation that prisoners express over small misuses of discretionary power—the peremptory treatment of their visitors, for example, or the overzealous application of the letter of the law in relation to important things like food, exercise, and mail. For these and other reasons it is in our view a serious but persistent mistake to regard the prison as a limiting case of the relevance of legitimacy.

In our attempts to reinstate the significance of legitimacy (and its erosions and absences) to prison studies in PPO and associated publications, we drew extensively on the work of the British political theorist David Beetham. In Beetham's view the modality of power which stands most in need of legitimation is not democratic discussion, which claims to be inherently self-legitimating, but force. For

> . . . the form of power which is distinctive to [the political domain]—organized physical coercion—is one that both supremely stands in need of legitimation, yet is also uniquely able to breach all legitimacy. The legitimation of the state's power is thus both specially urgent and fateful in its consequences. (Beetham, 1991:40)

Legitimacy and power are, on this view, two faces of the same problem. The content and strength of legitimating beliefs radically affect all parties in a system of power relations, and only legitimate social arrangements generate normative commitments toward compliance. Beetham (1991) thus argues that all systems of power relations seek legitimation. He contemplates very few exceptions, such as slavery. This is surely quite interesting from the vantage point of the present discussion. It might be argued that whether one thinks legitimacy is a relevant consideration in prisons comes down to whether you consider imprisonment to be more akin to slavery than to other, supposedly more contemporary institutions.

The particular content of legitimating beliefs and principles is extremely historically and culturally variable, but, Beetham contends, we can identify a common underlying structure which is very general (1991:22). According to Beetham's account, structure has three underlying dimensions or criteria in terms of which the legitimacy of any actually existing distribution of power and resources can be expressed and evaluated. Such criteria are almost never perfectly fulfilled, and each dimension of legitimacy has a corresponding form of nonlegitimate power. In outline, Beetham expresses his schema thus:

Criteria of legitimacy	*Form of nonlegitimate power*
i. Conformity to rules (legal validity)	Illegitimacy (breach of rules)
ii. Justifiability of rules in terms of shared beliefs	Legitimacy deficit (discrepancy between rules and supporting shared beliefs, absence of shared beliefs)
iii. Legitimation through expressed consent	Delegitimation (withdrawal of consent)

(From Beetham, 1991:20)

These three dimensions roughly correspond to the traditional preoccupations of three different academic specialists which have considered issues of legitimacy: first, lawyers (has power been legally acquired, and is it being exercised within the law?); next, political philosophers (are the power relations at issue morally justifiable?); and finally, social scientists (what are the actual beliefs of subjects about issues of legitimacy in that particular society?) (Beetham, 1991: 4ff). However, a central plank of Beetham's argument is that social scientists have been wrong to follow Max Weber (1968) in defining legitimacy as simply "belief in legitimacy on the part of the relevant social agents" (Beetham, 1991:6). To promote this view, Beetham argues, is to leave social science with no adequate means of explaining why subjects may acknowledge the legitimacy of the powerful in one social context, but not another (ibid: 10). Beetham accordingly argues for an alternative formulation of the social-scientific view of legitimacy—"a given power relationship is not legitimate because people believe in its legitimacy, but because it can be *justified in terms* of their beliefs" (ibid: 11).

How far does all of this really matter on the ground? And what is the relevance of Beetham's insistence on this seemingly rather fine distinction between his views and those of Weber? We can perhaps re-express some of what is at stake in this debate in much simpler terms. First, people in authority are generally well advised to follow the rules prescribed for their own behavior. Secondly, they should act in accordance with commonly agreed moral standards in the society in question. To the extent that they do these things they have a much better chance of having the legitimacy of their authority accepted than if they don't, even in the apparently unpromising setting of a high-security prison.

On a day-to-day level most prisoners accept that someone has to have power over them, on behalf of the State. What then becomes crucial is *the way* that that power is exercised. Some regime conditions can seem to prisoners to be deeply unfair (as the restricted regime at Albany did), and some decisions made by prison staff can seem, for example, capricious in outcome, or arrived at without properly listening to the prisoner, and in either case unfair. To the extent that such situations are ameliorated, however, prisoners are normally willing to admit that particular regimes, or particular kinds of staff behavior, are *fair* rather than unfair. In such contexts, we argued, prisons can indeed appear legitimate to prisoners. We further argued that it was important for many reasons, including political ones, to identify this dimension of power in prisons, as well as the more coercive dimensions.

We did not ever argue that in prisons prisoner compliance is simply the result of assent to the legitimacy of the regime. Naturally, we recognized that the situational controls available in a prison—cells, gates, secure corridors, and so on—are vital to the maintenance of order; and we recognized too the sometimes important role of incentives and disincentives, though in fact those are less-powerful weapons in prison than many outside observers initially imagine (Bottoms, 2003). In short, we always saw legitimacy as only one element in the overall production of order in prisons, but in our view a crucial one.

In PPO we record the pertinent question of one prison governor: "Does all this mean that legitimacy is just about pleasing the prisoners?" We argued—and the argument seems to have been generally accepted—that it does not. For—and this is the real significance of Beetham's conceptual distinction, noted above—the criteria of legitimacy are not just based on assent, they are also based on standards of fairness generally accepted in society at large. A prisoner appealing to those standards of fairness draws attention to a genuine legitimacy deficit that will resonate in wider political debate if it reaches forums such as a parliament, a public inquiry, or a court of law. A prisoner making far-fetched demands (such as—to take a real example—"don't patrol our exercise yard—you're invading our privacy") will have no impact on wider debates. Most prisoners intuitively understand this difference, and they know that only the first kind of claim is really about legitimacy. Among the implications of this are that it is not only the bare, objective facts of a prison regime (how many hours unlocked?, how much access to gymnasia or education?, and so on) that matter in prisoners' estimation of the fairness of their treatment. Their perceptions of the fairness of the staff in matters such as manner, even-handedness, and the quality of explanations given in case of problems are perhaps the most crucial factors of all in determining whether or not prisoners see the prison as operating in a legitimate manner.

Ten Years After: Some Developments in Theory, Research, and Intervention

We turn now to address some connections between our position and those of other researchers. We begin with some brief remarks on the wider criminological literature before turning to the views of some colleagues who have applied, extended, or criticized the account suggested in PPO. Given considerations of space there are some major issues that we cannot deal with adequately here at all and which we will have to postpone to another occasion. These include: the quite contentious issue of the bearing of questions of legitimacy on the privatization of prisons and corrections; the related but wider point of the development of the "new public management" or "managerialism"; and the shifting character of the public and political demands and expectations imposed on prisons, as on other institutions and services, today. The ways in which we measure success and failure, or demand accountability, have developed rapidly in the period since PPO was written, and continue to do so—with major possible implications for the meaning and relevance of legitimacy. Similarly there are very important questions concerning judicial intervention and the developing jurisprudence of the courts in Britain, Europe, the United States, and elsewhere, especially the application of the language of Human Rights to prisons. These too are matters that have moved on rapidly in the last decade and that deserve separate discussion. Finally, in this inventory of issues that we are *not* going to discuss, there are the many other uses of the notions of legitimacy and legitimation in the wider realms of political rhetoric and media discourse. Prisons, like other criminal justice issues, have often been intensely politicized over the last decade and more, with severe consequences both for the scale of incarceration and the conditions experienced by many prisoners. These dynamics are fundamental to understanding the wider context in which prisons issues are situated and presented to other audiences. Although these currents in the political culture constrain and direct the actions of politicians and administrators, and undoubtedly ripple through onto the landings and exercise yards, their primary reference is to influences that originate far outside prison as such. For now our focus must remain on the question of legitimacy as applied to the transactions that go on between prisoners, prison officers, and prison managers within institutions.

Despite this self-denying ordinance (and bearing in mind our comments on the transdisciplinary nature of Beetham's schema), there is no escaping the fact that legitimacy is fundamentally a political concept. It refers to the relations between parties who are very differently situated in a distribution of power, and to the capacity of the more powerful to constitute their position as authorized and justified, especially in the eyes of the less powerful. For all the multitude of ways in which prisons are special and unusual places, in which special and unusual practices go on, and special and unusual problems arise, this way of conceiving the problem ultimately emphasizes the continuity between the analytic terms that we need to understand prisons and those we apply to other settings and institutions.

For example, we have concluded on the basis of the line of thinking outlined above that there is an important sense in which the prison staff may be said to *embody*, in prisoners' eyes, the regime of a prison, and its perceived fairness. In this regard there is an important consonance between our work and that of Tyler and his associates on policing (but also with some work on less obviously linked themes in regulatory studies, such as tax compliance) (Tyler, 1990; Tyler, 2001a). This connection was already evident in PPO, but the body of work led by Tyler has developed to a remarkable extent since then (see, for example, Sunshine and Tyler, 2003; Tyler and Huo, 2002 and see generally http://www.psych.nyu.edu/tyler/lab/). Among the primary conclusions of Tyler and colleagues are that: People, including offenders, who find themselves treated fairly are more inclined to accept even unfavorable outcomes; citizens who view police officers and judges as lacking in legitimacy are less likely to follow their directives; citizens who view the law as not legitimate and unjust are less likely to obey it; the key antecedent of confidence in the police and courts is that these exercise their authority through fair procedures; even in high-crime areas people's confidence in the police is more strongly linked to whether they feel the police harass and demean citizens, and much less to whether the efforts of the police are in fact lowering crime (see, further, Karstedt, 2005; Sherman, 2002; Smith, 2007). These points have a special bearing on relations between police and members of visible minorities (cf. Fagan and Meares, 2000), and this is an issue that is additionally salient in the prisons of many countries. In both our work and in Tyler's, the issue of the subject's direct, interpersonal handling by particular agents of "the system" strongly shapes perceptions of the wider institutions involved.

In this respect the seemingly rather special issue of legitimacy in prisons in fact speaks strongly to concerns with the relationship between equity and effectiveness in criminal justice generally, and to a range of cognate questions regarding trust, confidence, credibility, propriety, and so on. We do not, however, accept that in the context of the prison, legitimacy is only or even primarily a *procedural* issue. Procedures are, of course, hugely important and prisoners are highly alert to any departure from proper form in the institution's handling of them. Nevertheless, prisons are places where everyone is a "repeat player." Prisoners and prison staff alike are in one another's enforced company for extended periods; and people know a good deal about one another's business. Prisoners are also in an especially dependent and often highly vulnerable situation with respect to the decisions of officials and the discretionary powers of prison staff. It follows that outcomes are often of particular significance. But so too are informal aspects of interpersonal conduct, even when no "decision" of moment is involved (see, further, Crawley, 2004; Liebling, 2004).

There have been a certain number of responses to and developments of our work in PPO. Some of these have been (more or less gently) critical; others have taken the discussion well beyond the point at which we stopped. We want to conclude by briefly commenting on a few of the more significant contributions.

Mary Bosworth has suggested that the account of legitimacy developed in PPO does not easily translate to women's prisons (indeed that PPO is somewhat insensitive to issues of gender and sexuality). There might be a range of empirical reasons for this. There is also a large theoretical literature that we do not directly consider in that text. To take only the former, the balance of power (or, more formally, the dialectic of control) in women's prisons may be so different as to discount many of the criteria of legitimacy that we say are crucial. Similarly, strategies of resistance may take distinct and perhaps less-apparent forms (Bosworth, 1999; Bosworth and Carrabine, 2001). We take this line of commentary very seriously and are inclined to concede on several points. Since all our own analysis took place within prisons for adult men (and only of one kind, in one country) we can in no way claim to have identified, still less explored, all possible dispositions. We cited, and may be seen as having endorsed, Beetham's argument that legitimacy is (almost) always a relevant term in social analysis. We hope our other claims were less general. Clearly there is much as yet unexplored scope for comparative analysis, between sectors and internationally. What is not so clear to us is whether the very different possible modes of domination and resistance that obtain in different prisons, at different times and places, among different populations, mean that in some cases legitimacy (and hence, let us not forget, its counterpart illegitimacy) is simply not an applicable notion.

A somewhat similar view is developed by Eamonn Carrabine (2004) in the course of his "genealogy" of the riot at Strangeways prison in Manchester—the event that precipitated Lord Woolf's major inquiry (Woolf, 1991; Sparks and Bottoms, 1995). Strangeways was (and is) a "local" prison, and not a "dispersal." During the period in question (up to and including 1990) it was also a famously "traditional" prison, one in which few of the complexities or sensitivities that we claimed to observe at Long Lartin, for instance, were apparent. In PPO we drew a distinction between power that is "taken for granted" and power that is "accepted as legitimate." and we noted that the distinction between the two could be a fine one. Carrabine accepts this, but he goes on to make this comment:

> The distinction [between 'taken for granted' and 'legitimate'] is crucial, for it could be argued that, in a number of ways, power in prisons represents

an inevitable "external fact" for prisoners—in which the experience of confinement is endured without any reference to some version of legitimacy.

Elsewhere, Carrabine makes the claim that for many prisoners, it is the apparently overwhelming power stacked up against them that secures their assent; thus, their assent is based on what he describes as "dull compulsion," rather than legitimacy.

We have two comments on these important claims. The first is that we were indeed aware of the power of dull compulsion. Indeed we used this term ourselves (1995:53), adapting Marx. Moreover, it arose for us in the context of the following question: "Are there, indeed, *any* conditions under which prison management could reliably call upon a recognition of legitimacy by prisoners . . . as distinct from mere acquiescence or dull compulsion?" (emphasis added). We were aware of this particularly in the Vulnerable Prisoner Unit (VPU) at Albany, in which were located long-term prisoners who had committed serious offences (such as sexual offences) but who required protection from fellow prisoners, either because of their offences (and the reactions that these tended to cause among "mainstream" prisoners) or because of events that had occurred in prison, such as getting into debt to other prisoners and not paying it off. Prisoners in the VPU correctly perceived themselves as largely powerless, and the level of challenge to staff that they posed was minimal. The events that led to the "restricted regime" at Albany had nothing to do with the prisoners in the VPU, but it was nevertheless decided that, on the grounds of equality, these wings should also be subject to the restricted regime in exactly the same way as the main prison. This was seen as doubly unfair by VPU prisoners, but in their powerless state they accepted the inevitable, knowing that any protest could lead to their being transferred to another prison, where conditions for them could easily be worse. "Dull compulsion" was therefore absolutely the main reason for the passive response of these prisoners who felt they had no choice but to put up with their fate.

Secondly, however, it seems very strange that Carrabine refers to prisoners enduring "the experience of confinement . . . . without any reference to some version of legitimacy." In the Albany VPU, for example, there were plenty of references to the perceived illegitimacy of the situation, but also an awareness that, given the power imbalance, nothing much could be done about it. As we observed, that produced some undesirable consequences, with some staff behavior being overweening, and unchecked by any serious challenge. But an absence of challenges to authority is not, in and of itself, evidence that prisoners endure confinement "without any reference to some version of legitimacy"; and in other prison contexts (where such challenges are more commonly made), there is plenty of evidence that the language of legitimacy is often used both positively and negatively. In short, Carrabine is absolutely right to draw attention to the role of "dull compulsion" as a motive for obedience in the prison setting, but wrong to downplay legitimacy to the extent that he has. Indeed we would tend to argue that to experience the conditions of one's existence as dully compelled is part-and-parcel of what it is to live under an illegitimate power.

Finally, we turn to the outstanding work of Alison Liebling. Liebling's remarks on legitimacy, as on any other aspect of the social life of prisons, merit the most careful consideration in view of her exceptional knowledge and understanding of them. We make no pretence here of summarizing Liebling's *magnum opus Prisons and their Moral Performance* (2004), still less her many other contributions (see also, Liebling *this volume*). These are far too wide-ranging and sophisticated to be encapsulated in that manner. Among other achievements, Liebling has devised more systematic and multidimensional methods of studying prisons than we or others had previously contrived. One product of this is to enable her to break down a notion such as legitimacy into rather more components than we had envisaged and to find that institutions vary on these dimensions in more surprising ways than we might have predicted. (We might not have anticipated that a prison could score highly on "fairness" but low on "respect," for example [Liebling, 2004:459].) At an early point in her discussion, Liebling states that:

> [Prisons] are places where relationships, and the treatment of one party by another, really matter. They raise questions of fairness, order and authority (others might say legitimacy), but also some other questions about trust, respect and well-being in an exceptionally palpable way. (op. cit.: xviii)

Among Liebling's points here is that there are very important aspects of the emotional texture of prison life, of people's emotional well-being, and interpersonal behavior that are not well encapsulated by the notion of legitimacy—hence her coinage of the more inclusive idea of "moral performance." Thus:

> Our scheme . . . operationalizes the key concept of legitimacy. But it also incorporates broader questions of personal development, psychological well-being, the delivery of pain, interpersonal treatment outside the flow of power, and meaning, not all of which are fully explained by or conditional upon power relations. (Liebling, 2004: 475)

In short, there is more to legitimacy than we might think and there is more going on than legitimacy anyway. We have already acknowledged that legitimacy is at bottom a political concept, concerned with the applications of power and with the critique of those applications. For Liebling this is its limitation. It prioritizes the dimension of power at the expense of the full range of moral questions, and emotional and existential complexities, that prisons present us with. As a way of putting legitimacy in its proper place and reminding us (should we need it) that it is very far from all that is at stake in the social analysis of incarceration, we accept these correctives. (Though we certainly would not accept that this was all that we discussed in PPO, should anyone suggest that.)

Nevertheless, legitimacy is, as Liebling acknowledges, a key concept. For us it is not just a variable of the same weight or kind as any other. This returns us to our main theme and hence offers a fitting point at which to conclude. Legitimacy can be studied as a property of social systems but it is also in an important sense their *goal*. The usual condition of most institutions—and certainly prisons—is to achieve only limited and partial legitimacy, to face resistance and contestation. Sometimes many institutions—and certainly prisons—descend into an outright crisis of legitimacy. Both sorts of problems, the chronic and the critical, ought to sensitize us to the nature and gravity of problems. Legitimacy is a term that has both descriptive and normative dimensions. It directs attention to how things work and fail to work. But it should also make us more sharply aware of the gap between things as they are and as they might be.

References

Advisory Council on the Penal System (1968). *The Regime for Prisoners in Conditions of Maximum Security* (Radzinowicz Report), London: HMSO.

Beetham, D. (1991). *The Legitimation of Power.* London: Macmillan.

Bosworth, M. (1999). *Engendering Resistance: Agency and Power in Women's Prisons,* Aldershot: Ashgate.

Bosworth, M. and E. Carrabine. (2001). "Reassessing Resistance: Race, Gender and Sexuality in Prison." *Punishment & Society,* 3, 4: 501–15.

Bottoms, A. E. (2003). "Theoretical Reflections on the Evaluation of a Penal Policy Initiative." In L. Zedner and A. Ashworth (Ed). *The Criminological Foundations of Penal Policy: Essays in Honour of Roger Hood.* Oxford: Oxford University Press.

Carrabine, E. (2004). *Power, Discourse and Resistance: a Genealogy of the Strangeways Prison Riot,* Aldershot: Ashgate.

Crawley, E. (2004). *Doing Prison Work.* Cullompton: Willan Publishing.

DiIulio, J. (1987). *Governing Prisons.* New York: The Free Press.

Fagan, J. and T. Meares. (2000). *Punishment, Deterrence and Social Control: The Paradox of Punishment in Minority Communities Columbia Law School, Public Law Working Paper No. 010.* New York.

Garland, D. (2001). *The Culture of Control.* Oxford: Clarendon Press.

Giddens, A. (1984). *The Constitution of Society.* Cambridge: Polity Press.

Karstedt, S. (2005). "Great Expectations: Enlightenment, Justice and the Invention of Institutions," plenary address to XIV World Congress of Criminology, University of Pennsylvania.

Liebling, A. (assisted by H. Arnold) (2004). *Prisons and their Moral Performance.* Oxford: Oxford University Press.

Scraton, P., J. Sim, and P. Skidmore. (1991) *Prisons Under Protest,* Buckingham: Open University Press.

Sherman, L. (2002). "Trust and Confidence in Criminal Justice," *National Institute of Justice Journal,* 248: 22–31.

Smith, D. J. (2007) "New Challenges to Police Legitimacy." In D. J. Smith and A. Henry, eds. *Transformations in Policing,* Aldershot: Ashgate.

Sparks, R. and A. E. Bottoms. (1995). "Legitimacy and Order in Prisons," *British Journal of Sociology,* 46, 1: 45–62.

Sparks, R., A. E. Bottoms, and W. Hay. (1996). *Prisons and the Problem of Order.* Oxford: Oxford University Press.

Sunshine, J. and T. R. Tyler. (2003). "The Role of Procedural Justice and Legitimacy in Shaping Public Support for Policing," *Law and Society Review,* 37, 555–589.

Tyler, T. R. (2001). "Trust and Law Abiding Behavior: Building Better Relationships Between the Police, the Courts, and the Minority Community." *Boston University Law Review,* 81, 361–406.

Tyler, T. R., and Y. J. Huo. (2002). *Trust in the Law: Encouraging Public Cooperation with the Police and Courts.* New York: Russell-Sage Foundation.

Useem, B. and P. Kimball. (1989). *States of Siege: US Prison Riots 1971–1986,* Oxford: Oxford University Press.

Woolf, Lord Justice. (1991). *Prison Disturbances: April 1990.* London: HMSO.

5

Why Prison Staff Culture Matters

Alison Liebling[1]

Professor of Criminology and Criminal Justice,
and Director, Prisons Research Center,
Institute of Criminology Cambridge, UK

I am not prepared to continue to apologise for failing prison after failing prison. I have had enough of trying to explain the very immorality of our treatment of some prisoners and the degradation of some establishments.

—(Prison Service Director General 2001)

In 1999 the Chief Inspector of Prisons for England and Wales declared in the preface to his Inspectorate report following a weeklong inspection that Wandsworth prison had a "culture of brutality." He was referring to a collective attitude among staff toward prisoners, detected by his team and described by prisoners, that he saw as intimidating and demeaning (HMCIP 1999). Wandsworth is a fairly "typical" Victorian local prison, with a radial design, a poor infrastructure, and a long history. It accommodates far more prisoners than it can cater for. It is regarded as difficult to manage, at least in part, because officers working there (as in other local prisons built during this era) tend to have cynical attitudes and to be fairly demoralized.

Most of the sociological literature on prison life restricts its attention to prisoner culture (interesting and important as this is). Few empirical studies of prison officer

[1]Special thanks are due to Helen Arnold, Sarah Tait, and Clare McLean for research assistance throughout the two research projects drawn on in this chapter.

105

culture exist, although there have been powerful "simulated prison" experiments showing how structural features of the prison induce hostility toward prisoners (Haney et al., 1973), and there have been dramatic examples of brutal prison cultures in recent history (e.g., Abu Ghraib, Guantanamo Bay, the early days of the Close Supervision Centers in England, and some segregation units). The term "culture" is common currency in official reports about prisons and prison life (see, e.g., Home Office, 1991, Prison Service, 2001; HMCIP, 2003; OICS, 2004), but there is little detailed empirical knowledge of its character or impact in the UK. U.S. scholars have argued that correctional officers as a group "hold values that are antithetical to helping inmates" (Lombardo, 1985: 79), but this view has been disputed by those who maintain that prison officers do not subscribe to a single view and that many are interested in expanding their human service role (e.g., Toch and Klofas, 1982).

Crouch and Marquart proposed that the "Fundamental Tenets of Guard Work" include the belief that security and control are paramount, and that social distance should be maintained from prisoners (Crouch and Marquart, 1980: 89–90). They suggested that officer culture is characterized by distrust of prisoners and administrators, authoritarian attitudes, and resistance to change (ibid.: 91-5). Lombardo, and Toch and Klofas, respectively, argued on the other hand that these perspectives are adopted by a subcultural minority rather than the majority of officers, and that two other subcultural groups existed: the "Lonely Braves," who held professional attitudes, but felt that few others did, and the "Supported Majority" who held professional attitudes and thought most others officers did too (Klofas and Toch, 1982; Lombardo, 1985). The negative minority tended to be the most vocal, however.

In this chapter I propose two things: first, that there is a collective working personality or officer culture detectable among prison officers in general. This "working personality" is related to the nature of the occupation and is composed of both positive and negative characteristics. Secondly, prisons differ significantly in the precise shape this culture takes (that is, the degree, intensity, and form of the negative aspects of staff culture). I argue that these differences have causes and consequences. This argument is tentative and exploratory, for my main point is that these important issues are generally neglected in prisons research. In proposing both similarities among staff and differences between prisons, I hope this chapter satisfies Mathiesen's plea for a better and more nuanced prison sociology. Most accounts of prison staff in particular, he suggests, over-concentrate on similarities and single case studies (Mathiesen, 1966).

The term culture as used here refers to a shared set of assumptions, values, beliefs, and attitudes that officers express, directly and indirectly, and which shape action to a greater or lesser degree. They provide working rules about "the way things are done around here." This includes the way staff respond to outsiders (civilians), senior managers, to each other, and to prisoners, what skills are prized, which posts are favored, how segregation units are run, how language is used, and so on. Culture provides a set of 'craft rules' about how and why things are done (Reiner, 1992). Schein argues that:

> [C]ulture is to a group what personality or character is to an individual. We can see the behaviour that results, but often we cannot see the forces underneath that cause certain

kinds of behaviour, Yet, just as our personality and character guide and constrain our behaviour, so does culture guide and constrain the behaviour of members of a group through the shared norms that are held in that group. (Schein 2004: 8)

Certainly, prison staff often refer to "the Wandsworth way," "the Wakefield way," the "Long Lartin ethos," or "the way we do things around here." New staff are often socialized into these ways of thinking and doing, and departures from the norm may be sanctioned (by ostracism or worse). Schein suggests that, just as with individuals, some of the assumptions operating in groups may be unconscious; others may be amenable to discovery or expression, however. Often, there are more powerful emotions underlying attachment to certain assumptions. He proposes that culture accounts for patterns in organizations, and that it underlies resistance to change, communication problems, and ineffective practices. It is wide-ranging, in that it influences all aspects of a prison officer's approach to his or her work. Culture tends to form around leaders, but the leaders may not be those in formal positions of power. They may be senior individuals, union representatives, or strong personalities on a wing. There may be conflicting cultures within a prison—for example between uniformed staff and psychologists, or between different staff subgroups (e.g., prison wings or even shifts).

The Prison Officer Working Personality

Prison officers are often described, rather like the police, as an inward-looking, solidary group, who (unlike the police) feel stigmatized by the nature of their work, and undervalued. Officers often feel powerful in the prison setting, and in social groups, in large numbers. They often drink together, and they identify strongly with one another. They depend on their colleagues for assistance at times of threat, and they bond both during their initial training and during testing incidents (such as disturbances, hostage-takings, or assaults). Officers often feel that only other officers understand what it is like to work on a wing, and that others have romantic, idealized views of who prisoners are and how they generally behave. The camaraderie of prison officer work is reinforced by the acute awareness that prisoners are unwilling recipients of the "services" they offer, that conflict is routine, and that a constant testing of formal and informal boundaries takes place. There are rapid, informal exchanges of news, gossip, rumor, and opinion between officers from different wings as they go about their daily business, escorting prisoners to and from the segregation unit, visits, the health care center, the gym, education department, and workshops. A form of desensitization takes place as staff become accustomed to drug-taking, self-harm, the threat of violence, and explosive reactions to bad news. Prison officers share with the police a tendency to feel their work has a public mission (public safety), to express cynicism and pessimism, due to the hard-nosed nature of their work, to be suspicious, conservative, macho, internally cohesive, and pragmatic (see Reiner, 1992, and Liebling and Price, 2001: 148). What works—to quell disorder, quiet a disgruntled prisoner, or avert a breach of security—is more important than "what is right" (Sparks et al., 1996). The primary allegiance of prison officers is to their peers and to their own safety.

The fact that prison officers wear uniforms is inevitably significant in reinforcing a sense of identity, and in distinguishing officers from managers and from civilian specialists. Senior and Principal officers wear "pips" (crowns on their epaulettes), so that it is immediately apparent to the eye who is who, among officer ranks. Officers attending full-staff meetings in prisons often cluster at the back of the room, leaving the front rows, and even the chairs, to the nonuniformed staff. This, together with their late arrival, expresses their primary commitment to life on prison wings (where the action is), their distance from (and often distrust of) senior managers, and their physical proficiency. There is an overlap between a distrusting stance toward senior managers and prisoners, and unionization, and it is often the case that officers who take up official union positions both locally and nationally tend to have more oppositional views toward senior managers in particular than their less-active colleagues.

Standard grade prison officers are arguably relatively low in the prison hierarchy (e.g., compared to prison doctors, or psychologists) but they have maximum street credibility, as they handle difficult prisoners, protect Governors from violence, and use highly prized Control and Restraint procedures to manage threats. Officers tend to make clear distinctions between the "rough" and "respectable" and to base these judgments on cues and stereotypes. These characteristics and behaviors are related to the nature of the job: Prison officers use authority and often face danger. The outcome of their encounters can be highly unpredictable, and being able to look confident in the face of danger is an important survival skill. Officers work in high-risk, place-based environments where the consequences of a wrong decision can be calamitous. They have a tradition-oriented investment in "what worked yesterday," and feel reluctant to trust in increasingly abstract, future-oriented management strategies which bear little relevance to their primary concern: making it through the day peacefully. All of these features of prison work make it highly likely that officers will over-use their authority at times, although empirical research suggests they actually under-use it most of the time in ways that can be highly skilled (Liebling et al., 1999).

The positive aspects of the prison officer working personality are, among other things, preparedness to work as a team, a problem-solving and decisive approach to their work, having "bottle" (confidence), being multiskilled and flexible, having a sense of humor, and being experts at talk and diplomacy. It is a pity that such skills and attitudes are not generally included in empirical studies of prison officer work. The literature on police and prison officer culture tends to refer to the negative aspects of staff attitudes. This is a narrow (and potentially misleading) approach to take. For the purposes of this article, I stick broadly to the parameters set by previous research (but see Liebling and Price, 2001 and Arnold, Liebling, and Tait, 2006 for a more appreciative approach). I shall return to possible ways forward at the end. It is important to note that staff attitudes toward prisoners can be too laissez-faire, and relationships too close, as well as too distant.

To what extent is it possible to empirically establish the existence of an officer culture or subculture? Lombardo suggested that one criterion would be group cohesion. Other criteria might include the expression of negative attitudes toward

TABLE 5.1 *Prison Officer Views on Relationships with Colleagues and Senior Managers[a]*

	Belmarsh %	Holme House %	Risley %	Doncaster %	Wandsworth %
Do you feel you have a good relationship with officer colleagues?					
Very good	73.7	66.7	59.2	84.8	82.4
Quite good	26.3	25.0	28.6	12.1	17.6
Do you feel you have a good relationship with senior management?					
Very good	0.0	20.8	12.2	24.2	17.6
Quite good	21.1	33.3	24.5	33.3	23.5

[a]For further detail on methods and results, see Liebling 2004.

prisoners and senior managers: the "them and us" perspective often identified in sociological depictions of the officer culture.

In a detailed study of the emotional and moral climates of five similar prisons in England, prison officers were asked whether they had a good relationship with (a) their colleagues and (b) senior managers or governor grades.[2] The five prisons concerned were mainly local prisons (Risley was an exception, but had been a local prison and had recently been rather unsuccessfully converted to a category C Training prison). They all held adult males. They ranged in their official performance rating or assumed quality from poor (Wandsworth and Belmarsh) to good (Holme House and Doncaster). Risley's performance was mixed (see Table 5.1). The officers' answers were as follows:

Officers overwhelmingly reported very good relationships with their peers (range 59.2%–84.8%). No officers described their relationships with colleagues as poor. Relationships with senior managers were less positive, with over a quarter of officers at one prison describing relationships with senior managers as "very poor" and small but significant numbers at three of the other four prisons describing them as "very poor" (8.2%, 12.1%, and 5.9%, respectively). It was common in all five prisons for staff to report very good peer relationships and mixed relationships with senior managers. This can be regarded as a general pattern, confirming the characterization of the officer working personality as internally cohesive and distrusting of administrators as described above. Differences of degree are significant, however. The prison with the poorest staff–management relationships, as seen by officers, was distinctive in many respects. The governor was female and young, the prison had a high-security function, and a "fatal error" had been made by this incoming governor at her first

[2]For further detail on methods and results, see Liebling, 2004.

staff meeting when she explained to the staff, as they recounted the tale, that prisoners mattered more than they did. Staff–prisoner relationships in this prison were formal and distant, and officers were largely unwilling to engage in the human services aspects of their role. When asked to whom their primary loyalty lay, staff at Belmarsh overwhelmingly reported that it lay with "officer colleagues" (84.2%). This reflected the general pattern (58.3% at Holme House, 34.7% at Risley, 69.7% at Doncaster, and 76.5% at Wandsworth) but was exaggerated at Belmarsh (and Wandsworth), with serious consequences for prisoners (see below).

Each prison had a distinctive culture, linked to indirectly expressed organizational goals. Belmarsh, for example, had security as its main organizational goal, Holme House prioritized "resocialisation"; Risley was mainly concerned with "survival" (it had been threatened with privatization); Doncaster was at the time somewhat "laissez-faire," with "respect" as a key organizational goal, and Wandsworth had "discipline" as its key goal. These five prisons were all working to the same official Prison Service statement of purpose, and each had a similar function. Their value cultures, however, were fundamentally different. Staff worked to very different models of what it meant to be doing the job well. Belmarsh and Wandsworth had traditional custodial goals, although of different kinds, one favoring security and the other discipline, and only Holme House had a rehabilitative goal. Doncaster was modeled on a humanitarian principle that people were sent to prison "*as* and not *for* punishment," but this had led to a slightly naïve stance on security among staff. Risley had lost sight of its formal purpose in its efforts to survive in the public sector. The emotional climates in each prison were distinctive, with staff and prisoners sometimes sharing an emotional condition (e.g., powerlessness at Belmarsh) and at other times, expressing opposing sentiments (e.g., confidence among staff, but disrespect and indignation among prisoners at Holme House). Prisoners were undergoing distinctive forms of imprisonment in each establishment (see, further, Liebling, 2004). Our interest at the time was in identifying which aspects of prison life "mattered most." This dimension—let us call it staff–prisoner relationships for short—was one area that mattered very much, according to prisoners.

The Significance and Measurement of Staff Attitudes

Three out of eight. Three out of eight officers are OK. The rest are just . . . won't give you the time of day. (prisoner, prison 1)

What helps you to feel safe here?
Just the friendliness of the staff, really . . . . You know, here they are very friendly. They were very reassuring when I first come in, you know, they weren't stand off-ish. They talked to you, they'd ask you questions, and that made you feel at ease, really. (prisoner, prison 4)

It seemed significant that in our early explorations of prison life and quality, how staff thought and felt about prisoners and managers influenced the quality of life for prisoners or the prison climate. There were links between these aspects of the quality of prison life (or the quality of their treatment) in each prison and levels of well-being among prisoners. Our portrayal of these dynamics in the study reported above was tentative, and so in a second, larger study we sought to describe and if possible quantify staff culture more systematically.

In a 12-prison before–after study of a specific suicide prevention initiative, then, we devised a detailed "quality of life" survey for staff (building on the first study, above) to explore whether staff perceptions of their role and treatment were related to prisoner evaluations and well-being. The intention of the new suicide prevention strategy was to effect cultural change in the five pilot sites (Eastwood Park, Feltham, Leeds, Wandsworth, and Winchester) as well as to change practices in relation to the identification, management, and care of at-risk prisoners.

The 12 prisons in the study included five high-risk (high-suicide rate) local prisons receiving substantial investment, five high-risk (high-suicide rate) local prisons not receiving substantial investment, and two high-performing "controls." The poorest prisons, with the highest suicide rates, were generally characterised by dissatisfied and alienated staff. Staff in general noted the difficulty in deriving job satisfaction from prison work, especially in high-turnover local prisons with inadequate resources. They described a context of understaffing, long hours, the monotony of tasks, difficulties in getting time off, and the morale-sapping tendency to see the same faces returning to prison over and again. The 12 prisons differed significantly, however, in their quality of life as perceived by prisoners, in levels of prisoner distress, and in the values and attitudes expressed by the majority of staff. Prison staff reported very different levels of job satisfaction, recognition, direction, and support, and these differences were related to their willingness to care for prisoners. Alienated staff in the poorest prisons were often over-preoccupied with the threat to safety that prisoners posed, even though the prisoners were no different from those in other prisons. Staff concerns about safety were often related to their own relationships with prisoners and senior managers, rather than to levels of risk. These "quality of life" and "cultural" differences were associated with the success or otherwise of implementation of the new suicide prevention strategy, as well as with levels of distress among prisoners.[3]

Tables 5.2 and 5.3 show some of the differences between the "good implementers" of the new suicide prevention strategy (Eastwood Park and Feltham) and the "poor implementers" (Leeds, Wandsworth, and Winchester). The staff results shown in Tables 5.2 and 5.3 are from a questionnaire distributed to a full-staff meeting in 2002, shortly before implementation began, and again in 2004 at the "after implementation" stage. Fairly marked differences of degree can be seen among staff in Table 5.2 (showing percentages, as this is more informative than mean scores, used below), with those at Eastwood Park and Feltham generally rating their enjoyment of work, the relationships with senior managers (governor grades), their level of support, and their satisfaction with their own levels of power and responsibility higher than the poor implementers. The prisoner questionnaire was also distributed in

[3]Mean levels of distress among prisoners were highly correlated with three-year moving average suicide rates for the relevant period in each establishment. See Liebling et al., 2005a; 2005b.

TABLE 5.2 *Staff Perceptions of the Quality of Their Working Lives, and Prisoner Experiences of Prison in Good vs. Poor Implementers*[a]

| | 2002 (2004) | | | | |
| | Good Implementers | | Poor Implementers | | |
	EWP %	FELTHAM %	LEEDS %	WANDSWORTH %	WINCHESTER %
Staff Questions					
I get a lot of enjoyment from my work in this prison	54	69	26	29	40
I look forward to coming to work in this prison	32	44	22	18	17
I trust the governor grades in this prison	35	21	12	5	8
I feel supported in my work by governor grades	35	32	15	10	6
The success I achieve in my working day is recognized and rewarded	24	23	20	8	15
The level of power and responsibility that prison officers have is about right	43	36	21	29	27
Prisoner Questions					
When I first came into this prison I felt looked after	27 (49)	30 (37)	30 (23)	22 (28)	24 (16)
Relationships between staff and prisoners are good	37 (56)	37 (42)	23 (31)	26 (31)	38 (35)
Life in this prison involves a great deal of suffering	56 (33)	51 (43)	42 (43)	45 (55)	48 (64)
This prison is good at providing care for those who are at risk of suicide	27 (37)	37 (51)	30 (30)	18 (35)	14 (20)
My experience of imprisonment in this particular prison has been stressful	63 (36)	53 (52)	40 (50)	58 (61)	62 (65)
Changes in Composite dimensions[b]					
Care for prisoners (2002–2004)	↑↑↑	↑	ns	ns	ns
Level of distress (2002–2004)	↑↑	ns	ns	ns	ns

[a]Percentage of staff/prisoners agreeing or strongly agreeing with the item.

[b]↑ = $p < 0.05$ ↑↑ = $p < 0.01$ ↑↑↑ = $p < 0.001$

ns = not significant.

TABLE 5.3 *Significant Differences between Good and Poor Implementers, 2002 and 2004*

	2002				2004			
	Good Implementers Mean Score	Poor Implementers Mean Score	Mean Score Diff	Sig	Good Implementers Mean Score	Poor Implementers Mean Score	Mean Score Diff	Sig
Staff Questions								
I get a lot of enjoyment from my work in this prison.	3.79	3.01	0.78	***	3.73	3.38	0.36	***
I look forward to coming to work in this prison.	3.37	2.76	0.61	***	3.44	3.06	0.38	***
I trust the governor grades in this prison.	3.05	2.42	0.63	***	3.20	2.79	0.41	***
I feel supported in my work by governor grades.	3.16	2.65	0.51	***	3.21	2.96	0.25	**
The success I achieve in my working day is recognized and rewarded.	2.84	2.50	0.34	***	3.01	2.78	0.23	**
The level of power and responsibility that prison officers have is about right.	3.16	2.90	0.26	**	3.23	2.98	0.24	**
Prisoner Questions								
When I first came into this prison, I felt looked after.	2.70	2.57	0.14	ns	3.16	2.59	0.57	***
Relationships between staff and prisoners are good.	3.07	2.87	0.20	*	3.34	2.92	0.42	***
Life in this prison involves a great deal of suffering.	2.69	2.81	0.12	ns	2.95	2.59	0.36	***
This prison is good at providing care for those who are at risk of suicide.	2.78	2.73	0.05	ns	3.25	2.74	0.50	***
My experience of imprisonment in this particular prison has been stressful.	2.47	2.60	0.13	ns	2.80	2.41	0.39	***
Composite Prisoner Dimensions								
Composite care dimension score	2.87	2.78	0.09	ns	3.10	2.78	0.32	***
Distress dimension score	2.81	3.00	0.19	**	3.05	2.90	0.15	*

*The mean difference is significant at the $p < 0.05$ level.

**The mean difference is significant at the $p < 0.01$ level.

***The mean difference is significant at the $p < 0.001$ level.

ns = not significant.

2002 (to 100 randomly selected prisoners at each site) and again in 2004, at the "after implementation" stage. What the prisoner results show, on the whole, is that the quality of life for prisoners improved significantly between 2002 and 2004, that levels of care increased, and that levels of stress and suffering decreased over this period (albeit from high levels, and more significantly at Eastwood Park, the better of the two implementers). The two "good implementers" were a female prison and a Young Offenders Institution, and levels of distress in those prisons tend to be higher than in adult male prisons. The levels of distress in the poor implementers with dissatisfied staff were therefore higher than expected before implementation, as well as after implementation. Prisoners in these prisons said, for example, "It's like shouting and shouting, and no-one's listening to a word you say" (Prisoner).

> If the staff are horrible to you, you end up feeling bad and you either end up going down the block for fighting or you just bottle it up and then it will come out in the end . . . there's no consistency. You can sense the glow in his voice, you know, "I'm in charge, put that fag out" – that gets on people's nerves. (Prisoner)

The environments in these prisons were described as "indifferent," "unresponsive," or "hostile."

More detailed analysis of the results suggested that adherence to a traditional culture varied significantly among the staff in our study and that this cultural dimension explained much of the variance among staff as well as much of the variance in perceived levels of care among prisoners. We look more closely at these findings below.

The Significance and Measurement of Traditional Culture

Studies of policing culture have found that close adherence to a traditional culture is significantly associated with increased likelihood of coercion (Terrill et al., 2003). Borrowing from this literature, we identified a number of items in our staff questionnaire that arguably reflected adherence to a traditional culture. They reflected staff attitudes toward senior managers, toward safety, and toward prisoners. A factor analysis showed that they clustered together reasonably reliably (.77). The items were:

> I trust the Governor grades in this prison (reverse scored)
> I feel a sense of loyalty to the Governor in this prison (reverse scored)
> I feel a sense of loyalty to the Prison Service (reverse scored)
> I feel safe in my working environment (reverse scored)
> I trust the prisoners in this prison (reverse scored)

The level of power and responsibility that prisoners have in this prison is too high.

Taking four of the 12 prisons in the study for illustrative purposes, the following Table 5.4 shows the distribution of officers one standard deviation above and below the mean on adherence to traditional cultural attitudes at each establishment. The

TABLE 5.4 *All Staff and Prison Officer Views on a "Traditional Culture" Scale at Four Prisons, 2002*

	Leeds Pilot %	Liverpool Comparator %	Wandsworth Pilot %	Swansea Control %
Very "Pro"				
All staff	14.6	18.5	9.0	30.8
Uniformed staff	11.2	6.7	3.2	13.0
Very "Anti"				
All staff	33.5	37.7	33.3	7.7
Uniformed staff	47.2	52.2	41.3	13.0

samples include all staff attending a full-staff meeting held for the purposes of the survey. The results are shown for all staff (including specialists) and for uniformed staff only. Very "Pro" means staff reporting positive attitudes toward managers, safety, and prisoners; very "Anti" means staff reporting negative views. The four establishments included three relatively poor performing establishments regarded as having "cultural problems," where prisoner quality of life was relatively low; and one relatively high performing local prison regarded as more progressive, where prisoners rated their quality of life relatively positively. The results are taken from the baseline or before stage of the research.

Taking the staff with positive attitudes first, the results show that the proportion of all staff reporting positive attitudes toward senior managers and prisoners was low. Even at Swansea, the high-performing prison, less than a third of all staff fell into this category. Among uniformed staff, the proportions were even lower, with a high of 13 percent at Swansea. This suggests two things. First, there is support here for a general tendency for uniformed officers in particular to express less than positive attitudes toward senior managers and prisoners, confirming the argument earlier that a basic working personality or cultural stance exists even in relatively good prisons. Prison officers are in general, it seems (at least in the 12 local prisons included in this study) unlikely to acknowledge, or hold, positive attitudes toward senior managers (see Paoline, 2003 and 2001 on the police in this respect).

Looking at the negative attitudes, a third of all staff at the three poorly performing prisons reported negative attitudes toward senior managers and prisoners, suggesting that negative views are by no means exclusive to uniformed prison officers. Swansea is the exception, with only 7.7 percent of all staff falling into this category. They are clearly outnumbered by the more positive staff, and evenly balanced by the small group of very positive uniformed staff. The picture at the three poorly performing prisons among uniformed staff is clear: Almost half of the uniformed staff at Leeds, over half at Liverpool, and two-fifths at Wandsworth reported negative attitudes toward senior managers and prisoners. This group vastly outweighs

TABLE 5.5 *All Staff and Prison Officer Views on a "Traditional Culture" Scale at Four Prisons, 2004*[a]

	Leeds %	Liverpool %	Wandsworth %	Swansea %
Very 'Pro'				
All staff	13.5	6.3	9.8	20.9
Uniformed staff	5.1	1.3	0.0	7.1
Very 'Anti'				
All staff	25.8	49.6	16.7	9.3
Uniformed staff	39.4	57.7	24.6	14.3

[a]For further detail on methods and results, see Liebling et al., 2005.

the very small group of staff reporting positive attitudes in each prison. On the wings, this is reflected in a kind of peer pressure experienced by what Toch and Klofas called the "Lonely Braves": enthusiastic staff trying to provide human services to prisoners, but against the cultural grain of the establishment. Such staff reported anxiety and exhaustion, and often described having to "go back to that prisoner later, when colleagues were not looking" to respond to requests. These figures show that attitudes among officers differ somewhat in their distribution, and that certain establishments can be characterized as having a mainly traditional or negative culture. If half of the uniformed staff working in a prison adhere to these negative attitudes, then prisoners' experiences in these prisons tend to reflect this general trend. At Swansea, the positive and negative groups are both relatively small and evenly balanced. Prisoners there reported a reasonable quality of life and a generally good atmosphere.

Two years later, after considerable investment and intervention at the three poorly performing prisons (Swansea was a "control" establishment in the study and so received nothing), the surveys were repeated.[4] The results looked as follows (Table 5.5):

Attitudes at Leeds and Liverpool had become more negative. At Wandsworth, the proportion of staff reporting negative attitudes had declined significantly, but with no corresponding increase in positive attitudes. Staff at Swansea reported broadly similar attitudes, with a slight decline in the size of the positive all staff group. Of the 12 prisons studied, the proportion of uniformed staff reporting positive attitudes toward senior managers and prisoners was highest at Swansea at Time 1, with the exception of a private prison, in which the proportion of uniformed staff expressing positive views was unusually high at Time 1 (at 27.9%) but this had fallen to 7.1 percent by Time 2.

[4]For further detail on methods and results, see Liebling et al., 2005a and b.

TABLE 5.6   *Prisoner Views on Their Prison Experience*

	Belmarsh %	Holme House %	Risley %	Doncaster %	Wandsworth %
My time here seems very much like a punishment					
Strongly agree	34.9	10.6	16.8	12.3	30.0
Agree	48.2	36.2	36.6	36.8	31.7
Staff in this prison have a lot of power and control over prisoners					
Strongly agree	37.3	37.2	22.8	16.7	41.7
Agree	53.0	52.1	43.6	44.7	50.0
My experience in this prison is painful					
Strongly agree	26.5	7.4	13.9	1.8	20.0
Agree	24.1	18.1	17.8	14.0	15.0
I feel tense in this prison					
Strongly agree	24.1	6.4	14.9	4.4	10.0
Agree	26.5	22.3	24.8	16.7	26.7

The Consequences of Cultural Differences

One of the distinctive findings of our original "measuring the quality of prison life" research at Belmarsh was that prisoners described their experience there as especially painful and punishing, compared to other prisons in that study. Staff saw prisoners as "dangerous subjects" who should be controlled and policed. They did not generally treat prisoners with respect. Disregard for their individual needs and circumstances created negative feelings, so when asked to agree or disagree with the following statements about the experience of prison life, we found that prisoners reported significant differences in important areas of prison life and well-being (Table 5.6).

Differences in prisoner well-being, measured using a seven-item scale, were directly related to levels of respect and fairness experienced (also measured using scales), which in turn were closely linked to the nature of staff–prisoner relationships. The manner in which prisoners were treated by staff determined the nature of the prison experience to a greater extent than material or regime provision. It is also apparent from the above table that the *amount* of power prisoners feel that staff have over prisoners does not differ significantly between prisons. What differs is the *way in which power is used*, and how this *feels*.

In the later suicide prevention study, we were able to establish the relationship between staff attitudes and prisoner distress more clearly, so that prisoner perceptions of staff–prisoner relationships, fairness, and respect were significant contributors to mean levels of distress, after controlling for prisoner differences in "imported vulnerability" (see, further, Liebling, et al., 2005a). Prisoners' feelings of safety (or lack of safety) were highly significant in explaining variations in distress between prisons. In turn, feelings of safety were determined by how staff responded to requests and difficulties. What made prisoners feel safe was "having someone to talk to" and "knowing that if you go to an officer with a problem, you won't be fobbed off" (prisoner). The way prison officers talked to prisoners, and what they did in response to requests for help were crucial. These relationships were mediated by the scale "traditional culture," so that where high proportions of staff adhered to traditional cultural attitudes, prisoners' perceptions of staff–prisoner relationships, fairness, and "care and safety" were lower, and levels of distress were higher. These findings are tentative and exploratory, but they suggest that staff culture exists, that it differs in its intensity, and that it has consequences for the quality of life for prisoners. Where improvements were found in cultural attitudes among staff over time, scores on a composite "care for prisoners" scale improved significantly (these improvements in levels of care are shown in Tables 5.2 and 5.3).

Those prisons where successful implementation of the strategy took place already had slightly better cultural attitudes among staff at the "before" stage of the research. At Wandsworth, cultural attitudes became less negative over the course of the research, but by 2004 did not pass the apparently critical threshold beyond which prisoners could report feeling that their individual needs were being met.

It looks, from our study, as though the balance of staff reporting positive attitudes has to be at least even for prisoners to feel their needs are taken seriously. An exploratory regression analysis showed that the scale "traditional culture" was associated with a range of staff views on feeling valued, job commitment, and levels of perceived safety. Staff had to feel that their needs were being met before they felt able or willing to take on the problems prisoners had. Where staff felt undervalued, alienated, or distrusting of senior managers, their adherence to traditional cultural attitudes was stronger. The result was that prisoners felt treated unfairly and with indifference. Staff attitudes, in other words, are linked to behavior, as studies of police culture have indicated, as well as to prisoner-related outcomes. Culture, then, is related to the likelihood of implementation of new policies, as well as to outcomes for prisoners. Where large proportions of staff hold negative attitudes toward senior managers and prisoners, they are unlikely to embrace or implement new policies. Prisoners in local prisons with few resources rely on front line prison staff for access to work, education, specialists, and telephones. Staff attitudes translate into regime qualities that can make the difference between a survivable experience of imprisonment and an unbearable one. Positive staff attitudes can make it more likely that prisoners who are susceptible to distress feel inclined to go on living. We hope to take these analyses further in future work. Finally, I look briefly below at some possible causes of these cultural differences.

The Causes of Cultural Differences

> Everything seemed to happen when the new Governor came here . . . about 18 months ago. Every day he was putting things out, he saw things which he didn't like, he'd put a notice out, 'this will change'. And it changed. It made things a lot better. I think it's working quite well, really. (Senior officer)

Police staff culture is thought to arise as a coping mechanism in response to a danger- ous occupational and ambiguous organizational environment (Terrill et al., 2003). Clearly, prison officers face problems in their work, including exposure to danger, a feeling of individual accountability when things go wrong, a sense of feeling invisible to and misunderstood by senior managers, and increasingly, inroads being made into their pay and working conditions in the face of private sector competition. Prison staff carry out unpopular work, with conflicting goals, behind the scenes. Their failures (escapes, suicides, disturbances) receive far more attention from the public and from managers and politicians than their successes. Under these conditions, prisons, staff tend to adopt an insular, conservative, and somewhat defensive posture, and to focus on their own safety. These general feelings and attitudes are more prevalent in certain establishments. As Terrill et al. argue, officers handle the strains in their working environment in different ways (2003: 1029). Prison staff attitudes may also be shaped by changes in the political and policy climate (i.e., by changes in the moral status of prisoners), by the local industrial relations climate, and by changes in function and role (e.g., losing their high security status). We were particularly interested in the finding that, even among difficult prisons with similar functions, some establishments had more positive and open staff cultures than others. In the prisons with poor cultures in our study, staff felt undervalued and over-preoccupied with control:

> Its weaknesses are the infrastructure of the building, staff that felt that they were scapegoats and being picked on and nobody loved them and there was no point in being here because you weren't going to get any support from management. The staff were considered the lowest of the low. So the self-esteem of the staff in some respects. I think there is still a cultural jump to get to the point where we can actually open everybody up (unlock prisoners) and the world is not going to fall apart, you know? (Governor)

Staff in these prisons could "completely kid themselves they are doing a good job" when in fact prisoners were locked up for most of the day. Prisons with more positive cultures tended to have confident staff (i.e., staff who felt comfortable with the level of power and responsibility they had), stable, united, and competent senior management teams, a clarity of function and a convincing direction, reasonable levels of trust between staff and their managers, and usually (although not always) they had reasonable physical and architectural conditions, They were also adequately resourced. Staff in these prisons worked cooperatively with specialists, seeing them as a means of support rather than a threat.

Changing a prison's culture took time, energy, and strong leadership. Effective line managers were important transmitters of moral messages from senior managers to front line staff. Staff had to be supported, but also held accountable and challenged on a regular basis. This took energy and nerve. Prison cultures seemed to deteriorate more rapidly and easily than they could improve. Attempting to change a prisons' culture could unleash resistance if staff felt threatened or unsafe. The 12 prisons in our study were full of strong characters, so it was better if the governor had at least as strong a character as the strongest informal prison officer leader. It was easier to improve a prison culture when staff were already benign (that is, not hostile). It was harder to work with staff who were deeply embedded in a cynical and defensive position. These prisons took several years, and often more than one governor, to "turn around." We last assessed the most difficult prison in our study one year ago, for the third time. There were indications that some significant positive movement had taken place. An influx of new entrant staff had arrived, and an intensive training course on "the role of the prison officer" was under way (see, further, Tait, in progress).

Conclusion

Empirical evidence suggests that a distinctive prison staff culture exists and that variations in this culture can be found. These variations may be related to establishment history and leadership. Attitudes and values form an important part of this culture and seem to be shaped in direct and indirect ways. It may be useful to characterize this culture as representing a moral and emotional climate, and to recognize that culture has consequences. Prison staff culture, like police culture, is complex and variegated, and is best studied using a combination of survey and observational methods.

Privatization has provided an opportunity to experiment with the deliberate shaping of distinctive prison staff cultures. Most of the 20 or so newly built prisons in England and Wales since the 1990s have been operated by the private sector, although one or two are operated by the public sector (e.g., Woodhill) or have been taken over by the pubic sector since opening under private management (e.g., Blakenhurst). Disentangling the effects of new buildings from new approaches to management is important, and it is clear that "traditional cultures" can be imported into new buildings by prison staff with public sector experience (e.g., Belmarsh). It is significant that private sector managers tend to recruit staff with little or no public sector experience, to discourage unionization, and work hard to set the tone of prisoner custody officer work. Despite these efforts, cultures in private sector prisons vary, with the best being characterized by respectful and professional attitudes toward prisoners, and the worst heading quickly toward the over-use of authority or the under-use of formal procedures. One deliberate consequence of private sector competition has been to render the external environment less secure, so that prison staff working in the public sector can no longer take their jobs or current working conditions for granted. This has inevitably led to both greater flexibility among some staff (in some prisons) and greater cynicism and resistance among others. Factors influencing the direction of change include relationships with senior managers, senior management ability, size of the establishment, the nature of the population, and other contextual matters (such as an influx of well-targeted resources).

Other important questions arise as to the significance of gender in staff culture (see Tait, in progress), the characteristics of effective senior management teams in shaping resistant staff cultures successfully, the causes of disaffection in individual staff members, the prospects of rehabilitation for the alienated, and the qualities shown by those who resist such disaffection, even when surrounded by colleagues with cynical attitudes. Such themes await future research.

This chapter has shown that it is possible to study these matters empirically, and that it is possible to learn a great deal about prisons, their differences, and their effects by exploring prison staff culture.

References _____

Arnold, H., A. Liebling, and S. Tait (2006). "Prison Officers and Prison Culture." In Y. Jewkes (Editor). *The Prisons Handbook*. Cullompton, Devon: Willan Publishing.

Crouch, B. and J. W. Marquart (1980). "On Becoming a Prison Guard." In B. Crouch (Editor). *The Keepers: Prison Guards and Contemporary Corrections*. Springfield, IL: Charles C Thomas.

Haney, C., C. Banks, and P. Zimbardo (1973). "Interpersonal Dynamics in a Simulated Prison." *International Journal of Criminology*, 1: 69–97.

HMCIP (1999). *HM Prison Wandsworth: Report on a Short Unannounced Inspection of HM Prison Wandsworth 13th–16th July, 1999*, London: Home Office.

HMCIP (2003). *HM Prison Wandsworth: Report of an Unannounced Inspection of HM Prison Wandsworth 20–24 January, 2003*, London: Home Office.

Home Office (1991). *Prison Disturbances, April 1990: Report of an Inquiry by the Rt. Hon. Lord Justice Woolf (Parts I and II) and his Honour Judge Stephen Tumim (Part II)*, London: HMSO.

Klofas, J. and H. Toch (1982). "The Guard Subculture Myth," *Journal of Research in Crime and Delinquency*, 19/2: 238–254.

Liebling, A. (2004). *Prisons and their Moral Performance: A Study of Values, Quality and Prison Life*. Oxford: Clarendon Press.

Liebling, A., C. Elliott, and D. Price (1999). "Appreciative Inquiry and Relationships in Prison," *Punishment and Society: The International Journal of Penology*, 1/1: 71–98.

Liebling, A., L. Durie, A. Stiles, and S. Tait (2005a). "Revisiting prison suicide: the role of fairness and distress." In A. Liebling and S. Maruna (Editors). *The Effects of Imprisonment*. Cullompton, Devon: Willan Publishing.

Liebling, A. and D. Price (2001). *The Prison Officer*. Leyhill: Prison Service and Waterside Press.

Liebling, A., S. Tait, L. Durie, A. Stiles, and J. Harvey, assisted by G. Rose (2005b). *An Evaluation of the Safer Locals Programme:* Project Report; Home Office.

Lombardo, L. (1985). "Group Dynamics and the Prison Guard Subculture: Is the subculture an Impediment to Helping Inmates?" *International Journal of Offender Therapy and Comparative Criminology*, 29(1): 79–90.

Mathiesen, T. (1966). "The Sociology of Prisons: Problems for Future Research," *British Journal of Sociology*, 17(4): 360–79.

Office of the Inspectorate of Custodial Services (2004). *The Diminishing Quality of Life at Hakea Prison 2001–2003*, OICS: Perth, WA.

Paoline, E. (2001). *Rethinking Police Culture*. New York: LFB Scholarly Publishing LLC.

Paoline, E. (2003). "Taking Stock: Toward a Richer Understanding of Police Culture." *Journal of Criminal Justice*, 31: 199–214.

Prison Service (2001). *Prison Service Review*. London: Prison Service.

Prison Service Director General (2001). *Speech to Prison Service Conference*, Nottingham, February 2001.

Reiner, R. (1992). "Police Research in the United Kingdom." In N. Morris and M. Tonry (Editors). *Modern Policing*, Chicago: University of Chicago Press.

Schein, E. H. (2004) *Organizational Culture and Leadership*, 3rd edition, San Francisco: Jossey-Bass Publishers.

Sparks, R., A. E. Bottoms, and W. Hay (1996). *Prisons and the Problem of Order*. Oxford: Clarendon Press.

Tait, S. (in progress) "Prison Officer Culture and Care for Prisoners in One Male and One Female Local Prison." Ph.D. thesis (due October 2007), Cambridge University.

Terrill, W., E. A. Paoline III, and P. K. Manning (2003). "Police Culture and Coercion," *Criminology*, 41(4): 1003–34.

Toch, H. and J. Klofas (1982). "Alienation and Desire for Job Enrichment Among Correction Officers," *Federal Probation*, 46(1): 35–47.

6

Culture, Performance, and Disorder: The Communicative Quality of Prison Violence

Elaine Crawley, PhD

Senior Lecturer in Criminology
University of Salford, UK

Peter Crawley, MA

Associate Lecturer
Open University, UK

Introduction

In previous work, Elaine Crawley has shown that life in prison, for both inmates and prison staff, is overwhelmingly *domestic* in nature (Crawley, 2004a, 2004b). For a researcher entering prisons for the first time, the main impression may be one of unfamiliar routines and practices with the ever-present possibility of violence. Researchers have commented, for example, on the need to become accustomed to particular smells, incomprehensible routines, and terminology, all against a high level of background noise. However, greater familiarity with the prison—and with the social interactions that take place within it—allows the prison sociologist to appreciate that it might best be understood as a *domestic* space. Moreover, many prison officers, when asked, may compare their workplace to other domestic and quasi-domestic spheres such as the family home, a children's home, a school, a hospital, or (in the case of dealing with elderly inmates) an old-people's home (see Crawley, 2004a, pp. 254–6).

The domestic, routinized, and, in certain respects, rather unremarkable nature of life in prison (once the inherent *unnaturalness* of the prison as institution has been acknowledged) contrasts sharply with the ways in which prisons are presented in popular factual accounts (particularly those in the UK's tabloid press) and in contemporary (highly dramatic) fictional accounts of prison life such as those constructed in movies (e.g., *Brute Force* and *Midnight Express*). Almost universally in these representations, prison life is depicted as brutal and brutalizing, with an unending stream of violent inmate-on-inmate violence and constant antagonism between prisoners and prison officers. At the same time, the media is able to maintain a contrasting depiction of the prison as a place of "rest and recreation"; a safe, "cushy"[1] haven where all prisoners are assumed to enjoy the supposedly unearned "privileges" of in-cell television, computer games, free association, "luxury" food, "better" education[2] facilities (i.e., better than those enjoyed by school children), and better training for employment on release. Indeed, a recent introduction to English prisons (Coyle, 2005, pp. 104–5) comments that the UK media generally provide two contrasting pictures of prison life: One is of a "dangerous environment where there is an ever-present threat of violence and brutality" (from staff and inmates alike), while the other is of the prison as "holiday camp" in which prisoners "can lie in bed all day if they so choose, are well fed and provided for."[3]

A number of criminologists writing about the prison (e.g., Sparks, Bottoms, and Hay, 1996; Crawley, 2004a; Coyle, 2005) have recognized that *concern* about violence—or perhaps more correctly, the potential for violence—is ever-present in prisons, and that concern about violence (potential and real) dominates staff discussions about the maintenance of order. They also note, however, that such discussions fail to acknowledge the relative *absence* of actual violence in day-to-day prison life. Indeed, describing the social, ethnic, and demographic mix in prisons, Coyle (2005, p. 139ff) notes that although groups and individuals who would not normally mix "are thrown into close proximity. . . [ ]. . . one is entitled to be surprised, not that disorder occurs in prisons from time to time, but that it occurs so infrequently."

Given recent increases in the number of people in prison in the UK, the painful and emotional nature of imprisonment, the domestic and claustrophobic nature of the prison setting, and the limits on available resources, prisons suffer surprisingly few *collective* disturbances. Although a variety of problems and difficulties arise on a day-to-day basis, these are generally settled (or at least die down) relatively quickly. Generally speaking, most prisons' days are—for both staff and prisoners—humdrum,

---

[1]See, for example, 'No cushy prison option for burglars' *The Guardian*. (UK) September 23, 2003.

[2]As Sparks et al. (1996:24) note, "much of the populist animus against 'cushy' regimes fell on the dispersal system and other relatively privileged long-term prisons such as Grendon" ('Jail Perverts Live in Luxury' *Sun*, May 9, 1994).

[3]See, for example, 'Prison with a Holiday Camp Regime.' Telegraph.co.uk 27.05.06.

domestic, and routine (Crawley, 2004a, 2004b). Occasionally, however, serious problems do arise, and these are more difficult to solve. Sometimes, for example, in the case of a prison suicide, they are impossible to solve, and prison officers must simply deal with the situation as it stands (see Crawley, 2004a, p. 156). As we know, violent resistance from prisoners also occurs, but interestingly it is the *possibility* of violence that generates anxiety among uniformed staff (Crawley, 2004a. p. 133). Much more rarely—at least in the UK—prisoners engage in collective disorder. When such disturbances do occur, however, they can have both negative and positive effects. In contrast to most of the literature on prison violence, this article is concerned to highlight the *positive* outcomes of prison riots.

Our aim, in this article, is to suggest a different way of thinking about those episodes of individual and collective violence which take place in prisons. In our view, it is important to capture the *nuances* of prison violence in a way which succeeds in describing both the mundane background "noise" of low-level violence *and* the occasional "peaks" of more violent events. So how can the prison sociologist (1) convincingly demonstrate the significant differences between the types of violence that take place in prisons and (2) explain the *etiology* of prison violence, the *effects* violence can have on prison cultures, occupational identities, regimes and morale, and of equal importance, (3) the *capacity* of violence to act as a catalyst for (positive) change? In this article we attempt to answer these questions.

The persistence of violence in contemporary western societies remains a significant, and interesting, social phenomenon (van Binsberg, 1995; Thornton, 1995). The anthropologist van Binsberg (1995, p. 1) suggests this is in part due to the social sciences' debt to Hobbes who "defined social life [as] not essentially violent in itself, but rather as an alternative to violence. . . [ ]. . . Violence was regarded as the exception, the uninvited guest, relegated to deviant behaviour and political and military crises in our own society, and to the remote periphery of exotic places." On this view, peaceful coexistence is regarded as the norm, with individual episodes of violence constructed primarily as the result of individual pathology. Collective episodes, such as the prison riot, are constructed as manifestations of a form of temporary madness.[4]

In their overview of the criminological literature on violent crime, criminologists Levi and Maguire (2002, pp. 810–1) reflect on the history of attempts to explain violence in society. They list, in turn, a number of approaches to the study of violence, including the biological, the sociobiological, the psychological, and the psychoanalytical. Importantly for the approach we wish to take in this chapter, Levi and Maguire borrow from the psychological literature the concepts of *instrumental* and *expressive* violence. Instrumental violence is, of course, the type most familiar to criminologists and sociologists of deviance: violence used to obtain a direct economic benefit—to gain property or cash by robbery, to keep other drug dealers off

[4]Interestingly, when talking about their participation in violent incidents, prison officers very often invoke the image of "the red mist" coming down.

one's "patch," and so on. Expressive violence, on the other hand, can be viewed as "emotionally satisfying violence without economic gain,"[5] such as domestic violence or street fighting. However, we want to argue that violence, in addition to being instrumental and expressive, is also *communicative* in that a violent episode can transmit meaning to an audience far wider than its intended recipient.

The Sociology/Social Anthropology of Violence

Before we say anything further on violence within the closed environment that is the prison, we want to briefly note how anthropology (which has its origins in Western studies of "exotic places") has regarded order and disorder in small-scale—and often, incidentally, enclosed—societies. Although (or perhaps because) anthropology began by looking exclusively at non-Western and premodern societies, "order," "violence," and "warfare" have always been significant topics of study (Barfield, 1997; Dunbar; Knight and Power, 1999; Hendry, 1999). More recently, anthropologists have also begun to focus on the existence of such phenomena within industrialized Western societies, and to view our institutions and practices through an anthropological lens. With this in mind, we began to consider whether anthropology can provide prison sociologists with useful ways of thinking about individual and collective acts of violence in contemporary Western institutions such as the prison.

To take one example of an anthropological approach, Roberts's (1979) work on order and disputes begins with the assumption that although there must be order in any society, disputes are inevitable. He points to the widespread occurrence of the *permitted* exercise of interpersonal violence in society, that is, where a limited amount of violence is recognized *by all sides to the dispute* as an appropriate response.[6] On occasion, it may require a more *ritualized* and/or organized staging of interpersonal violence to bring about a resolution. Roberts cites two examples of extreme forms of ritualized violence, one from New Guinea, the *tagba boz,* in which men from opposing sides line up clasping their hands behind their backs. They proceed to kick each other's shins until one side withdraws. The other example is found among certain Eskimo groups who either sit opposite each other and engage in head-butting or stand up and deliver straight-arm blows to each other's heads. In either case, the battle continues until one side falls over. These examples may be characteristic of premodern societies, but we think it may be possible—and indeed fruitful—to treat incidents of violence in prisons in a similar way, that is, as both highly

---

[5]However, as Levi and Maguire acknowledge, a reputation for extreme and perhaps unpredictable, *instrumental* violence ensures that violence, when it comes, is also *expressive* and *communicative*. Such a reputation will ensure that the number of occasions on which actual violence is required will be few.

[6]Of course, the injured party may not accept this as adequate resolution and long-standing grievances and feuds may result which poison relations for some time.

ritualized and *expressive*, but also *functional*[7] in the sense of either asserting a social order or restoring a social order once disrupted. They are also *communicative* in that the display and its outcome quickly become known throughout the community—and that includes a community such as a prison.

Rethinking Prison Violence

In this chapter, then, we take a route somewhere between the anthropological, sociological, and criminological approaches outlined above to explore the *symbolic meanings* that prison violence has for those engaged in it. We examine (albeit only briefly given limits on space) (1) how, when, and why violence is employed; and (2) the ways in which prison violence is *communicative* and how violence can bring about positive change. To do this, we interweave our sociological/anthropological understandings of violence and conflict with comments made to us by prison officers when asked to reflect on the meanings and outcomes of the violent episodes they have either witnessed or have themselves been involved in. The empirical works we use as illustrative examples are drawn from the findings of a large ethnographic study (Crawley, 2004a, 2004b) on the "doing" of prison work. This research involved two years of sustained observations of, and interviews with, prison officers in six prisons in England.[8]

In the discussion that follows we consider both the formal and informal responses to individual prisoner dissent used by prison officers, and highlight the ways in which the latter are underpinned by the more "traditional" (i.e., illiberal) occupational cultures of uniformed prison staff. We then want to go on to suggest that—perhaps contrary to a commonly held assumption that riots can only be destructive, dysfunctional events—collective disorder can actually be *functional*, both for prisoners and for prison staff. We propose that unless there are serious staff casualties, and as long as prison staff can quickly regain control, a prison riot can both reinforce and reinvigorate staff solidarity and provide a catalyst for change. In addition to "clearing the air" (see Crawley, 2004a)—collective disturbances can generate a new set of ground rules, new policies, and new working practices within prisons. As we will show, while collective disorder may be instrumental in the development of more "legitimate" regimes for prisoners,[9] it can also provide a new context for the reinstatement of staff authority. Since in the end, prison officers always "win" in riots, collective disorder can be important in reinforcing (or repairing if necessary) staff morale. Indeed, as we shall see below, when prison staff feel that they are losing

---

[7]In small-scale societies, violence has to be ritualized (even violence between adjoining and competing social groups) because small communities simply cannot afford to risk population depletion through unnecessary bloodshed.

[8]These six prisons included three Young Offender Institutions (Lancaster Farms, Stoke Heath, and Portland (the latter of which had a therapeutic community) and two adult prisons (Garth and Wymott) the latter of which had a "special" regime, i.e., a sex offender treatment wing and a wing for elderly prisoners.

[9]The 1990 riot at Strangeways in Manchester, England, led to significant changes to the regime.

control of prisoners (see Crawley, 2004a for further elaboration), and a riot ensues—following which most prisoners are transferred out and the prison's operational procedures examined—the riot itself may be viewed in a positive light by staff. Moreover, prison disturbances which achieve a lot of media coverage (e.g., the protracted riot at HMP Strangeways in Manchester, England in 1990) give officers a rich fund of "war stories" which they are able to draw upon to generate esteem among fellow staff. This may remain the case even when, later, they have moved to comparative "backwaters" within the prison estate. Disorder—especially collective disorder—is symbolic and highly dramatic. Consequently, participation in such events, whether as prison officer or prisoner, provide opportunities for the construction of a courageous identity through stories of endurance and resilience in the face of danger and risk.

Prisons are emphatically *not* places where inmates are cowed into submission. On the contrary, order is maintained on a daily (even an hourly) basis by a process of compromise and accommodation (see Sykes, 1958) between prisoners and prison officers.[10] Crawley (2004, pp. 19–21) shares Sykes's view of the operation of power in prisons, and expands on his analysis to develop an empirical examination of what happens when the benign "compromise and accommodation" break down and the *process* by which they break down. There is evidence (see Crawley, 2004a) that illicit officer-on-inmate violence occurs simply because some officers (albeit a small minority) refuse to acknowledge that order is based on negotiation. Instead, they retain the (outmoded) belief—a belief deeply rooted in the intensely macho and militaristic occupational cultures of prisons in the 1970s and '80s—that the prison officer is 'the law' in prisons (Livingstone and Owen, 1995). There is also evidence that the incidence of staff-on-inmate violence (and also inmate-on-inmate violence) has a strong relationship to the (widely differing) occupational cultures of individual prisons (Crawley, 2004a). With regard to the latter, there is no doubt that among both prison officers and prisoners in English prisons, certain establishments have a reputation for being more violent than others.

Responses to Prison Disorder

We turn now to a brief discussion of responses to disorder in prisons, but before we do so we wish to make/restate a number of key points:

- The day-to-day maintenance of order depends on appropriate "performances" by both prisoners and prison staff, within which a certain amount of one-on-one violence may be tolerated. When a prison suffers *collective* disorder, however, everything that prison officers had previously relied on breaks down, especially,

---

[10]Prison officers are reliant on inmates' cooperation because (1) they are outnumbered, and (2) they lack any effective system of rewards and punishments. The prison officers' priority is to carry out the bureaucratic tasks associated merely with "running" a prison. Hence, far from being in an all-powerful position, they require the cooperation of inmates.

of course, prisoners' recognition of staff authority and their adherence to rules and routines.

- In prisons, both individual and collective disorder tends to occur when prisoners do not perceive the regime (including the behavior of staff) to be *legitimate*.
- There may be disagreement among prison officers as to what constitutes "order" and how to achieve it. There may also be disagreement as to what constitutes "proper control"; indeed, what counts as negotiation for some officers may be seen as the "appeasement" of prisoners by others.

Dissent[11] in prison may present itself in a variety of forms. "Everyday" dissent includes (1) prisoner-on-staff assaults (some serious, others less so) and (2) prisoner-on-prisoner assaults. In the prisons of England and Wales, attempts have increasingly been made to deal with dissent *proactively*, that is, through good prison management. Proactive management of dissent depends on forward planning and introducing consistency and predictability into the regime (Barclay, Skerry, Sneath & Webster, 1994). As Barclay et al. note, two reports—Dunbar's (1985) *A Sense of Direction* and the *Woolf Report* (1991)—developed concepts which are applicable to the management of dissent. The former pointed to the need to achieve "dynamic security"[12] while the latter emphasised the need to strike a balance between security, control, and justice. Both are concerned with the day-to-day management of dissent. Sometimes, however, proactive strategies to manage dissent are ineffective and staff must resort to *reactive* strategies.

When prisoners do not conform, and control breaks down, officers have a number of responses at their disposal to try to regain it. The first, and most obvious response, is for the officer to simply talk to the prisoner, since uncooperative behavior may often stem from feelings of anxiety, from fall-outs with other prisoners, or from receiving bad news. Another response available to the officer is to put the prisoner "behind his door" (i.e., impose lock-down) until he quiets down. If such measures fail, more formal, reactive mechanisms are set in train. Dissent could also, on occasion, be managed medically. According to one officer: "*It was a case of jump on where you could . . . and we used the wicker suit and large doses of muscle relaxant.*"

Methods of controlling resistant prisoners in UK prisons have changed significantly over the years. The formal reactive response used throughout the 1960s and 1970s—what some officers called the "melee of fist, staves and feet"—was replaced in 1983 by a "technology of the body" known as *Control and Restraint* (*C&R*), a reactive response, which is (or is supposed to be), clinical, methodical, and strategic. C&R is intended to remove the likelihood of injuries being caused to a recalcitrant

---

[11]Dissent in prisons can broadly be conceived as any episode or expression of nonconformity to generally accepted and established rules or practices. Although dissent may start at a simple level as verbal attacks, it often spirals into more complex conflict situations which are difficult to manage (Barclay et al., 1994:158).

[12]"Dynamic security," i.e., security resulting from well-developed staff–prisoner relationships and an active regime is recognized by many prison managers as more important than physical security in the maintenance of control. Dynamic security is characterized by strong, visible leadership and good communication; control depends upon staff knowing what is going on (Dunbar 1985).

prisoner, for example in the general melee of prison officers simply piling into the prisoner's cell. It uses controlled actions aimed at minimizing physical injury, according to laid-down rules of authority and accountability. Generally speaking, the introduction of C&R has reduced the level of injuries to both staff and prisoners. Abusive and inappropriate methods for dealing with prisoners do, however, persist and, as Crawley (2004a) notes, are still put into practice on occasion.

Violence, either individual or collective, represents the most extreme disruption to the normal ordering of the prison. For prisoners to be "disorderly" is for prisoners to *be openly emotional*—to shout, scream, break things, and to engage in physical violence, either because they are distressed, because they are having difficulties relating to certain prisoners or prison officers, or because they are dissatisfied with their treatment. Arguably, much of what has been "won" by prisoners collectively (in terms of improved conditions and the acknowledgment by the courts of their legal rights) has been won through the use of overt violence (see, e.g., Livingstone and Owen, 1995; Woolf 1991; Scraton, Sim, and Skidmore, 1991). Prisoners know this, and the threat of being disorderly is a powerful tool in their relations with prison officers and prison governance.

Disgruntled prison officers, on the other hand, do not need to resort to emotional expression to get what they want. If what they want is an orderly prison [as opposed to a prison in which they feel that prisoners have "got the upper hand" and they themselves feel unsafe (see Crawley, 2004a)] they know that in the last resort they can make that happen, at least on a temporary basis, for example, by issuing a lock-down order whereby all prisoners remain in their cells. If what they want is better working conditions, increased pay, or greater acknowledgment of their efforts, they can engage in consultations with their managers and the Officers' Association (in the UK this body is the Prison Officers' Association or POA). If such talks fail, officers can, *in extremis,* deliberately restrict the regime (see Fitzgerald and Sim, 1982) so that prisoners will become resentful and express *their* emotions instead—in the last resort by rioting.

If what a prison officer wants is to "teach a lesson to" a particular prisoner, then emotion (particularly anger) may well be physically expressed (see Crawley, 2004a). Even here, however, there is likely to be a significant *performative* component to this expressed anger, and the time and place will be carefully chosen. For example, while violence may be meted out to individual prisoners in the confines of their cells, and out of view of other prisoners (and, indeed, other officers), there remains a strong *communicative* element. The distinctive *sounds* made during such assaults[13] (there are likely to be thuds, shouting, and, on the part of the prisoner, cries of distress) communicate a particular message to other prisoners, prisoners who might also be contemplating resistance to the regime. The communicative quality of violence is particularly intense when the perpetrators of violence are in a group. As this

---

[13]During research conducted by Elaine Crawley in Scotland, prisoners who had been transferred to the Barlinnie Special Unit from prisons such as Inverness spoke of the beatings they endured while defined as Scotland's most "difficult" and "dangerous" prisoners. On numerous occasions they had no option but to sit in their own cells listening to the screams of fellow prisoners being assaulted, and then to wait to see if it was their turn next (Crawley 1995).

senior officer put it: *At Manchester, the, heavy mob—which was just a collective term for whoever was free at the time—was quite impressive. And they sent out a very clear message; 'If you behave yourselves, you've got nothing to fear from us, but if you come on strong, this lot will come for you.'*

An important aspect of such "performance," recognized by prison officers and inmates alike, is therefore the communication of where power lies in the prison. Incidents such as these will also either establish or reestablish both informal and formal modes of dealing with resistance, and they may also function as bonding ceremonies for the prison officers involved. Violence on the part of the prisoner allows a prisoner to express physically what he[14] previously could not express verbally—for example that the regime is unreasonable and heavy-handed or in some sense *illegitimate*. Violence on the part of prison officers, in contrast, communicates that, they, not the prisoners, are in charge.

Tales of Bravery and Violence: Prison Officers' "War Stories"

Among serving prison officers in prisons in the UK (and we have no reason to believe this is not also the case in other countries) "war stories" circulate about previous violent episodes in which they have been involved. As with all war stories, the more dramatic and violent these episodes were, the more persuasive—and there is inevitably some elaboration in the telling. In addition, it is clear that violent episodes that attract widespread media coverage and result in the government enacting new pieces of legislation (e.g., an additional 10-year sentence to rioting prisoners for the offence of "prison mutiny") provide the most satisfying of such stories.[15] In talking to officers, Crawley (2004a) found little inclination to talk about contemporary episodes of violence, although we know from newspaper reports that violence in prisons continues to happen. Rather, they uniformly spoke of violence as elsewhere (at "another prison") and in the past (things are "different" now). Most long-serving officers expressed themselves glad that they had "got past the days of blood and snot on the landings"; apocryphal stories (illustrative but not necessarily entirely truthful) about the methods of subduing uncooperative prisoners still survive and are retold on the landings. These tales are replete with words such as *bravery, fear, blood, pay-back,* and *desert*. The oldest tales tell of groups of staff protecting themselves with old mattresses and using whatever means they could to restrain prisoners.

The introduction of C&R has allowed officers to talk of prisoner violence in terms of how they respond to it now and how "things were done" in the past (i.e., with little thought to prisoner injury and a lot of thought to "paying the prisoner

[14]The majority of prisoners are male; hence the majority of prisoners who engage in prison violence are male.

[15]In the UK the riot at HMP Strangeways was the most serious and widely reported.

back"). Crawley (2004a) found that long-serving officers, particularly those nearing retirement, were often willing to talk very frankly about staff-on-inmate violence, even about episodes of violence they themselves had been involved in. According to these officers, before the introduction of C&R the removal of uncooperative prisoners from their cells was carried out in a "chaotic" as well as brutal fashion, as illustrated by the following comments from prison officers:

> There was much more rough-and-tumble before C&R. The methods of subduing an inmate have changed; all you could rely on before was numbers. You just all piled on!

> There were no set guidelines for dealing with violent inmates before C&R came in. You just gave inmates a hammering.

> C&R put an end to a lot of staff-on-inmate violence . . . All you had before was MUFTI, which involved, basically, a mattress and about ten officers [each] with a helmet and a big stick.

> Previously, we had no strategy for dealing with it ['trouble' from inmates]. It was just a mass fight.

> 'Staff just piled in and did as much damage as possible to the inmate.'

Numerous officers reported that in these circumstances injuries to prisoners were often deliberately inflicted, and that the removal of a prisoner to the segregation unit provided an opportunity for some officers to "settle old scores." Those who had worked in the UK Prison Service in the 1970s commented that offering violence to prisoners was never questioned—it was simply what one did: *"Risley was a brutal regime. We'd beat them up and throw them in the corner of the cell, and if they looked at you, you'd beat them up a bit more. We didn't know any different then."*

However, even when they did "know different," many staff simply carried on, sometimes with the full knowledge of their managers:

> [When I worked at Strangeways], some officers went further than shouting and bawling; they used physical force on a fairly regular basis. (How did they get away with this?) They got away with it 'cos those in charge turned a blind eye.

The regime in place at HMP Strangeways up until 1990 has, of course, been discussed a great deal (see, especially, Woolf, 1991). It was a regime in which antagonism between staff and prisoners was intense, and where "pay back" was commonplace. Describing the occupational culture of Strangeways in that period, this senior officer commented:

> . . . If an alarm went off, a melee ensued—you'd get officers running 300 yards just to get a punch in! (Really? Why?) Oh yeah. Cos they had this macho image they wanted to live up to. I've never seen that in the whole of the five years I've been at this prison. You get physical force, but not brutalising of inmates for the sake of it.

The following quote from a long-serving officer who worked at Strangeways at the time of the riot illustrates the *communicative* quality of staff violence, and leaves us in no doubt that violence was intended as both *an individual and general* deterrent:

> *Hand on heart, I've never seen un-called-for violence in this jail, but traditionally, if a prisoner 'performed' [i.e. played up] you bounced him off every wall on the way to the block! That was to show others, as well as him, that officers wouldn't put up with that.*

These examples illustrate what seems very clear to us: that aggressive displays such as these are, to use Pierce's (1940) term, both *iconic* and *indexical*. Weaponry, costumes—in this case riot gear (black uniforms, helmets with full-face visors, batons)—and the rhythmic thudding of running feet demonstrate the threat posed to those who refuse to conform in prisons. This threat is signaled both to the rule-breaker and the potential rule-breaker; it sends out a message to all that rule-breakers will be dealt with.

Riots as Repair Work

The most exhilarating form of "action" available to prison officers is responding to a riot situation (Crawley, 2004a). A major disturbance is, for prison officers, both a highly symbolic and functional event. It makes (dramatically) explicit the notion of "us" and "them" and in so doing coalesces a staff group that may be demoralized and fragmented into a cohesive force with a communal aim—that of overpowering "the enemy." In such situations, petty squabbles and rivalries are forgotten and teamwork is to the fore; whatever their earlier differences with colleagues, prison officers are ready to do whatever it takes to regain the establishment and look after each other. After the Strangeways riot, officers' tales about their feelings *before* ("When you're on the bus[16] going to the prison you're shitting yourself because you don't know what to expect"), *during* ("at Strangeways you could hear the helicopters overhead and see the spotlights flashing by the windows") and *after* the operation to retake a prison are important for the maintenance of occupational cultures and for raising morale. In attempting to theorize the significance of the riot for achieving as well as maintaining staff solidarity, it is fruitful, we think, to borrow from anthropology the concept of the "ceremony of aggregation," whereby the riot becomes a ceremony "in which social relations that have been interrupted are about to be renewed" (Radcliffe-Brown, 1952, p. 243; but see also Kuper, 1983).

[16]The Prison Service of England and Wales must be prepared for incidents of serious conflict with prisoners, and it is for this reason that the Service ensures that a sufficient number of officers are trained in C&R to an advanced standard. When a collective disturbance takes place in a prison, three-man teams trained to such a standard are combined. When a disturbance occurs elsewhere, that is, in another prison, six teams of three (18 officers) are initially sent from establishments nearest the one in difficulty. If the disturbance worsens, officers must be bussed in from prisons farther afield.

The aftermath of a riot may also demonstrate the power of collective action to effect social change. Prison riots are usually followed by a period of relative calmness in the prison, and a process of "taking stock" by prison staff. This is particularly likely to be the case if large numbers of prisoners have been "shipped out" to other prisons leaving behind a significantly higher ratio of prison staff than was previously the case. Riots are generally followed by an internal (external in the case of serious and/or prolonged disturbances) enquiry and a published report. This all contributes to the "taking stock" period when prison managers have time to reflect on the causes of the riot, and how riots might be avoided in the future. It is also a time when prison officers are in the strongest position to restate long-standing concerns, and to renegotiate their working conditions.

We do not want to suggest, however, that violence in all its various guises is *always* functional rather than dysfunctional. On the contrary, while riots usually communicate prisoner dissatisfaction, and thus have the express aim of improving prison regimes, prison violence in its *illicit* forms—in particular the brutalizing of individual prisoners by uniformed staff—can produce extremely *negative* outcomes for all concerned. Such outcomes—including increased levels of suspicion, resentment, anger, and fear and a confirmation of the unequal distribution of power—are negative not only for the psychological and physical health of prisoners but also for the psychological and physical health of uniformed staff. Nonetheless, illicit violence does still *communicate;* most obviously in the prison it communicates the illegitimate character of the prison staff and the illegitimate use of their power.

We have already suggested that riots can be beneficial to the morale of prison staff. As our empirical evidence shows, when officers feel that their interactions with prisoner relations are no longer "right" (i.e., when they feel that the prisoners are outside their control) they may actually wish for a riot, because they know that it will put an end to the status quo and create a space for change. Indeed, when the governor of one of the prisons in this study commented that staff stress levels had fallen since the most recent riot at his establishment, we asked him, hesitantly, if that meant that the riot had had some positive results. He agreed that this was indeed the case: *"We felt so fed up about the place we felt like giving the inmates a box of matches. But in the end, they got their own matches [and the prison was much better afterwards]."*

Similarly, from a male officer working in the same prison at the same time: *"The riot was the best thing that happened to us."*

Riots are also significant events for the identification of "suspect" staff:

If things go well, staff feel they can rely on each other again in similar situations. They're very quick to make derogatory remarks about their colleagues though . . . For example, if they are asking for staff to go to a riot [at another prison], and one declines, some officers will be quick to claim he has 'bottled out.'

Prison riots generate a mixture of emotions among prison officers. They generate apprehension and real fear among prison officers, who remain also acutely aware of the anxieties which grip their families while riots are taking place. However, despite this, many officers find riots exciting—even good fun:

> *Riots are very stressful for wives, but brilliant for male officers . . . In riots, you know that you can't lose. If there's a chance of that, you wait for reinforcements. Basically you're a highly organized and trained team versus a rabble.*

Prison officers explicitly acknowledge the polarizing effect of riots; in such circumstances the staff–prisoner relationship becomes explicitly one of "them and us" (Crawley, 2004a). They also noted the lightening of the atmosphere once the trouble is over, and the sense of excitement and relief once the trouble is over. The following comment from a Principal Officer is, in our view, illustrative of all these issues: *[When there's a riot] Its 'Them and Us' without any doubt then. . . . [afterwards] there's a good buzz about the place . . . with sandwiches and that.*

Concluding Comments

As we have said, of course, riots are *not* everyday occurrences. Rather, many prisons usually manage to "go on" from week to week, from month to month, and from year to year with relatively few serious conflicts between prisoners and staff. When conflict does occur, it is usually at the individual, rather than the collective level. Moreover, conflicts in prisons are not solely prisoner–staff conflicts. On the contrary, disagreements between individual officers, groups of officers, and between officers and their managers constitute a significant degree of conflict in every prison in this study, and these divisions are rooted in the ideologies and working practices and styles of individual members of uniformed staff.

In this chapter we have attempted to provide a different perspective on prison conflict. We have done so by drawing on an anthropological literature which recognizes conflict, interpersonal and collective, as being integral to human societies—particularly small-scale and enclosed societies. We feel this approach foregrounds the *meanings* violent confrontations (both interpersonal and collective) embody, and begins to properly account for the *communicative* nature of violence more generally. We believe these aspects of violence in relation to the prison tend to be neglected in sociological, political, and legal discourses, which generally overlook the communicative and functional dimensions of disorder in prison settings.

References

Barclay, A., K. Skerry, E. Sneath, and R. Webster, (1994). Management of dissent in prison. In E. Stanko (Editor). *Perspectives on violence*. London: Quartet Books.

Barfield, T. (Editor). (1997). *The Dictionary of Anthropology*. Oxford: Blackwell.

Coyle, A. (2005). *Understanding Prisons: Key Issues in Policy and Practice*. Milton Keynes: Open University Press.

Crawley, E. (2004a). *Doing Prison Work: The Public and Private Lives of Prison Officers*. Cullompton: Willan Publishing.

Crawley, E. (2004b). "Emotion and Performance: Prison Officers and the Presentation of Self in Prisons." *Punishment and Society*, 6 (4), 411–27.

Crawley, E. (1995). "Dangerous Prisoners or Dangerous Prisons: A Case Study of Barlinnie Special Unit." Unpublished dissertation. Keele University, England.

Dunbar, I. (1985). *A Sense of Direction*. London: HM Prison Service.

Dunbar, R., C. Knight, and C. Power (Ed). (1999). *The Evolution of Culture*. Edinburgh: Edinburgh University Press.

Fitzgerald, M. and J. Sim. (1982). *British Prisons*. Oxford: Blackwell.

Foucault, M. (1977). *Discipline and Punish*. Harmondsworth: Penguin.

Hendry, J. (1999). *An Introduction to Social Anthropology: Other People's Worlds*. Basingstoke: Macmillan Press.

Kuper, A. (1983). *Anthropology and Anthropologists*. London: Routledge.

Levi, M. and M. Maguire. (2002). Violent crime. In Maguire, M., Morgan, R., and Reiner, R. (Editors). *The Oxford Handbook of Criminology* (3rd ed.). Oxford: Oxford University Press.

Livingstone, S. and T. Owen. (1995). *Prison Law*. Oxford: Clarendon Press.

Mathiesen, T. (1965). *The Defences of the Weak*. London: Tavistock.

Radcliffe-Brown, A. R. (1952). *Structure and Function in Primitive Society*. London: Cohen and West.

Roberts, S. (1979). *Order and Disputes*. Harmondsworth: Penguin.

Scraton, P., J. Sim, and K. Skidmore. (1991). *Prisons under Protest*. Milton Keynes: Open University Press.

Sparks, R., Bottoms, A. and Hay, W. (1996). *Prisons and the Problem of Order*. Oxford: Oxford University Press.

Sykes, G. (1958). *The Society of Captives*. Princeton, NJ: Princeton University Press.

Thornton, R. (1995). *The Peculiar Temporality of Violence (Seminar no. 1)*. Anthropology Department, University of the Witwatersrand, South Africa.

van Binsberg. (1995). *Introduction to the Present Conference and Papers. (Seminar no. 1)*. Anthropology Department, University of the Witwatersrand, South Africa.

Woolf, Lord Justice. (1991). *Prison Disturbances 1991*. London: Her Majesty's Stationery Office.

7

The National Institute of Corrections' Institutional Culture Change Initiative: A Multisite Evaluation

James M. Byrne, PhD, Professor
University of Massachusetts Lowell

Don Hummer, PhD, Assistant Professor
Penn State Harrisburg

Faye S. Taxman, PhD, Professor
Virginia Commonwealth University

Introduction: The Empirical Foundation of Culture Change Initiatives

A number of recent, comprehensive reviews of the research on the causes of various forms of prison violence and disorder (e.g., Byrne and Hummer, *this text*, Edgar et al, 2003; Bottoms, 1999; Liebling, 1999; Braswell, Montgomery, and Lombardo, 1994; Adams, 1992) have examined the impact of prison "culture" on the level of order and control within the prison. However, much of the research identified in these reviews consisted of case studies and/or nonexperimental research studies of poor quality. In addition, most studies focused on inmate (not staff) culture; and with few exceptions, no attempt was made to link changes in inmate (or staff) culture to changes in prison violence and disorder. In fact, there is no body of existing scientific evidence that can be referenced to support the dual notions that (1) prison "culture" is one of the primary causes of prison violence and disorder, and that (2) changes in prison culture (i.e., movement from a negative to a positive culture) will result in improvements in the performance of prisons in the control of violence and disorder.

We begin our examination of the ongoing series of culture change initiatives sponsored by the National Institute of Corrections by offering this unequivocal, negative assessment of the empirical adequacy of research on prison culture for a reason: to highlight the importance of quality research in this area. The evaluation highlighted in this chapter represents one of the few objective, independent, assessments of prison culture currently available (see Byrne and Hummer, *this volume*). While the results of our evaluation of the NIC initiative are important to consider, we recognize that much more—and much higher quality—research needs to be conducted before we can offer an assessment of whether culture change—inmate, staff, and/or management culture change—will result in lower levels of violence and disorder in prison.

It is clear that the conceptual framework underlying the National Institute of Corrections' culture change initiative was developed—by necessity—based on the combined *experiences* of NIC staff and its contracted service providers; it was not designed based on an evidence-based review of the research on "best practices" in this critical program/policy area. At the time of the development of the NIC initiative, this type of evidence-based review was simply not available.

Because the NIC project was designed based on the *experience* of NIC staff and service providers, not on a review of research of "best practices," it is important to consider the context of that experience. For several years, NIC received repeated requests for assistance from corrections managers across the country concerning a variety of inmate, staff, and management problems (e.g., staff sexual misconduct, excessive use of force, inmate misconduct/drug use, staff retention). When traditional strategies (often based on training and education) did not appear to work, NIC program developers decided to try a different approach, based on the notion that in many prisons, the "presenting" problem was actually a symptom of a more serious underlying problem: the negative prison culture that existed in these institutions. According to NIC program developers, the underlying assumption of the Culture Change Initiative is straightforward: If negative prison culture is a primary cause of various forms of prison conflict, violence, and disorder, then it certainly makes sense to focus on "culture change" as a primary solution to this problem. While there are certainly myriad possible strategies that can be included in this type of broad, organizational change initiative, the four interventions described in the following section represent NIC's preliminary attempt to develop reliable and valid assessment protocol and then test three possible interventions (of varying scope, duration, and intensity) designed to positively change the culture of selected prisons.

Defining Institutional Culture

An obvious starting point to our review was to ask NIC program developers how they define prison culture generally, and how they distinguish positive from negative prison culture. Prison (or institutional) culture has been defined in a variety of ways, but in this initiative, it refers to "the values, assumptions, and beliefs people hold that drive the way the institution functions and the way people think and behave" (NIC's working definition of institutional culture 2003). Although NIC program developers did not explicitly define either positive or negative prison culture, it appears that "negative" prison culture was believed to be associated with a variety of staff-related (staff morale, staff sexual misconduct, lack of diversity); management-related (ineffective communication, convoluted mission, lack of leadership); and offender-related (racial tension, prisoner drug use, escapes) problems. The NIC initiative targeted both staff and management culture as their primary focus, based on the following key assumption: *"If we change staff culture, inmate culture will follow"* (Corcoran, 2004, personal communication). This is an interesting research question, which has not been explored by researchers studying either staff culture (e.g., Carrol, 2003), or inmate culture (e.g., Toch and Maruna, 2005; Edgar, O'Donnell, and Martin, 2003).

Based on this assumption, NIC has designed a strategy that targets staff (and management) culture; the "inmate culture" issue is not addressed directly. However, NIC program developers contend that changes in staff culture will affect inmates in two specific ways. First, staff attitudes toward specific types of offenders (e.g., sex offenders) and groups of offenders (e.g., minority offenders) will be changed positively as a result of this initiative. Second, as a result of these attitude changes it is expected that staff behavior will also change in a number of important respects. For example, both staff tolerance of prisoner-on-prisoner violence (e.g., inadequate staff response to allegations of sexual assault) and the use of force by staff on inmates (i.e., institutional violence) are expected to decrease as a result of this initiative. The idea that rates of violence and disorder in prison can be lowered *without* specifically addressing inmate culture is a central tenant of this NIC–ICI initiative. We discuss the implications of this design choice in the conclusion of our review.

A Description of NIC's Institutional Culture Change Initiative

The NIC-sponsored culture change initiative included four different program components: (1) assessment of institutional culture, (2) promoting positive corrections culture, (3) strategic planning and management, and (4) leading and sustaining change. Each initiative has been designed as a stand-alone program, and all are short in duration. For example, the "Assessment" initiative is designed to be a 3- to 5-day intervention; promoting positive corrections culture is a 3-day training session; strategic planning and management is designed to vary by site, but is likely to involve between 5 and 15 days (on- and off-site); and leading and sustaining change involve approximately 15 days (consulting effort [on/off-site]) per year. While the "dosage" level of each intervention is minimal, several sites received more than one intervention. This natural variation allows the research team to assess the individual and combined effect of these four interventions. Table 7.1 highlights site-specific combinations of the four interventions developed for this initiative. Between September

TABLE 7.1   *National Institute of Corrections' Institutional Culture Initiative (NIC/ICI) Site Matrix**

	Assessment	PPCC	Leading & Sustaining Change	Strategic Planning
Site 1	yes	yes	yes	no
Site 2	yes	yes	no	**
Site 3	yes	no	no	no
Site 4	yes	no	yes	no
Site 5	yes	no	no	no
Site 6	yes	no	yes	no
Site 7	yes	no	no	no
Site 8	yes	no	yes	no
Site 9	no	yes	no	no

*Includes all sites identified by NIC between September 15, 2003 and September 15, 2005, where NIC-funded ICI interventions were initiated. However, for three sites included in our review, the initial assessment was actually conducted one year prior to the initiation of our evaluation (sites 2, 6, and 8).

**No strategic planning initiative was conducted during our evaluation period; this was a pretest site.

15, 2003 and September 15, 2005, nine separate sites were selected for one of more of the four initiatives we evaluate in this report [Note: *At the request of NIC, the names and locations of these prisons will not be included in this chapter.*] In addition, NIC is currently in the process of selecting sites for a new wave of interventions, based on follow-up with the initial pool of "Assessment Sites," as well as the identification of new sites for one or more ICI interventions. We should also point out that a distinction has been made by the evaluation team between work *publicly* funded by NIC during the study period (9/15/03 to 9/15/05) and work in the exact same area contracted *privately* with one of the two contractors selected as service providers. [*Note: at NIC's request, the names of service providers are also not included in this chapter*]. Our evaluation focused exclusively on those intervention sites (and interventions) funded by NIC during our review period.

Examination of Table 7.1 reveals that during our evaluation review period, one site received three interventions, four sites participated in two interventions, and four sites were assessment-only sites. However, one of the four "assessment-only" sites was the pretest site for the strategic planning initiative, which has yet to be initiated. For the purpose of our impact evaluation, we have examined the three initiatives tested at the nine prison sites highlighted in Table 7.1. All nine sites were "assessed" (although only six of these assessments were completed during our review "window"); three sites received the PPCC training; and four sites were selected for the "leading and sustaining change" initiative. Although obviously still in the development phase, we have included the fourth intervention (strategic planning) in our assessment of the level (and quality) of overall program implementation, since it was included in our original evaluation plan.

Initiative 1: Assessing Institutional Culture   The National Institute of Corrections selected a program implementation group to conduct a number of assessments of prison culture throughout the country over the past few years. *Assessing institutional culture* was designed not only as an individual initiative, but also as the first step of the NIC–ICI process to identify other interventions (e.g., Promoting Positive Prison Culture, Leading and Sustaining Change, Strategic Planning and Management) that may be suitable for addressing the organizational culture issues. The assessment team (consisting of four to five members from various backgrounds and specialties) works onsite at the facility for 4 days to assess and analyze the culture of a prison including the underlying beliefs and values of staff. One tool that the implementation group uses to assist in the assessment process is the Organizational Culture Assessment Instrument—Prisons (OCAI-P), a survey consisting of two sets of six questions that asks staff how they feel about the facility currently and then how they would prefer that the facility operate.

Using the assessment tool, the implementation team surveys a number of staff members that serve various functions within the facility, while also interviewing other staff and management directly to develop a balanced view of the organization's culture. Following 3 days of on-site work, the assessment team presents their findings to prison management and staff, highlighting their assessment of institutional culture and offering their initial recommendations. Based on the response of the institution to this review, one or more of the following culture change strategies were initiated at the facility: (1) promoting a positive prison culture, (2) strategic planning and management, and (3) leading and sustaining change. The decision on *which* strategy to employ was made by NIC project staff, in conjunction with the warden at each facility.

However, NIC program developers did not design a specific follow-up protocol for the allocation of subsequent culture-related interventions at assessment sites. Without such basic review criteria, it is difficult to determine *why* some sites were "assessment-only" sites, while other sites received one or more additional services funded through this initiative. Adding to the confusion about site selection for multiple NIC-funded interventions are two factors: first, NIC designated some sites for additional culture-related services using separate technical assistance funds; second, some sites received additional services from the two subcontractors selected for this initiative using separate funding. In both instances, these activities are not included in our implementation review, although they may certainly affect our impact assessment.[1] The program implementation group has conducted dozens of assessments of institutional culture, but only nine of these assessments were conducted in sites included in our 2-year review (September 15, 2003 through September 15, 2005). However, the same group has conducted several other assessments that were funded either through

---

[1]For the next wave of culture-related NIC initiatives, we strongly recommend that NIC develop explicit guidelines for linking these initiatives, based on the types of problems identified. In addition, NIC will also need to examine the issues raised when subcontractors assisting in site selection, even in an advisory role, are doing the same work (in this case, culture change) both publicly and privately.

NIC technical assistance funds or privately, using institutional funds. These assessments are not included in our evaluation, because they are not funded directly through the NIC–ICI initiative. Our review is based on an examination of the assessment reports that the implementation group provided to these facilities, as well as the observational data collected by the evaluation team doing site visits to several sites during the assessment process. It should also be noted that the decision on whether a particular site would be a NIC/ICI site or a privately funded intervention was unclear.

Table 7.2 lists the presenting problems provided to NIC by facility administrators to request a cultural assessment. The decision to do a cultural assessment in a particular prison was made by NIC with input from the program implementation group. A comparison of the total requests for assistance (from prison administrators/wardens) and the subgroup of selected sites did not reveal any clear criteria for selection by NIC or the implementation team (e.g. by presenting problem, source of request–i.e., central office vs. warden). However, interviews with program implementation group members revealed that three important criteria were considered: (1) significance of culture issue (e.g. persistence and/or seriousness); (2) diversity of institutional setting (e.g. by security level, size, urban/rural location, and gender); and (3) the perceived cooperation level of central office and the warden.

The implementation group's plan for assessing a prison requires a team of four to seven consultants to conduct an on-site review for 3 to 5 days. The on-site review included observations by team members of inmate-staff interactions across all shifts, the use of focus groups to discuss presenting/ongoing issues at the institution, and meetings/interviews with the warden and management team. To meet the needs of each institution scheduled to be assessed, the implementation team selected consultants that had expertise in areas that fit the presenting problems of the institution. Typically, implementation team staff lead the review, with the assistance of two outside consultants, including former wardens or correctional officials. It does appear that the implementation group's reliance on in-house staff, rather than external experts with specific training in ethnographic research (or as sociologists), limited the intended multidisciplinary nature of the on-site assessment process. To obtain a multidisciplinary assessment of prison culture, the program implementation group would need to expand its pool of consultants to include a wider range of backgrounds (psychologists, sociologists, etc.), which was their original strategy for conducting these on-site assessments, according to the review/background materials (Carrol, 2003).

The assessment instrument used by the program implementation group is a modified version of the well-respected and public domain tool developed by Cameron and Quinn, (1999), titled the *Organizational Culture Assessment Instrument (OCAI)*. The implementation team went through an extensive review process to select an assessment tool to be used as part of this review process; Dr. Ken Cameron was an advisor to the implementation team and recommended the tool that he and Quinn developed for private sector agencies. With permission from the authors, the implementation group adapted this assessment to be used in correctional settings primarily in the prison system by creating the *Organizational Culture Assessment Instrument—Prison*

TABLE 7.2 *Requests for Assistance through the NIC/ICI*

Institution	Reason for Request
Site 1	A high level of use of force incidents against inmates.
Site 2	Pervasive staff sexual misconduct at all levels of staff (correctional officers and support staff up to a deputy warden) and racial discrimination and disparate treatment of people of color—African-American employees in particular.
Site 3	High rate of positive drug urinalysis tests, staff over-familiarity with inmates, a lack of consistent institutional leadership, low morale, and a poor relationship with the Central Office.
Site 4	Problems included a disconnect with Central Office due to minimal visits to the facility by Central Office staff, a high positive rate of inmate drug use, staff over-familiarity with inmates, and a lack of institutional leadership.
Site 5	(1) Recent history of staff sexual misconduct; (2) multiple institutional missions; (3) staff recruitment and retention difficulties; (4) high utilization of overtime by security staff; and (5) acquired a negative reputation as the Department's "problem" institution.
Site 6	(1) Lack of line staff and supervisors' experience in basic correctional philosophy and practice; (2) multiple disconnects between individual units and the institution as a whole; (3) lack of experience and leadership among supervisors; and (4) inmate idleness. Site 6 was not initially selected due to its relatively brief history. It was later selected to pilot test the efficacy of a modified version of the culture assessment protocol and its ability to provide meaningful assistance to relatively newer facilities where the institutional culture had not yet become solidified, and the organization required assistance more in the spirit of "prevention" and "early intervention" rather than "treatment." At this site, abbreviated protocols were used.
Site 7	Multiple institutional problems.
Site 8	High rates of staff sexual misconduct.
Site 9	High staff turnover, low staff morale, inmate idleness and violence, and a lack of institutional leadership.

(OCAI-P). The program implementation group altered the language of the instrument to make it applicable to correctional institutions. Like the OCAI, the OCAI-P assesses the profile of organizations along a continuum representing competing values: stability and control versus flexibility and discretion, and internal versus external focus. The OCAI-P along with interviews and observations were used to illustrate the relationships of subcultures within an organization.

According to Cameron Quinn, the OCAI-P is designed to identify "competing values" in an institution where the current and desired states are not the same. It is a tool to assist in the assessment process that provides information to the implementation team regarding the degree to which the values of the institution and the fit with the individuals who work in that institution are in agreement. According to the implementation group, because the concept of a culture reflects "the system of values, beliefs and norms held in common by a group of people, the tool identifies the degree to which this occurs through reporting the scores in each dimension as well as the degree to which the current and desired state are similar" (quote from program implementation group assessment report, included in Byrne, Taxman & Hummer (2005)).

The OCAI-P produces a profile of the institution's current and preferred culture types formed by surveying six distinct characteristics of the organization: (1) Dominant characteristics—what the overall prison organization is like; (2) organizational leadership—the style and approach of the administration including the warden; (3) management—how employees are treated by their supervisors/management; (4) organizational glue—bonding mechanisms that hold the organization together; (5) strategic emphasis—the mission and vision that drive the prison's strategy; and (6) success criteria—how success is defined, and what gets rewarded and celebrated. It should be noted that the instrument does not provide a score for each of these constructs but rather presents a score for four separate dimensions of culture:

- *Family culture*—focuses on internal maintenance with flexibility, concern for people and sensitivity to customers;
- *Dot com culture*—focuses on external positioning with a high degree of flexibility and individuality
- *Market culture*—focuses on external positioning with a need for stability and control;
- *Hierarchy culture*—focuses on internal maintenance with a need for stability and control-culture types.

By using these cultural "types" as an analytic framework, the assessment team provides a profile of the current and preferred culture at each institution they visit, which they highlight in their final presentation to the warden and staff. However, it should be noted that the assessment team utilizes both objective survey data and subjective assessments based on team member observations, interviews, and focus group discussions in their evaluation of a particular prison's prevailing culture.

Initiative Two: Promoting Positive Corrections Culture   *Promoting Positive Corrections Culture* is designed as a 3-day training session to teach prison staff about organizational culture; in the process, participants will examine (and learn about) the organizational culture of their own prison. According to program developers, the overall goal of this course is to provide staff at the facility an opportunity to assess their culture and then begin to formulate a plan to improve it. Once a "core group" of staff is trained, they are then responsible for disseminating the information throughout the facility to other staff. Staff will attempt to identify and write a mission statement (or action plan) for the facility, identify their current and desired values and beliefs, and develop a strategy for improving the culture to attain their desired outcomes and monitoring progress toward those goals. This relatively short intervention strategy (3 days) can be viewed as one step in a long-term organizational change process.

According to NIC program staff, this curriculum has been well received by the field; as a result, it has been used both as a follow-up to assessment and to introduce the "culture" issue to many institutions. The curriculum has undergone several changes, especially as a result of feedback by a set of trainers that were trained to "deliver" the training (i.e., a train the trainers program). Additionally, the curriculum has been used in several different ways—to begin the change readiness process, to train trainers within a prison setting, and to assist wardens in beginning to consider a new vision for their organization. There appear to be a number of merits to this curriculum, including its potential use as a tool to prepare the wardens for the change process (e.g., its flexibility in format, length, and in its application to different target groups), and to prepare both line staff and management for a concerted, large-scale culture change initiative.

Initiative Three: Strategic Planning and Management   *Strategic Planning and Management* is a third initiative designed to affect change within the culture of a correctional facility. During our evaluation period, no site had been selected for this initiative, although the protocol has been pretested. The purpose of this initiative is to provide staff of the facility with an opportunity to create a strategic plan or "map" of responses by the facility to different situations, or problems within the prison, and then to assist in the development of an action plan designed to change the culture of the selected facility. This strategy was designed to allow each facility to develop their own policies and procedures and their own mission/vision statements about where they want the facility to go (in terms of culture change) and how they plan to get there (i.e., a plan of action incorporating one or more culture change initiatives). Following the creation of a planning team (representing all facets of employment within the facility), staff identify a specific strategic planning process/model, develop a response methodology, prepare a guide for staff, and develop an evaluation process to monitor any progress made. The project is designed to (1) familiarize the staff with the "tools and techniques" of strategic planning and management, and (2) assist in the implementation of a concrete action plan targeting problems related to prison culture. The duration (and intensity) of this initiative has not been predetermined, but it is expected that project staff will be on-site for "blocks" of days over several months. Although we were unable to assess the implementation and impact of this strategy, it makes sense to consider the potential utilization of strategic planning tools and techniques as a culture change strategy.

Initiative Four: Leading and Sustaining Change   One final strategy that is available through the NIC–ICI is the *Leading and Sustaining Change* initiative. This strategy's purpose is to develop the skills and competencies for change in the specific leadership at a facility. The Leading and Sustaining Change strategy is designed to provide the leadership of a particular prison (e.g., warden) or prison system (e.g., commissioner) with an advisor to help craft responses to culture-related management issues. In many instances, this initiative will be a follow-up to the completion of an on-site assessment of institutional culture. In these prisons, a "change advisor" will serve as an outside consultant to the warden at select facilities to assist leadership in changing the organization's culture. The change advisor (in conjunction with leadership) will identify areas in which staff need assistance and select approaches that will help increase staff's understanding and competencies in the area of culture change. The overall goal of the initiative is to develop a fuller understanding of the culture within the prison and the implementation of a "plan of action" to move the prison toward their desired goals.

The feature that distinguishes the "Leading and Sustaining Change" initiative from the "Strategic Planning" initiative is the use of external change advisors with expertise in organizational development and change, but not necessarily in prisons, to facilitate the change process. The idea behind this initiative is that prison managers need to think "outside the box" for a change, because the long-standing approach taken by NIC—relying on the expertise and experience of former and current corrections managers as consultants—has not worked particularly well, according to NIC staff. This strategy has been designed to work with only those facilities that are viewed by NIC as "ready for change" and that have expressed a willingness to change their culture. Because the change advisor works directly with the warden and management team of a prison, the initiative is a good example of a "top-down" change strategy. The four selected prisons with change advisors have their expertise for approximately 10 to 15 days per year. The change advisors complete their work with the warden and "change team" via on-site activities, telephone follow-up, and report preparation.

We have conducted interviews with the current change advisors to learn about their activities and efforts. The phone interviews revealed that the selected change advisors were experienced in the area of organizational change, had a background working with a wide range of public and private sector organizations (although none had prior experience with prisons or correctional institutions), and viewed the issues faced by corrections managers as quite similar to the issues faced by managers in other large organizations. (see Byrne, Taxman, and Hummer, 2005).

Evaluation Design

Our evaluation design included two basic components: an implementation assessment, and an impact evaluation. First, we assessed both the level and quality of implementation for each of the four initiatives developed by NIC, based on our review of available program documentation and our direct on-site observations of these initiatives. The results of this review are needed to answer a basic evaluation question: Was each program implemented as designed? It should be obvious to even the casual observer that we *cannot* evaluate the impact of the NIC initiative unless we have a clear understanding of what *exactly* was implemented under the auspices of "institutional culture." As we discuss in the conclusion of this chapter, it is critical to examine the linkages between/among program design, implementation level/quality, and the assessment of each program's (and/or combinations of programs) impact.

Figure 7.1 depicts the key features of our impact evaluation, which utilizes a pre/post interrupted time series design to examine the impact of each intervention (or intervention combination) on the level of violence and disorder in prison. For each site, a comparison is made (utilizing ARIMA [Auto Regressive Intergraded Moving Average] modeling techniques) between the pattern of incidents at this facility (monthly total incidents; monthly totals, by incident type) during the period *before* the NIC initiative was begun (between 6 and 12 months, depending on data availability at each site), and the period beginning with the start of the first intervention at the facility (the start-up date) and continuing for at least 1 year. The use of interrupted time series as a program evaluation strategy is fairly standard; a review of the evaluation research literature reveals that this method has been used in the past to evaluate a wide range of criminal justice interventions, including mandatory sentencing, gun control, intensive probation supervision, and most recently, the "Operation Ceasefire" policing initiative. While the use of this type of quasi-experimental design does not represent the most *rigorous* evaluation design choice available, it was the most appropriate (and rigorous) evaluation design at our disposal, given (1) the exploratory nature of the intervention, and (2) the amount of funding available to conduct the evaluation.

The evaluation of this NIC–ICI required two types of data collection. To evaluate the initiative definitively, it was critical to measure *both* the *implementation* and the *impact* of each of NIC's four major strategies. The preference for the evaluation was both a strong implementation component (including on-site observation, assessment instrument validation, review of selection process, examination of presenting problems by prison administrators, and selected interviews with subcontractors involved in each component of the initiative) and a comprehensive impact evaluation (including collection and review of monthly incidents reports, disposition/sanction data, offender background data, monthly grievance reports [and dispositions]; and quarterly collection and review of survey data to gauge changes in staff/management perception of prison culture and prison problems).

Using a combination of existing data sources (e.g., *Census of Federal and State Correctional Facilities, 2000,* ACA's survey of riots, disturbances, violence, assaults, and escapes, etc.), the evaluation team developed a protocol to collect and analyze baseline data directly from participating institutions on both the level and rate of prison incidents (including both individual and collective violence by inmates

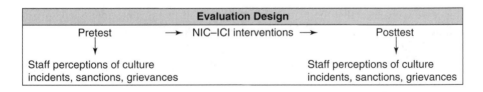

FIGURE 7.1   Evaluation design of the National Institute of Corrections' Institutional Culture Initiative.

and staff) during the study period. We have collected baseline indicators that will allow us to track the impact of these interventions over time (6–12 months prior to implementation and at least 1 year after start-up). However, data availability (and data quality) has varied from site to site, which will make it difficult to fully assess the impact of the NIC initiatives at these sites.

Because many of the NIC-sponsored initiatives involve "soft" changes in the culture of prisons, we decided to use an approach similar to Liebling (1999), in her study of the "moral performance" of prisons in England to measure the climate and culture within an institution. The most direct method to do this is through staff and administrative surveys, which were distributed to a random sample of prison staff on a quarterly basis, beginning at the start of the first on-site initiative. (Note: sample size varied from site to site, given such factors as facility size and staffing levels; survey administration also varied from site to site for a different set of reasons, which we discuss later in the report.) The survey tool includes the following components: (1) a modified version of the Cameron and Quinn Organizational Culture Assessment Inventory—Prisons (OCAI-P); and (2) the Sweeney and McFarlin (1997) scale of organizational justice to measure procedural justice and distributive justice. The data collection plan called for data to be collected quarterly for 1 year past the initial assessment or any NIC–ICI. (Note: site-specific variation in the length/ timing of the initial and follow-up survey administration is discussed later in this article).

Assessing the Level and Quality of Implementation

The difficulties inherent in culture change initiatives are highlighted in our initial findings regarding both the level and quality of implementation for each of the four NIC initiatives. Although the results of our implementation assessment are only presented in summary form in this article (due to space limitations), a more detailed review is available from NIC's information center (Byrne, Taxman, and Hummer, 2005). Our evaluation findings on level and quality of implementation can be divided into three categories: (1) conceptual framework, (2) implementation level, (3) and implementation quality.

Conceptual Framework

Our review revealed that the National Institute of Corrections has identified "prison culture" as a major impediment to ongoing attempts to reform prisons *and* as a potential cause of various forms of prison violence and disorder (including interpersonal, intrapersonal, collective, and institutional violence and disorder). To address the prison culture problem, NIC—in conjunction with private (for profit) vendors—has developed a culture change initiative that targets both the staff and management of prisons for services. Importantly, the NIC initiative was designed based on a simple premise: "If you change staff culture, inmate culture will follow." When reviewing

NIC's four initiatives, a clear distinction can be made between NIC's *staff-centered and management-centered* strategies and the *inmate-focused* violence/disorder reduction strategies proposed by Edgar (*this text*) and others (see, e.g., Lifers' Public Safety Steering Committee, 2004).

Based on our review, there appear to be a number of significant design flaws that need to be addressed by NIC program developers. First, our review revealed that there is no body of empirical evidence to support the notion that there is a direct relationship between negative prison culture and prison performance (see Liebling, *this text*; and Byrne, Hummer, and Taxman, *this text*, for a detailed review), and/or that "inmate culture" is directly related to the dominant staff (or management) culture identified in prison. Second, there is no clear definition of the specific problems to be addressed at each of the prison/intervention sites, and the linkage between identified problems and recommended interventions. It appears that this strategy was developed based on the assumption that regardless of the particular presenting problem (e.g., high staff turnover, sexual misconduct, racial tensions, institutional violence), the "solution" was the same: initiate one or more of the culture change interventions at the targeted prison. We suspect that all four initiatives would be significantly improved by the incorporation of the types of "best practices" reviews now widely used in the public sector and in other parts of the criminal justice system. It seems fairly obvious that regardless of the prevailing institutional culture, different problems will have different solutions; less obvious is the recognition that in prisons today, we may "solve" one problem (e.g., interpersonal violence will be reduced using segregation) but create another (e.g., intrapersonal violence, collective violence will increase in these locations) as a consequence (Sparks, 1999).

A third problem we identified in our review of the conceptual framework for the NIC initiative was that the "dosage level" for two of the initiatives (strategic planning and management and leading and sustaining change) is set much lower than normal for this type of work. For each initiative, a single consultant/change advisor will work with prison management for up to 15 days a year; in many cases, this consulting work will be done off-site, using phone calls, e-mails, and conference calls. A much larger project, including a significant on-site commitment, appears to be needed for this type of large-scale, organizational change effort.

Finally, our review revealed that NIC did not establish clear criteria for the selection of specific prison sites, the number of initiatives used at each site, and the timing/sequencing of multiple initiatives. This lack of precision was likely due to changes in NIC project administration, as well as the inevitable changes that occur in the ongoing development of a new initiative. Without clear selection criteria, the NIC project became much more difficult to evaluate. Similarly, specific components of *each* intervention changed during the course of this evaluation, which leads to problems in multisite evaluations of this kind, because an intervention (e.g., leading and sustaining change) initiated in one jurisdiction may look quite different across sites. From the service provider/vendor's view, such changes are inevitable in the early stages of a new initiative. However, these changes may effectively render a new initiative "evaluation-proof," because if the results of the evaluation are mixed or even negative, the vendor/service providers can simply point out that the "program has changed" during the evaluation (or since it was completed). In this regard, innovation becomes a powerful—and effective—buffer against negative evaluation.

Implementation Level

Overall, our review revealed that the NIC Culture Change Initiative was implemented in a manner generally consistent with the design originally proposed by NIC. Both the assessment and the PPPC initiatives have been fully implemented at the targeted number of sites, while the "leading and sustaining change" initiative had start-up problems (three of four sites did not begin work until year 2 of our evaluation), and the "strategic planning and management" initiative has remained in the development stages for the duration of our evaluation (years 1 and 2). Because the implementation level was higher for both the PPPC workshops and the assessment initiatives, we have more complete impact data available from prison sites selected for these initiatives. However, we should point out that the format of the PPPC workshops changed from site to site during the implementation phase, suggesting shifting goals for the workshop. In addition, the vendor conducting assessments of institutional culture changed its on-site review protocol during the second year of the initiative; in year 2, the assessment team placed less emphasis on survey findings and more emphasis on the qualitative assessments of the assessment team in preparing their report and offering recommendations.

Implementation Quality

Our implementation assessment identified a number of potential problems with the NIC initiative, but these problems appear more closely linked to the *design* of the initiative (e.g., low dosage, staff qualifications) than its actual implementation. We briefly highlight the identified problems next, but a more detailed discussion and review are found in our final NIC evaluation (Byrne, Taxman, and Hummer, 2005):

Assessment Initiatives:
- The "assessment" process initially placed too much emphasis on survey data that are unreliable, due to sample size constraints.
- The assessment team was not able to include the diverse group of reviewers (e.g., ethnographers, sociologists) described in the original program model.
- The final assessment report provided to each prison did not include specific, problem-oriented strategies and/or specific recommendations for follow-up work on culture change issues through the initiative.
- The timing of the initial assessment was often scheduled several months after the request for services, which raised the likelihood that "Things would be different" when the assessment team arrives on site (e.g., new management, new problems).
- The criteria for the selection of sites for NIC-funded assessments was unclear, especially given the potential availability of state/local funding at some sites; if

available, the assessment work could be contracted directly with the (for profit) organization assisting NIC staff with the site selection decision.

Promoting Positive Corrections Culture:

- There was no clear linkage between the 3-day, promoting positive corrections culture program and the other three initiatives. In particular, there needs to be additional work on how the culture "styles" identified using the OCI (Organizational Culture Inventory) will be used to distinguish positive from negative culture; and in the process, on how to determine whether a particular institutional culture facilitates—or impedes—the prison's ability to address the presenting problems identified during the training session.
- Due to the unclear linkage between the dominant culture styles identified using the OCI instrument and performance, its use as the "center piece" of the PPCC training program is problematic.
- We have not assessed whether the quality of the PPCC varies by the facilitator selected for a particular site, but this is always a concern when multiple facilitators are employed in this fashion.

Leading and Sustaining Change:

- The contractor appears to have identified a qualified group of change advisors for each of the first four intervention sites; these change advisors have a strong background in organizational development.
- There appears to be some confusion over role definition (e.g., advisor, facilitator, O.D. consultant), which may be addressed by increasing the amount of consulting days allotted for each site, and in the process, requiring a greater proportion of contracted work to be performed on-site. Further role clarification will be needed even if this change is implemented.
- The organizational development activities initiated at each of the four sites (e.g., change committee meetings, development of "plans of action" to address culture-related issues) have been limited, at least to date (Byrne, Taxman, and Hummer, 2005).
- By design, change advisors have been selected from outside the corrections arena, based on their work on organizational change issues in the public and private sector. The overall quality at the LSC initiative would likely be improved if change advisors could be teamed with experts in evidence-based practices in corrections settings. The linkage between accurate problem definition (via assessment and/or LSC advisor reassessment) and evidence-based selection of intervention strategies is critical.

Strategic Planning and Management:

- Our review of pretest experiences suggest that there may be a "dosage" issue; a much greater time commitment appears to be needed on site.
- Strategic planning and management can easily be integrated into the "plan of action" currently used as part of the LSC initiative.

- There appears to be no need for both an LSC and a strategic management initiative; components of both designs should be integrated into a single initiative, thereby increasing the funds available for *on-site* organizational development.
- Direct linkages need to be made between all three primary change strategies (assessment, PPCC, strategic planning/LSC).
- The current strategic planning manual does not include a "problem-oriented" approach to organizational change in prison settings; it also does not include an evidence-based review of "best practices" in the areas of prison management likely to be addressed in the initiative (e.g., classification, programs, situational context, the link between incidents and sanctions.)

Overall, we found that both the implementation level and quality were sufficient to allow us to examine the potential *impact* of three of the four culture change initiatives (strategic planning and management was not implemented during our review period) developed by NIC. We present the results of our impact assessment in the following section.

Evaluating the Impact of NIC's Institutional Culture Initiative

We begin our description of the impact evaluation by briefly describing data collection procedures and the method of analysis utilized in our impact assessment. Initial findings are highlighted, focusing on (1) changes in staff perceptions of institutional culture, and procedural justice and (2) changes in the incident levels reported at selected impact sites during the pretest, posttest review period. As we noted above in our implementation review, a more detailed presentation of findings is included in our final evaluation report to NIC (see Byrne, Taxman, and Hummer, 2005).

Two separate data collection efforts were undertaken during this evaluation. First, we collected objective data on the number of reported incidents at each prison, the types of sanctions that were imposed for each incident type (e.g., violence, disorder), and where available, inmate (and staff) grievances. In all our analyses of these objective data, the unit of analysis is the incident, the sanction, and/or the grievance, rather than a particular offender. Table 7.3 summarizes our data collection efforts; to date, we have collected data on these objective indicators from seven sites.[2]

---

[2]The collection of these data involved gaining permission from individual prison and/or statewide data systems after careful attention to human subjects/confidentiality issues. Importantly, no individual-level, offender-specific identifiers are included in our data file. Although pretest data collection, coding, and analysis are complete at several sites, we were still in the process of collecting posttest (or postintervention) data at the time of final report submission to NIC (OCT, 2005), due to a variety of factors, including: (1) intervention start-up dates, (2) data availability, (3) state-level evaluation review/human subjects protection protocol, and (4) the decision of one site to "pull-out" of the culture change initiative. See Byrne, Taxman, and Hummer (2005) for more detailed review.

TABLE 7.3 *National Institute of Corrections' Institutional Culture Initiative (NIC/ICI) Data Collection Matrix*

	Objective Data Collection		Survey Data Collection*		
	Pretest Data	*Posttest Data*	*Time 1*	*Time 2*	*Time 3*
Site 1	1987 incidents 106 grievances	4458 incidents na	na	na	40 staff surveys
Site 2	in progress in progress	na na	88 staff surveys	41 staff surveys	15 upper management surveys
Site 3	224 incidents 217 grievances	176 incidents 103 grievances	25 staff surveys	na	na
Site 4	566 incidents na	na na	93 staff surveys	101 staff surveys	73 staff surveys
Site 5	269 incidents na	na na	46 staff surveys	31 staff surveys	na
Site 6	474 incidents 170 grievances	na na	na	na	na
Site 7	463 incidents 105 grievances	na na	na	na	na
Site 8	Data collection protocol being developed	—	—	—	—
Site 9	Data collection protocol being developed	98 staff surveys	—	—	

At sites 1, 6, and 8, initial assessment occurred before evaluation began. At site 3, no time 2 or time 3 data could be collected due to institutional resistance. At site 5, no time 3 surveys were conducted due to institutional resistance.

na = data not available.

— = data not scheduled to be collected.

* = we are currently collecting staff perception data at three sites. Only one site (site 7) has not continued with ICI, while two other sites have just recently been added (sites 8 and 9).

In addition to objective data collection, we have collected preliminary survey data from prisons on staff (and management) perceptions of prison culture. To examine the impact of the initiative on *changes* in staff perceptions over time, we designed a survey protocol that calls for administering the surveys—on site—on a quarterly basis (beginning—whenever possible—in the first month of the initiative). A review of Table 7.6 reveals that we were less successful collecting staff perception data than objective (incident, sanction) data. Nonetheless, data were available to examine staff perceptions of culture at six sites.

These survey data are less complete than we anticipated, due to difficulties associated with gathering a random sample of staff from existing agency staffing lists, and problems related to administering the survey on-site during an *ongoing* NIC culture change initiative. Despite the data collection shortfalls we have described, it is still possible to offer a preliminary assessment of the "impact" of the NIC initiatives on both staff perceptions of culture, and the number of reported incidents during the prepost period.

The method of analysis we use to examine changes in staff perceptions at selected review points (Time 1 (start date), Time 2 [approximately 4 months after start-up], and Time 3 [4 months after time 2 review]) is a t-test for significant differences ($p < .05$) in the average scores ($\bar{X}$) given by survey responses to each of the four culture dimensions included in the OCAI-P survey instrument: family, Dot.Com, Market, and Hierarchy. Our analysis of pretest, posttest changes in the number of incidents (monthly) at each prison uses an ARIMA modeling technique that is appropriate for this type of multiple intervention, interrupted time series analysis. Separate ARIMA models have been developed and tested for each intervention site. Because sites vary not only in the number of interventions employed (one, two, or three), but also in the length and timing of the pretest, postintervention period, we will be able to examine the impact of these design decisions on our objective outcome measures: incidents, sanctions, and grievances.

The Impact of the NIC Institutional Culture Change Initiative on Staff Perceptions of Prison Culture

We highlight the results of our initial review of changes of staff perceptions of prison culture in Table 7.4. In the first site we examined (site 4 in Table 7.2), two separate change initiatives were introduced: Assessment, and Leading and Sustaining Change. Both of these interventions had been initiated by the time of our time 3 review (July 2005), so it is at this point that we would anticipate the largest "overall" effect (T1 vs. T3 mean differences) of the combined intervention. Surprisingly, the only statistically significant difference in mean scores between T1 and T3 was in staff perceptions of the family dimension, which appeared to *diminish* in importance over time. During this same 1-year period, staff perceived the culture becoming more hierarchical. Because there is no evidence that *either* dimension is associated with improved organizational performance, we are limited in the inferences that we can draw here about organizational culture and organizational change. However, it does appear that staff perceptions of the prison's "culture" did change over time at this site.

Further examination of Table 7.4 reveals that for site 5 (an assessment-only site), no statistically significant differences were found between the mean scores of survey respondents at time 1 (October 2004), and time 2 (May 2005), although at this site it appears that the organization was becoming less hierarchical and more "like a family" over time. Because only *one* intervention was introduced at this site, one possibility to be considered is that initial improvements following assessment were diminishing over time; if we had conducted follow-up surveys a few months earlier at

TABLE 7.4 *Results of OCAI-P Surveys—Staff Perceptions of Current Organizational Culture; Mean Scores on Scales Measuring four Dimensions***

Site 4				F	sign.
	Time 1	*Time 2*	*Time 3*		
Family	118.05	116.16	100.62	3.996	<.05 (t1, t3)
Dot.com	102.90	85.55	104.77	6.829	<.01 (t1, t2)
				5.060	<.05 (t2, t3)
Market	157.13	155.51	150.53		
Hierarchy	219.52	239.75	240.42		

Site 5		
	Time 1	*Time 2*
Family	118.24	132.32
Dot.com	82.15	97.45
Market	132.93	136.06
Hierarchy	226.85	188.87

*Significance levels ($p < .05$) only included for statistically significant differences in mean scores (T1, T2, T3) for each site.

this site, we may have identified the initial effect. However, small sample sizes ($N = 46$, T1; $N = 31$, T2) are a more likely explanation for the findings reported here. Overall, our preliminary analyses do not offer strong, initial support for the hypothesis that the intervention(s) introduced at these two sites resulted in significant changes in staff perceptions of the importance of the four culture dimensions measured using the OCAI-P instrument. Obviously, these analyses are preliminary and should not be viewed as evidence that the initiative doesn't work; but it does engender speculation.

The second component of the survey instrument evaluated dimensions of organizational justice. Sweeney and McFarlin (1997) delineated the key concepts of procedural and distributive justice as indicators of perceived organizational fairness and equity. Procedural justice refers to the decision-making process of rewards and benefits of an organization while distributive justice pertains to the actual allotment of benefits to members of the organization. Secondary organizational justice dimensions include views of management (Learning), fairness of punishment, equity of treatment, accountability of members of the organization, and extent of member contributions in decision-making (Control).

Table 7.5 shows that at site 4 (Assessment and Leading and Sustaining Change site), employees were significantly more positive about "procedural justice" issues at their facility, meaning that they viewed the management/operation of the prison as fairer and more objective. This change in perception occurred after the initial assessment was done at the facility, but perhaps more importantly, the change in perception was sustained through follow-up data collection. The same held true for perceptions of "distributive justice"—that is, one's views of their own performance and rewards

TABLE 7.5 *Results of Prison Culture Surveys—Staff Perceptions of Sweeney and McFarlin (1997) Scale of Organizational Justice; Mean Scores on Scales Measuring and Seven Dimensions**

Site 4 Dimension/Subscale	Time 1	Time 2	Time 3	F	sign.
Procedural	3.0976	3.2966	3.3015	5.00	<.05 (t1, t2)
Justice				5.09	<.05 (t1, t3)
Learning	2.8513	3.1192	3.0456	6.651	<.05 (t1, t2)
Distributive	3.0000	3.1639	3.1807	5.247	<.05 (t1, t2)
Justice				5.474	<.05 (t1, t3)
Punishment	3.6452	3.6312	3.6723		
Treatment	3.4301	3.3465	3.5642		
Accountability	3.7161	3.6594	3.7600		
Control	3.3247	3.3100	3.5013		

Site 5 Dimension/Subscale	Time 1	Time 2	F	sign.
Procedural Justice	3.4264	3.1017	4.105	<.05
Learning	3.0213	2.8611		
Distributive Justice	3.2194	3.0215		
Punishment	3.6023	3.5833		
Treatment	3.1307	3.2222		
Accountability	3.6000	3.5200		
Control	3.2636	3.4889	5.177	<.05

*Significance levels ($p < .05$) only included for statistically significant differences in mean scores (T1, T2, T3) for each site.

for positive job performance. Employees were more likely to believe that their hard work would be recognized by the administration after assessment and this perception was also sustained through follow-up in July (2005).

A more positive view of management ('Learning subscale') occurred also at this facility between the assessment and the "leading and sustaining change" initiative. However, in contrast to the discussion above, these positive views were *not* sustained through the follow-up period (summer 2005). The data indicate that employee attitudes had reverted back to near preassessment levels. Other dimensions in the Table 7.5 show no significant changes over time.

While site 5 (assessment-only site) also had significant attitudinal changes with regard to "procedural justice," the shift in perceptions was the *opposite* of that at site 4. Employees at site 5 perceived procedural justice to be declining over time, during the change initiative. We must be more cautious in the interpretation of these data, as site 5 has only two waves of survey data available. The only additional significant finding from site 5 is a shift in perception to a more control-oriented view of managing problem inmates or utilizing protective custody. Again, interpretation of this finding (and whether the significant findings from this institution are associated) should be facilitated with additional data-collection phases.

The Impact of the NIC Institutional Culture Change Initiative on Violence and Disorder in Prison

A trend analysis of total incidents at site 1 (*this site had all three NIC culture change initiatives during our review period*) during the 23-month period from May 2003 to March 2005 (Figure 7.2) shows a drop in inmate misconduct immediately following the implementation of each new phase of the ICI. For example, the mean number of reported incidents per month for the 6 months immediately preceding the assessment stage of the project was 351.2. The mean dropped to 292.3 in the 6 months immediately following the assessment, and decreased even further to 240.8 in the 8 months following implementation of PPCC. Figure 7.2 presents the trend line for the number of total incidents by month.

A similar view of the data for violent incidents only (Figure 7.3) shows a pattern that appears relatively unchanged through the implementation period. The mean number of violent incidents prior to assessment was 44.2. That figure increased slightly, but not significantly, after assessment to 50.2 and then levels off in late 2004/early 2005 at an average of 41.25 violent incidents reported per month.

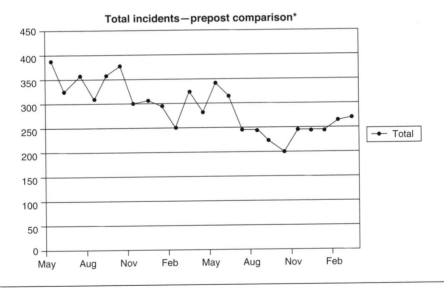

FIGURE 7.2   Total incidents at site 1, May 2003–February 2005.

*November 2003—Assessment of institutional culture.

January 2004—Leading and sustaining change.

August 2004—Promoting a positive corrections culture.

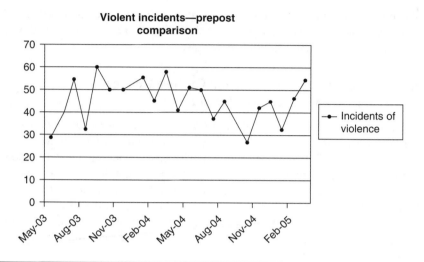

FIGURE 7.3   Violent incidents at site 1, May 2003–February 2005.

November 2003—Assessment of institutional culture.

January 2004—Leading and sustaining change.

August 2004—Promoting a Positive corrections culture.

Similar trend analyses were not performed for other subcategories of incidents (such as property offenses, drug/contraband possession, or sex offenses) because the numbers of such incidents were typically very low overall and, commonly, several months had no such offenses. Also, administrative violations, which make up the bulk of the total incidents reported at this facility, were not separated out due to the redundancy in analyzing these infractions and total incidents simultaneously. The trends for administrative violations and total offenses mirror one another; thus there is no need to review each separately. (See Figure 7.4 for a graph of administrative violations and note the similarity to total offenses from Figure 7.2).

To test whether the differences in the number of total incidents is significant over time (or more specifically between the preimplementation phases and after implementation of the ICI), ARIMA was utilized to measure mean differences in incidents by month for the 23 full months of data we possess for site 1 (the multiple intervention site). The moving average (Auto Regressive Integrated Moving Average) is calculated as a constant over the 23 iterations, in this case months. The *t*-ratio is the variance from the average at the beginning of the time series and the end. During the pretest phase, the number of incidents is higher than at the end of the time series—as visually demonstrated by Figure 7.1 above, but significance cannot be determined without additional regression analysis of the data over time. The results of the first ARIMA run are presented in Table 7.6.

The *T*-ratio indicates the difference in the average of the continuous variable (number of total incidents) between time 1 (May 2003) and time 2 (March 2005).

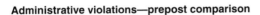

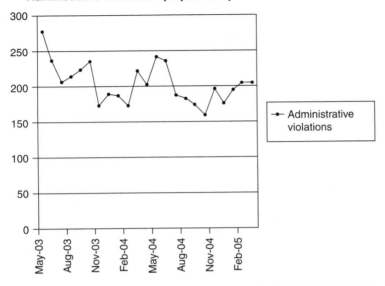

FIGURE 7.4 Administrative violations at site 1, May 2003–February 2005.

November 2003—Assessment of institutional culture.

January 2004—Leading and sustaining change.

August 2004—Promoting a positive corrections culture.

The analysis confirms the significant drop in total incidents from the pretest phase through the latest month of posttest data. It is important to keep in mind that this significant result represents an *initial effect*, and that a *sustained effect* can only be confirmed with forthcoming data from this facility. As a check on the modeling used in this analysis, a similar time series was performed on the 17 months of posttest data only (not shown, but available from the authors) to test whether a significant difference in total incidents occurs *during* the implementation phase itself, thus possibly confounding the results above. An analysis over the 17 posttest iterations (months) revealed no significant mean differences in total incidents reported monthly during

TABLE 7.6 *Time Series (ARIMA) Analysis of Total Incidents at Site 1, May 2003–February 2005*

	Estimate	*Standard Error*	*DF*	*T*	*Prob (T)*	*AR(1)*
Total incidents	−5.80469	1.239715	20	−4.68	0.0001	0.1658
Constant	361.0283	17.06726	—	21.15	0.0000	—

TABLE 7.7   *Time Series (ARIMA) Analysis of Violent Incidents at Site 1, May 2003–February 2005*

	Estimate	*Standard Error*	*DF*	*T*	*Prob (T)*	*AR(1)*
Violent incidents	−0.155596	0.3009579	20	−0.51	0.6108	−0.021
Constant	46.785568	4.1247497	—	11.34	0.0000	—

this time period, demonstrating that the significant difference is exclusive to the pre- and posttest phases of the ICI. A similar analysis was conducted on the subcategory of violent incidents reported over the same time period at site 1. As shown in Figure 7.3, the trend analysis showed no change in effect between the pre- and posttest phases of the ICI. To confirm, another ARIMA analysis was performed using only reported incidents of violence. Results are presented in Table 7.7.

The mean number of offenses decreased from time 1 to time 2, but not significantly so, leading to the tentative conclusion that the ICI has not reduced institutional violence at this prison, at least in the initial stage of the evaluation. As mentioned previously, more data would have to be collected to conclusively determine impacts of the strategies in terms of both incident reduction and sustainability. It is also important to point out what the preceding analyses *cannot* indicate. The data used in this evaluation have been collected using a quasi-experimental design method. Without a control group for comparative purposes, it is impossible to determine if the significant effects demonstrated here, or those potentially revealed in future analyses, may be causally linked to the ICI alone. It is entirely possible that significant effects may be resultant from intervening variables such as a change in inmate or staff composition, changes in policy that affect incident reporting practices, or a change in data collecting for incident reports just to name a few.[3] We must be extremely cautious also in basing conclusions on data from one institution. Time will allow for future waves of data from site 1 as well as similar analyses of data from other institutions included in the NIC–ICI.

Conclusions

Overall, our review revealed significant problems related to both to the design of the initiative and the level and quality of implementation that NIC will need to address as they move forward with this initiative. Modifications in the design in two of the

---

[3]We present our findings using incident levels rather than rates; however, there were no significant changes in prison populations at these sites during our initial review period.

initiatives (Assessment and PPCC) during the course of the evaluation render an overall assessment of impact more difficult than we originally anticipated. Perhaps most importantly, our review of implementation underscores the value of clearly defining the problem (i.e., developing a problem-oriented approach to addressing prison violence and disorder) and then linking specific interventions (and intervention combinations) to the problem(s) being addressed. The lack of overall "linkage" between/ among these four separate initiatives appears to be a significant potential design flaw that will need to be addressed by program developers.

Our preliminary review of the *impact* of the NIC culture change initiative revealed a statistically significant drop in overall inmate misconduct during the course of the project at the one multiple intervention site for which complete prepost comparison data were available. At this prison, the mean number of (officially) reported incidents dropped from a high of 351.2 incidents (in the 6 months before the first NIC assessment we conducted) to a low of 240.8 reported incidents per month (in the 8-month period after the implementation of the last on-site culture change intervention (PPPC). The results of time series analyses confirmed a significant drop in overall reported incidents immediately following each new "phase" of the NIC initiative at this prison. However, the subgroup of reported violent incidents (a mean of 44.2 per month pretest vs. 41.25 posttest) dropped only slightly during our assessment period, which suggests that the NIC initiative did not have the same effect on violence (interpersonal) as on other forms of inmate misconduct. Separate analyses of staff *perceptions* of institutional culture and organizational justice revealed mixed results, with sites showing changes in both areas, but in opposite directions. Overall, these preliminary results suggest that despite the design and implementation problems we noted earlier, there appears to be a potential link between prison culture and prison performance that needs to be explored further, using more rigorous evaluation designs (see Lieblong, *this text*).

Our review of the research on institutional culture generally—and culture change in particular—has revealed that "culture change" initiatives, such as the ones we describe here, do not have a strong empirical foundation (Bottoms, 1999). Moreover, there are a variety of innovative problem-solving strategies (e.g., the situational prison control strategies described by Wortley [2002]), that do appear to be based on a much firmer empirical foundation. The challenge for NIC and other agencies interested in culture change (both staff and inmate-based) is to develop an array of *evidence-based* problem-solving strategies and then integrate these strategies into current staff-based culture change initiatives (e.g., strategic planning, leading and sustaining change). Ultimately, we suspect that specific problem-solving interventions designed to reduce the levels of violence and disorder in prison will need to address issues related to both staff and inmate cultures. Without close attention to institutional culture, the latest wave of prison reform initiatives will not be successful, in large part because they will not be implemented as designed.

References

Adams, K. (1992) "Adjusting to Prison Life." In *Crime and Justice: A Review of Research,* Vol. 16. Chicago, IL: University of Chicago Press.

Beck, A., Hughes, and Harrison (2004) "Data Collections for the Prison Rape Elimination Act of 2003." *Bureau of Justice Statistics Status Report* (June 30, 2004) Washington, D.C.: U.S. Department of Justice, Office of Justice Programs.

Bench, L. L. and T. D. Allen. (2003). "Investigating the Stigma of Prison Classification: An Experimental Design." *Prison Violence* 83(4): 367–382.

Bogue, B. (2004). *Implementing Evidence-Based Practice in Community Corrections: The Principles of Effective Intervention.* Washington, DC: National Institute of Corrections. Available at: www.cjinstitute.org

Bottoms, A. E. (1999) "Interpersonal Violence and Social Order in Prisons." In M. Tonry and J. Petersilia, Eds, *Prisons.* Chicago: The University of Chicago Press, pp. 205–281.

Braswell, M. C., R. H. Montgomery, Jr., and L. X. Lombardo, Editors. (1994). *Prison Violence in America,* 2nd. edition. Cincinnati: Anderson.

Byrne, J., Taxman F. and Hummer, D. (2005). "The Development, Implementation, and Evaluation at NIC's Institutional Culture (Change) Initiative" Final Report to the National Institute of Corrections, Oct. 2005.

Cameron, K. and Quinn R. (1999). *Diagnosing and Changing Organizational Culture.* Addison-Wesley.

Camp, S. D., G. G. Gaes, N. P. Langan, and W. G. Saylor. (2003). "The Influence of Prisons on Inmate Misconduct: A Multilevel Investigation." *Justice Quarterly* 20(3): 501–533.

Carroll, L. (2003). "Institutional Culture." Unpublished paper.

Dumond, R. (2000). "Intimate Sexual Assault: The Plague That Persists," *Prison Journal* 80: 407–14.

Dumond, R. (2003). "Confronting America's Most Ignored Crime Problem: The Prison Rape Elimination Act of 2003." *Journal of the American Academy of Psychiatry and the Law* 60. 31(3): 354–360.

Edgar, K., I. O'Donnell, and C. Martin (2003). *Prison Violence: The Dynamics of Conflict, Fear and Power.* Devon, UK: Willan Publishing.

Gaes, G. and A. Goldberg (2004). *Prison Rape: A Critical Review of Literature.* Working Paper, National Institute of Justice, Office at Justice Programs, Washington, DC.

Gilligan, J. (1996). *Violence: Reflections on a National Epidemic* New York: Random House.

Hensley, C., R. Tewksbury, and T. Castle. (2003). "Characteristics of Prison Sexual Assault Targets in Male Oklahoma Correctional Facilities." *Journal of Interpersonal Violence* 18: 595–606.

Liebling, A. (1999). "Prison Suicide and Prisoner Coping." In M. Tonry and J. Petersilia, Eds, *Prisons.* Chicago: The University of Chicago Press, pp. 283–359.

Liebling, A. and S. Maruna. (2005). "Introduction: The Effects of Imprisonment Revisited." In A. Liebling and S. Maruna, Eds, *The Effects of Imprisonment* Devon, UK: Willan Publishing, pp. 1–29.

LIS, Inc. (2000). *Sexual Misconduct in Prison: Law, Agency Response, and Prevention.* Washington, DC: U.S. Department of Justice.

McCorkle, R. C., T. D Miethe, and K. A. Drass. (1995). "The Roots of Prison Violence: A Test of the Deprivation, Management, and 'Not-So-Total' Institution Models." *Crime and Delinquency* 41(3): 317–331.

National Institute of Corrections (NIC). (2003). Institutional Culture Initiative, Program Meeting, Washington, DC.

National Research Council. (2004). *Fairness and Effectiveness in Policing.* Washington, D.C.: National Academy Press.

O'Donnell, I. and K. Edgar (1998) "Routine Victimization in Prisons" *Howard Journal of Criminal Justice* 37: 266–279.

Reisig, M. D. (1998) "Rates of Disorder in Higher-Custody State Prisons: A Comparative Analysis of Managerial Practices." *Crime and Delinquency* 41(2): 229–244.

Reisig, M. D. and N. P. Lovrich. (1998). "Job Attitudes among Higher-Custody State Prison Management Personnel: A Cross-Sectional Comparative Assessment." *Journal of Criminal Justice* 26(3): 213–26.

Riveland, C. (1999) "Prison Management Trends, 1975–2025" In M. Tonry and J. Petersilia, Eds, *Prisons.* Chicago: The University of Chicago Press, pp. 163–203.

Sparks, R., A. Bottoms, and W. Hay. (1996). *Prisons and the Problem of Order.* Oxford: Clarendon Press.

Stephan, J. and J. Karlberg. (2003). *The Census of State and Federal Correctional Facilities.* Washington, DC: U.S. Department of Justice.

Struckman-Johnson, C. J. and D. L. Struckman-Johnson. (2000). "Sexual Coercion Rates in Seven Midwestern Prison Facilities for Men." *Prison Journal* 80: 279–390.

Sweeney, P. D. and D. B. McFarlin. (1997). "Process and Outcome: Gender Differences in the Assessment of Justice." *Journal of Organizational Behavior* 18: 83–98.

Taxman, F. and J. Byrne. (2001) "Fixing Broken Windows Probation." *Perspectives* 25(2): 23–29.

Toch, H. (1992). *Living in Prison: The Ecology of Survival.* Washington, DC: American Psychological Association.

Walters G. D. (1998) "Time Series and Correlational Analyses of Inmate-Initiated Assaultive Incidents in a Large Correctional System." *International Journal of Offender Therapy and Comparative Criminology* 42(2): 124–132.

Welch, M. (2004). *Corrections: A Critical Approach* (2nd. edition). New York: McGraw-Hill.

Wortley, R. (2002). *Situational Prison Control: Crime Prevention in Correctional Institutions.* Cambridge, UK: Cambridge University Press.

Wright, K. With J. Brisbee and P. Hardyman. (2003). *Defining and Measuring Corrections Performance: Final Report.* Washington, DC: U.S. Department of Justice.

8

Prison Culture and the Treatment and Control of Mentally Ill Offenders

Arthur J. Lurigio

Departments of Criminal Justice and Psychology
Loyola University Chicago

Jessica Snowden

Department of Psychology
Loyola University Chicago

I've been in the S.H.U. [secure housing unit] for over 6½ years where I've been locked in a cell for 23 to 24 hour a day, 7 days a week. In March of 2002, I had a mental breakdown because of being in S.H.U., and I attempted suicide by swallowing 150 pills. I was saved and sent to Central New York Psychiatric Center (CNYPC) for treatment where I stayed for about 7 weeks. I was then discharged and sent to Wende Correctional Facility. . . .Upon my arrival at Wende I was put in an observation cell in the mental health unit, where I was kept for 25 days in a stripped cell. I was mistreated and denied everything. There was no heat in the place. I was put in a dirty, bloody cell. I was jumped and assaulted by correctional officers and was left unattended to by the mental health staff. In the time I was there, I continually requested to be sent back to CNYPC for further treatment because I went into a relapses and could not bear being locked in a cell 24/7 again. . . .I'm writing this letter in hopes that someone will do something about the way these people in the mental health department here treats people, after I'm gone, because I simply cannot carry on no more like this. I hope that my death will bring about some good; if not at least I'll finally find some peace. C. X., New York, July 28, 2002. (Human Rights Watch, 2003, p. 37)

Nearly 35 years ago, Abramson (1972) noted that more and more people with *serious mental illness* (*SMI*) were being routed through the criminal justice system instead of the mental health system. Since then, data have suggested that the mentally ill are arrested and incarcerated in numbers that surpass their representation in the general population as well as their tendencies to commit serious crimes or be arrested (Council of State Governments, 2002). In light of these data, mental health advocates and researchers have asserted that people who have been cared for in mental health agencies and psychiatric hospitals are being shunted more frequently into jails and prisons (Teplin, 1983).

Prisons have now become de facto mental hospitals in the United States (Benson, 2003). Since the 1980s, get-tough crime control policies produced a precipitous growth in the use of incarceration and have made correctional facilities less inclined to view themselves as the center for rehabilitative services and more as the locus for punitive containment. Ironically, the shift away from treatment coincided with an increase in the numbers of inmates who require behavioral healthcare services, including HIV counseling, mental health intervention, and substance abuse treatment. Prisons are ill-equipped to deliver such care. As Benson (2003) pointed out, "They weren't built to deal with mentally ill people; they were built to deal with criminals doing time" (p. 23).

The number of mentally ill prisoners is substantial and growing, but treatment resources are scarce. Even when budgets allow for growth in the size of treatment staff, the availability of suitable providers can still remain woefully inadequate. Many mental health professionals are repelled by the prison environment; they see it as oppressive, regimented, and inhospitable to the basic principles of psychiatric care (Fagan, 2003). And so, the prison system has a mental health crisis on its hands: a sizeable population with a variety of clinical needs, a shortage of treatment providers, a prevailing philosophy that is antithetical to humane care, and institutional imperatives that place inmate control over their adjustment and well-being (Fagan, 2003).

This chapter focuses on the handling of prison inmates with SMI and is divided into four major sections. The first discusses the two principal factors that led to the involvement in the criminal justice system of large numbers of persons with SMI. It also briefly examines evidence for the "hydraulic hypothesis." The second presents findings on the prevalence of mentally ill prisoners in the United States and notes the limitations of our current estimates of the size of this population. The third describes standards of care for incarcerated persons with SMI and recent national data on the treatment of inmates with SMI. The fourth reviews the procedural and staffing issues in prisons (i.e., prison culture) that impede the delivery of effective mental health services.

1. Background: The movement of the mentally ill from the mental health system to the criminal justice system.

People with SMI enter the criminal justice system, and people involved in the criminal justice system enter the mental health system, through a variety of pathways, including "crisis services, departments of social services, human services agencies, educational programs, families, and self-referrals" (Massaro, 2003, p. 2). For most mentally ill offenders, SMI complicates rather than causes their involvement in the criminal justice system (Draine, 2003).

The disproportionately high number of people with SMI in correctional facilities is associated with the rising number of discharges from state hospitals, the passage of restrictive commitment laws, the splintering of treatment systems, the War on Drugs, and the deployment of order-maintenance policing tactics. (See Lurigio and Swartz [2000] for a full discussion of these factors.) Perhaps the two most important factors that have led to the reportedly large numbers of persons with SMI involved in the criminal justice system are the dramatic shift in mental health care related to the closing of state psychiatric hospitals and changes in crime control policies related to drug law violations.

Deinstitutionalization

A fundamental change in mental health policy, known as deinstitutionalization, relocated the hub of care for patients with SMI from psychiatric hospitals to community mental health centers. Deinstitutionalization is a major contributor to the processing of the mentally ill through the criminal justice system (Grob, 1991). After World War II, state mental hospitals nationwide began to release thousands of psychiatric patients to community-based facilities for follow-up treatment and services. As a result, the number of patients in state mental hospitals nationwide was substantially reduced from 559,000 in 1955 to 72,000 in 1994 and to fewer than in 60,000 in 2000 (Center for Mental Health Services, 2002). The length of the average stay in psychiatric hospitals and the number of beds available also declined sharply (Kiesler, 1982). Although the motivation for this change was driven by clinical experience and compassion—the idea that the mentally ill would be better served in the community—deinstitutionalization was an ill-fated policy with unbidden consequences.

The deinstitutionalization movement was fueled by media accounts of patient abuse and neglect, the development of effective medications to treat SMI, federal entitlement programs that paid for community-based mental health services, insurance coverage for inpatient psychiatric care in general hospitals, and antipsychiatry polemics written by researchers and academic scholars (Sharfstein, 2000). Deinstitutionalization, however, was grossly underfunded and never properly implemented. The policy provided for appropriate outpatient treatment for a large percentage of the mentally ill but it failed to care adequately for individuals who had limited financial resources or social support, especially those with the most severe and chronic mental disorders (Shadish, 1989). The lack of dollars and resources for the mentally ill in the community eventuated in the incarceration of an increasingly larger number of people with mental illness.

The failed transition to community mental health care had the most tragic effects on patients who were least able to handle the basic tasks of daily life. Public psychiatric hospitals became treatment settings for the indigent. Their patients became younger because new medications obviated the need for extended periods of hospitalization. Before these medications were discovered, psychiatric patients could remain in the state hospital for decades and be released when they were elderly. New money-saving measures and hospital policies shifted the costs of care from state budgets, which paid for hospitalization, to federal budgets, which paid for community-based mental health services. Unlike earlier generations of state mental patients, those who were hospitalized during and after the 1970s were more likely to have criminal histories, be addicted to drugs and alcohol, and tax the patience and resources of families and friends (Draine, 2003). In addition, newly implemented, restrictive commitment laws made it difficult to involuntarily hospitalize persons with SMI who had no insight into their illness and no desire for treatment (Lurigio and Swartz, 2000).

The shortage of affordable housing aggravates the problems of people with SMI and interferes with the provision of mental health treatment. An estimated 20 percent to 25 percent of the adult homeless population is afflicted with SMI (Council of State Governments, 2002). The characteristics of the mentally ill, therefore, resemble those of many criminally involved persons: poor, young, and estranged from the community (Draine, 2003; Steadman, Cocozza, and Melick, 1978). As the Council of State Governments (2002) noted, "Without housing that is integrated with mental health, substance abuse, employment, and other services, many people with mental illness end up homeless, disconnected from community supports, and thus more likely to decompensate and become involved with the criminal justice system" (p. 8).

In short, many persons with SMI fall into the clutches of the prison system because of the dearth of mental health treatment and other community services (Grob, 1991). Links between the criminal justice and mental health systems have always been tenuous, and the mentally ill who move from one system to the other frequently fail to receive enough treatment or services from either. Therefore, as their mental health deteriorates, they become both chronic arrestees and psychiatric patients (Lurigio and Lewis, 1987).

The rise in the number of persons with SMI in the nation's prison population affirms Penrose's (1939) notion that a relatively stable proportion of persons are confined in industrialized societies (i.e., as the census of one institution of social control—the mental hospital—goes down, the census of another—the prison—goes up). Penrose's seminal work has been cited by several authors who have written about the criminalization of the mentally ill (e.g., Cote, Lesage, Chawky, and Loyer, 1997).

Akin to Boyle's law in physics, which describes the constant relationship between volume and pressure for an ideal gas, Penrose's theory—also referred to as the "hydraulic hypothesis"—posits that a constant number of psychiatrically disordered persons require institutional care in industrialized or western societies. If psychiatric hospitals are unavailable or unwilling to treat the mentally ill, then they will be housed in other institutions (e.g., prisons and jails). The movement of the mentally ill from one long-term care facility to another has been termed "transinstitutionalization."

Direct evidence for the hydraulic hypothesis is mixed and based on correlational studies. For example, using census data from several states, Palermo, Smith, and Liska (1991) reported an inverse relationship between the number of the mentally ill persons in jails and prisons and those in psychiatric hospitals. They concluded that correctional facilities have become repositories for people with serious mental health problems. In contrast, Teplin and Voit (1996) reviewed studies on the imprisonment of the mentally ill and were unable to find definitive support for the hydraulic hypothesis. Similarly, Steadman, Monahan, Duffee, Hartstone, and Robbins (1984) analyzed imprisonment data in six states, comparing the numbers of prisoners with previous psychiatric hospitalizations in 1968 and 1978. The investigators concluded that the purported movement of the mentally ill from state hospitals to state prisons was unsupported by the data. Despite the lack of hard data in support of transinstitutional-ization, most policy analysts and advocates cite the closure of psychiatric hospitals and the absence of follow-up care as a primary causal agent in the growth of people with SMI in the correctional system (Council of State Governments, 2002).

War on Drugs

Since the late 1980s, people possessing and selling illegal drugs (who also have high rates of drug use) have been incarcerated with greater frequency and for longer prison terms than they were previously (Lurigio, 2004). Drug offenders constitute one of the fastest-growing subpopulations in correctional facilities (Beck, 2000). A fairly large proportion of these offenders have co-occurring mental illnesses, contributing to the number of mentally ill individuals in the criminal justice system (Swartz and Lurigio, 1999).

Like dolphins among tuna, many mentally ill, drug-using persons have been caught in the net of rigorous drug enforcement policies (Lurigio and Swartz, 2000). Several studies show that persons with SMIs who use illicit drugs are more prone to violence and more likely to be arrested and incarcerated than those who do not (Clear, Byrne, and Dvoskin, 1993; Swanson, Estroff, Swartz, Borum, Lachinotte, Zimmer, and Wagner, 1997; Swartz, Swanson, Hiday, Borum, Wagner, and Burns, 1998). Hence, the current War on Drugs, which started in 1988 with the passage of the Anti-Drug Abuse Act, and the high rate of comorbidity between drug misuse and psychiatric disorders can account partially for the large numbers of persons with SMIs in our nation's prisons. Fragmented drug and psychiatric treatment systems often fail to provide fully integrated care for persons with co-occurring disorders, compounding their problems in both areas and elevating their risk for arrest and incarceration (Lurigio and Swartz, 2000).

2. Prevalence Studies: Estimating the size of the mentally ill prisoner population.

Studies of the prevalence of persons with SMIs in prisons suggest that "at any given time, 10 percent to 15 percent of state prison populations are suffering from a major mental disorder and are in need of the kinds of psychiatric services associated with these illnesses" (Jemelka, Rahman, and Trupin, 1993, p. 11). Lovell and Jemelka (1998), for example, estimated that the percentage of persons with SMIs in prison is between 10 percent and 20 percent. Studies that compared the prevalence of SMI among prison inmates with the prevalence of SMI in the general population have produced inconsistent results. For example, Collins and Schlenger (1983) reported that the prevalence of SMI was lower among prison inmates than among persons in the general population whereas Hodgins (1990) found higher lifetime prevalence rates of psychiatric disorders among prisoners than among members of the general population.

According to Pinta (2000), data on the prevalence of SMI among inmates are inconclusive and have limited utility for prison mental health services planning, research, and policy. Studies of mental illness in the prison population have reported inconclusive results because of differences in how mental illness was defined and assessed in those studies and when their data were collected (Clear, Byrne, and Dvoskin, 1993). For example, Collins and Schlenger's (1983) earlier findings are based on data collected before the heavy influx of the mentally ill into the criminal justice system. More recent estimates of the prevalence of SMI within the prison population are significantly higher than those found in the general population (Robins and Reiger, 1991). Specifically, rates of SMI among prisoners are estimated to be three to four times higher than rates among the general population (Ditton, 1999).

The most reliable studies of mental illness among state prisoners have found that 15 percent suffer from an SMI (Jemelka, Rahman, and Trupin, 1993). Pinta (1999) reviewed studies of SMI among state prisoners and also reported an average prevalence rate of 15 percent. Based on the 15 percent estimate, at midyear 2004, 224,494 state and federal prison inmates were suffering from an SMI (Harrison and Beck, 2005).

Ditton (1999) conducted a nationwide survey of the prevalence of SMI among state prison inmates. Similar to Pinta's (1999) conclusion, she found that 16 percent of prisoners reported that they had an emotional or mental condition or had spent a night in a mental hospital. Compared with the rest of the prison population, Ditton (1999) reported that a higher percentage of mentally ill inmates were in prison for a violent crime and a lower percentage of mentally ill inmates were in prison for a drug offense. Ditton (1999) also found that mentally ill inmates were twice as likely as other inmates to report lifetime histories of physical and sexual abuse. They were also more likely to report homelessness in the 12 months before they were arrested for the crime that led to imprisonment. In addition, mentally ill inmates reported lengthier criminal histories than did inmates who were not mentally ill.

The number of individuals with SMI in the prison population is three times the number of mentally ill individuals in psychiatric hospitals (Human Rights Watch, 2003). Estimates suggest that at least 50 percent of prisoners with mental illness have co-occurring psychiatric and substance use disorders, and 25 percent of prisoners with mental illness are thought to be severely mentally ill (i.e., suffering from major depression, bipolar disorder, and schizophrenia) (PBS, 2006). In a study of the prevalence rates of specific disorders in prison, Pinta (2001) found that 13.8 percent of the inmates had posttraumatic stress disorder, 5.7 percent had generalized anxiety disorder, 4.7 percent had cognitive disorder, 4.4 percent had panic disorder, and 3.2 had somatoform disorder. Prevalence estimates in prisons for the most serious mental illness range from 1.5 percent to 4.4 percent for schizophrenia; from 3.5 percent to 11.4 percent for major depression; and from .7 percent to 3.9 percent for bipolar disorder.

According to Ditton (1999), nearly 30 percent of women in state prisons have a diagnosable mental disorder. White women in state prisons have the highest rates of mental illness, especially white women inmates under age 24, who have a mental illness prevalence rate of 40 percent. For all women in prison, another study reported that 24 percent have been previously treated with psychotropic medication, 70 percent have a history of substance abuse, and approximately 60 percent suffer from depression (Singer, Bussey, Li-Yu, and Lunghofer, 1995). The prevalence of other common disorders reported by female prisoners includes mood disorders (43%), anxiety disorders (42%), and psychotic disorders (11%) (Parsons, Walker, and Grubin, 2001).

3. Mental Health Care and Polices in Prisons

> At one point and time in my life here in prison I wanted to just take my own life away. Why? Everything in prison that's wrong is right, and everything that's right is wrong. I've been jump, beat, kick and punch in full restraint four times. . . . Two times I've been put into nude four points as punishment and personal harassment. . . . During the time I wanted to just end my life there was no counseling, no programs to attend. I was told if I didn't take my psych meds I was "sol." Three times I attempt suicidal by way to hang myself. I had no help whatsoever days and week and months I had to deal with myself. I was just kept into a lock cell ready to end my life at any given time. Each [time] I would try to hang myself it never work[ed] out. I cut my arms. I really was going thru my emotions and depression. . . . I would rather live inside a zoo. The way I've been treated here at this prison I couldn't do a dog this way." R.U., Nevada, June 4, 2002 (Human Rights Watch, 2003, p. 16).

Inmates with SMI need a variety of services, including mental health screening, intake assessment and classification, treatment, and discharge and reentry planning (Counsel of State Governments, 2002). Unlike jails, prisons must be prepared to provide longer-term services to the mentally ill. A 1988 survey of mental health services in prisons conducted by the Center for Mental Health Services (CMHS) found that only 2.5 percent of inmates were receiving psychiatric care (Swanson, Morrissey, Goldstrom, Rudolph, and Manderscheid, 1993), which is well below the approximate rate of 10 percent to 20 percent of prisoners who require such services.

Nearly 20 years after the CMHS survey, mental health polices and programs have become more common in state prison systems. For example, a national survey of state correctional facilities found that, overall, 2 percent of the inmates (in a confinement facility, not a community-based facility) were receiving mental health care at midyear 2000. Nearly 10 percent overall were being treated with psychiatric medications, 13 percent were receiving counseling or therapy, and less than 2 percent were cared for in a dedicated mental health unit. The percentage of inmates who were receiving psychiatric medications varied from 5 percent to 20 percent (Beck and Maruschak, 2001).

With respect to prison policies, more than nine out of ten correctional facilities reported that they screen or assess inmates at intake for mental health problems; 80 percent reported that they provide medication and therapy for inmates with SMI; and nearly two-thirds reported that they provide 24-hour mental health services. Policies that establish these services were most likely to be reported by maximum-security facilities and least likely to be reported by minimum-security facilities (Beck and Maruschak, 2001).

Among state prison inmates who were identified with mental illness, Ditton (1999) found that 60 percent received mental health services of any kind while serving their current prison sentence; 24 percent reported that they were admitted to a mental hospital or treatment program; 50 percent reported that they had taken medication; and 44 percent reported that they had received counseling or therapy. Nearly 70 percent of female inmates with mental illness reported that they received mental health treatment in prison, compared with 60 percent of male inmates with mental illness.

The landmark case of *Ruiz v. Estelle* (503 P. Supp. 1265.1323 [1980]) set forth standards for "a minimally adequate mental health treatment program." These standards included the systematic mental health screening and evaluation of inmates; the capacity to ensure that treatment involves more than just inmate segregation; the provision of individualized treatment by trained mental health professionals; the maintenance of accurate and complete mental health records; the supervision and review of prescriptions; and the identification of inmates with suicidal tendencies (Jemelka et al., 1993).

The basic components of psychiatric care enumerated in *Ruiz v. Estelle* were certainly well-intentioned guidelines for mental health services, but their vagueness makes them difficult to translate into definitive practices or programs. This vagueness results in prison-based mental health services that differ widely in both the quality and quantity of services provided to mentally ill prisoners (Lovell and Jemelka, 1998). State prison systems must develop and disseminate clearer blueprints for humane and effective care for inmates with SMI. These blueprints should build on and extend standards of prison health care and incorporate the input of mental health professionals, prison administrators, legal experts, and consumers of mental health services.

According to the American Civil Liberties Union (2002), prisons must provide prisoners with adequate medical treatment, which includes adequate mental health care. Under the Eighth Amendment, lack of medical care to inmates constitutes cruel and unusual punishment; however, the standard of cruel and unusual punishment requires officials to show "deliberate indifference to serious medical needs of prisoners" (Collins, 2001 pp. 30–33). The Supreme Court's recognition of a prisoner's right to mental health treatment is obvious; however, what constitutes "deliberate indifference" and "serious medical needs" is not (Collins, 2001). Therefore, the Supreme Court's attention to this issue does little to guarantee that prisoners with mental illness will receive adequate mental health services.

For prisoners who require mental health services, the basic question is: What level of treatment is considered acceptable? (Collins, 2001). For example, is merely prescribing psychotropic medication adequate treatment? Or must an inmate receive counseling, psychotherapy, and psychiatric rehabilitation? If so, how much of these services should they receive? Although the Supreme Court has ruled that prisoners should receive mental health care, no specific legal parameters have been set to specify the nature and extent of sufficient services. To fill this void, the National Commission on Correctional Health Care (NCCHC) has written the following standards regarding the provision of prison mental health care:

> Prisons must have procedures for screening and identifying mentally ill prisoners; a range of mental health treatment services, including appropriate medication and other therapeutic interventions; a sufficient number of mental health professionals to provide adequate services to all prisoners suffering from serious mental disorders; adequate and confidential clinical records; protocols for identifying and treating suicidal prisoners; procedures to ensure timely access by prisoners to necessary mental health services; and different levels of care, from emergency psychiatric services and acute inpatient wards, to intermediate levels of care, to "outpatient services." (National Commission on Correctional Health Care, 2003, p. 10).

Most prisons have formulated mental health polices, but not all are in full compliance with the NCCHC standards. Researchers have found that the majority of prisons afford prisoners with no or substandard mental health treatment. For example, only 61 percent of inmates in state or federal prisons who had a diagnosable mental disorder received psychological treatment (Human Rights Watch, 2003). At its most basic level, mental health services should consist of initial intake assessments, special mental health evaluations, crisis intervention services, brief counseling services, individual psychotherapy, and records maintenance and review (Fagan, 2003).

In the majority of prisons, there is an insufficient number of qualified mental health professionals on staff to address inmates' treatment needs (Benson, 2003). Because of understaffing, a high rate of turnover occurs among the overburdened, prison-based mental health professionals and leads to poor mental health service delivery. As a result, simply too few professionals are available to identify prisoners with SMI and to monitor their treatment (American Psychiatric Association, 2000). In the cases of *Madrid v. Gomez* (889 F Suppl.1146 [1995]) and *Jones 'El v. Berge* (164 F Supp.2nd 1096 [2001]), the courts cited a number of deficiencies in the mental health treatment of prisoners, such as poor screening and assessment techniques, an overall dearth of psychiatric services, and a high prisoner-to-mental health staff ratio.

4. Prison Culture and the Provision of Mental Health Care

The prison culture views mentally ill inmates as manipulative and malingering. Prisoners must ask repeatedly for services and have to wait several months before receiving attention. They can be dismissed as "fakers" or "crazies" who should be forced to compel with the institutional regimen (Rhodes, 2004). Prisoners are frequently denied treatment, and mental health staff shortages dictate that only the most severely ill prisoners are seen for mental health care. Hence, prisoners might feel compelled to exaggerate their symptoms in order to receive treatment. In short, the prison culture forces many inmates to prevaricate about their symptoms or to suffer in silence, which interferes with proper diagnoses and care (Rhodes, 2004).

Involuntary treatment and doctor–prisoner confidentiality issues loom large in prisons. Legally, prisoners have the right to refuse treatment as long as they are competent to do so (Collins, 2001). However, in the highly authoritarian setting of the prison, few prisoners actually know that treatment refusal is an option and are therefore unlikely to exercise this right. Prison rules about confidentiality are even less well defined than those that govern the right to refuse treatment. Psychologists are obliged to break confidentiality in cases in which inmates are a danger to themselves or others. But it is unclear what access prison officials have to mental health records (Collins, 2001). Prisoners might feel uncomfortable disclosing information, and treatment could be less effective as a consequence.

Treatment often occurs when a mental health professional visits a prisoner's cell, where there is no privacy, which could prevent prisoners from fully disclosing information about their mental health needs (Rhodes, 2004). Prisoners who receive mental health treatment have few confidentiality protections. For instance, they might receive daily mental health treatment that requires them to leave their cell and report to a mental health unit. The stigma of asking for help could put them at risk of being victimized by other inmates. Thus, inmates who could benefit from mental health treatment might be hesitant to request such treatment (Rotter & Steinbacher, 2001).

Social Structure of Prison

The social structure of prisons affects prisoners' mental health. For example, the stress of incarceration as well as the multiple, unspoken rules of conduct in prisons can exacerbate existing mental health problems. Similarly, prisoners who have been previously sexually or physically abused can be retraumatized by the unsafe surroundings and regimented control that they experience in the prison environment (Connor, 1997). The fear for their personal safety is warranted; inmates with SMI are at increased risk for victimization in prison often because they are unable to make the adaptations necessary to protect their personal safety (Rotter and Steinbacher, 2001).

Prisoners behave in accordance with an "inmate code," which includes unspoken rules about inmate behavior toward one another. One aspect of this code is to disregard another inmate's problems. Specifically, a prisoner might notice that a fellow inmate's mental health is deteriorating but the "code" prevents the prisoner from notifying staff. Furthermore, belonging to a group can be critical for survival in prison. Many inmates with mental illness avoid joining a group because of social anxiety, paranoia, or poor interpersonal skills and are victimized because they have no protection from other inmates (Rotter and Steinbacher, 2001).

Discipline

Prison rules are not designed to be responsive to the signs and symptoms of mental illness, and prisoners with SMI can find it difficult to comply with prison rules and codes of conduct because of the profound cognitive and emotional deficits that frequently accompany SMI (Kondo, 2003). "Their idiosyncratic behaviors often alienates them from other offenders (thereby leaving them isolated), creates housing dilemmas, and management difficulties for correctional staff, and may lead to liability issues for correctional administrators" (Fagan, 2003, p. 7). Prison officials often use disciplinary measures against such prisoners, even though mentally ill prisoners are unable to control their behaviors. Segregation is used to punish these individuals, which can seriously aggravate the symptoms of psychiatric illness (Coid et al., 2003).

Utilizing disciplinary measures against individuals with SMI, whose actions are a direct result of their illness, not only can worsen their mental health problems but it can also decrease their chances for parole and lengthen their prison sentence. According to the Human Rights Watch (2003), inmates with SMI spend an average of 15 more months in prison than inmates without mental illness and are often denied parole because of their disciplinary record.

Researchers have suggested that prisoners with mental illness receive disciplinary segregation at a higher rate than prisoners without mental illness (Haney, 2003). According to one study, the use of mental health services before entering prison was unrelated to whether or not an inmate was placed in disciplinary segregation. However, both men and women who had received disciplinary segregation were more likely to have requested, and been refused, psychological treatment while in prison. Women who were placed in disciplinary segregation were more likely to have received mental health services while in prison than women who were not placed in disciplinary segregation (Coid et al., 2003).

Regarding their current mental health status, both male and female prisoners in disciplinary segregation were more likely to have antisocial and paranoid personality disorders. Women were more likely to have borderline personality disorder, and men were more likely to have a narcissistic personality disorder, compared with prisoners who were not segregated. Moreover, both women and men who were segregated were more likely to have substance use disorders and higher rates of psychopathy than prisoners in the general prison population (Coid et al., 2003), which suggests the need in prison for integrated programs to treat persons with co-occurring disorders.

Prisoners with mental illness are overrepresented in solitary confinement (Human Rights Watch, 2003). They can find it difficult to comply with the strict rules of the prison facility, and correctional officers perceive them as being intentionally disruptive or intransigent. Thus, prison staff will sometimes place the individuals with mental illness in solitary confinement as justifiable punishment, which is the default option for "disruptive, troublesome, or inconvenient mentally ill prisoners" (Haney, 2003, p. 143; Cockburn, 2001). The effects of such confinement have been described as follows:

> The lack of human interaction and the limited mental stimulus of 24-hours-a-day life in
> small, sometimes windowless segregation cells, coupled with the absence of adequate

mental health services, dramatically aggravate the suffering of the mentally ill. Some deteriorate so severely that they must be removed to hospitals for acute psychiatric care. But after being stabilized, they are then returned to the same segregation conditions where the cycle of decomposition begins again (Human Rights Watch p. 3).

Most mental health professionals and correctional staff view solitary confinement as deleterious to mental health. The literature is replete with studies that demonstrate the adverse consequences of solitary confinement, which include depression, panic attacks, insomnia, hallucinations, paranoia, rage, self-mutilation, and suicidal ideation and behavior. The degree of mental health deterioration depends, in part, on the inmate's mental health before entering solitary confinement (Haney, 2003). Solitary confinement has the most deleterious effects on prisoners who have preexisting mental health problems; they are "at greater risk of having this suffering deepen into something more permanent and disabling" (Haney, 2003, p. 142).

The amount of time in solitary confinement also greatly affects mental health; the effects of long-term isolation are especially devastating (Haney, 1993). Prisoners have to "earn" their release from solitary confinement by displaying good behavior. This is often impossible for prisoners with SMI whose psychiatric problems are attributable to their isolation. As a result, prisoners with mental illness spend much more time in solitary confinement, with average stays of 5.2 years, and with time ranging from 1 month to 17 years (Human Rights Watch, 2003).

Appropriate mental health services are generally lacking for all prisoners. Thus, it is not surprising that prisoners in solitary confinement receive even less adequate psychiatric care. Segregation worsens the mental health conditions of all prisoners, not just those who also have displayed signs and symptoms of mental illness. Hence, the majority of individuals in segregation could benefit from mental health treatment. Both mental health professions and corrections officers believe that prisoners exaggerate their symptoms and need for mental health services in order to be removed from segregation. Therefore, many segregated prisoners who truly need mental health care receive none. For those who receive mental health treatment while in solitary confinement, mental health professionals generally visit the cell front and have a cursory exchange with the prisoner (Earley, 2006).

The effects of segregation coupled with the lack of mental health treatment have led to high rates of suicide among prisoners in segregation. Nearly two-thirds of individuals who commit suicide while in prison do so during segregation. In prison, attempting self-harm is viewed as breaking prison rules and is therefore often punished. Thus, the culture of prison exacerbates symptoms of SMI by segregating inmates and punishing them for self-harm and other symptoms and signs of SMI (Haney, 2003).

Suicide and self-mutilation are common in prison because of the high rate of offenders with SMI and the absence of available mental health treatment. Although the exact rates of self-harm are unknown, estimates suggest that the suicide rate among prison inmates is 2.5 times that of individuals in the general population. The majority of the individuals who commit suicide had a diagnosable mental illness, which suggests that proper identification and adequate treatment can help decrease the suicide rate (Metzner and Hayes, 2006).

Prison Employees

Correctional officers have the most extensive contact with inmates but they typically have little or no training in identifying and handling mentally ill prisoners. Correctional officers are generally the first prison staff members to witness the signs and symptoms of mental illness and make decisions about referring inmates for mental health treatment. However, correctional officers can often misinterpret the manifestations and expressions of mental illness and be reluctant to refer inmates for mental health treatment. Actual symptoms of mental illness can be regarded as prisoner malingering or acting out (Human Rights Watch, 2003).

The lack of training for correctional officers on handling mentally ill prisoners can result in the excessive use of force. Confronting a mentally ill inmate without proper training escalates prisoner misbehavior, which then leads to further control, constraint, and disciplinary action. These actions can spiral out of control to the point at which mentally ill prisoners have been seriously injured or killed. Correctional officers are justified to use force when necessary, but proper training in the handling of mentally ill prisoners could help decrease the use of force toward these individuals (Ellis, 2003).

The prison culture may also change the perspective of mental health professionals; they can begin to adopt views that are similar to prison officials, interpreting the signs and symptoms of SMI as exaggerations or malingering (Rhodes, 2004). Even prison officials and mental health professions who accurately identify mentally ill prisoners are forced to limit treatment to those with SMI or at high risk for suicide because of the paucity of mental health resources (*Madrid v. Gomez* 889 F Suppl.1146 [1995]).

Conclusions

Inadequate mental health treatment for prisoners with mental illness guarantees that these individuals are going to face the same problems at release as they did when entering prison, which leads to an increased risk for recidivism and reincarceration (Singer, Bussey, Li-Yu, and Lunghofer, 1995). As the Human Rights Watch (2003) concludes "The penal network is thus not only serving as a warehouse for the mentally ill, but, by relying on extremely restrictive housing for mentally ill prisoners, it is acting as an *incubator* for worse illness and psychiatric breakdowns" (p. 3). Thus, the current culture of the prison does little to alleviate prisoners' mental health problems and may actually aggravate them.

In order to provide appropriate treatment for the mentally ill in prisons, they should be evaluated for mental illness and those identified should have immediate access to appropriate treatment and rehabilitative services in the least restrictive environment necessary to meet their mental health needs. In addition to receiving comprehensive appropriate services, prisoners should have adequate records kept to ensure continued mental health care when being transferred to another facility. Furthermore, prisoners should be helped to gain access to mental health services after being released from prison (Council of State Governments, 2002).

Although guidelines for improving mental health treatment for prisoners are beginning to be well established, more resources must be allocated for prison-based mental health treatment. Changing the culture of the criminal justice system to focus not only on the control of persons with SMI, but also on their treatment, is a critical component in improving their mental health status while they are in prison as well as helping them avoid future incarcerations after they are released.

References

Abramson, M. F. (1972). "The Criminalizing of Mentally Disordered Behavior: Possible Side-effects of a New Mental Health Law." *Hospital and Community Psychiatry, 23,* 101–107.

American Civil Liberty Unions (2002). *Medical Care for Prisoners.* Retrieved February 10, 2006 from http://www.aclu.org/prison/medical/14767res20031113.html.

American Psychiatric Association (2000). *Psychiatric Services in Jails and Prisons,* 2nd Edition. Washington, DC: APA.

Beck, A. J. (2000). *Prisoners in 1999.* Washington, DC: Bureau of Statistics.

Beck, A. J. and L. M. Maruschak. (2001). *Mental Health Treatment in State Prisons, 2000.* Washington, DC: Bureau of Statistics.

Benson, E. (2003). "Rehabilitate or Punish." *Monitor,* 34, 23–26.

Center for Mental Health Services. (2002). *Mental Health, United States, 2002: National Mental Health Statistics.* Washington, DC: Substance Abuse and Mental Health Services Association.

Clear, T., J. Byrne, and J. Dvoskin. (1993). The Transition from Being an Inmate: Discharge Planning, Parole and Community-based Services for Offenders with Mental Illness. In: H. J. Steadman & J. J. Cocozza (Editors). *Mental Illness in America's Prisons.* Seattle: National Coalition for the Mentally Ill in the Criminal Justice System (pp. 47–63).

Cockburn, A. (July 15, 2001). "Commentary: Insane in the SHU Box." *Los Angeles Times*, p. M5.

Coid, J. et al. (2003). "Psychiatric Morbidity in Prisoners and Solitary Cellular Confinement, I: Disciplinary Segregation." *Journal of Forensic Psychiatry and Psychology,* 14, 298–319.

Collins, J. J. and W. E. Schlenger. (1983). The Prevalence of Psychiatric Disorders among Admission to Prison. Paper presented at the Annual Meeting of the American Society of Criminology.

Collins, W. (2001). Legal Issues in Provision of Jail Mental Health Services. In: G. Landsberg & A. Smiley (Editors). *Forensic Mental Health: Working With Offenders with Mental Illness.* New Jersey: CVI (pp. 30-1–30-33).

Connor, H. (1997). "Women's Mental Health and Mental Illness in Custody: Exploring the Gap between the Correctional System as It Is Presented and the Correctional System as It Is Experienced." *Psychiatry, Psychology and Law,* 4, 45–53.

Cote, G., A. Lesage, N. Chawky, and M. Loyer. (1997). "Clinical Specificity of Prison Inmates with Severe Mental Disorders: A Case Control Study." *British Journal of Psychiatry,* 170, 571–577.

Council of State Governments (2002). *Criminal Justice/Mental Health Consensus Project.* New York: Author.

Ditton (1999). *Mental Health and Treatment for Inmates and Probationers.* Bureau of Justice Statistics. Retrieved February 20, 2006 from http://www.ojp.usdoj.gov/bjs.

Draine, J. (2003). Where Is the Illness in the Criminalization of the Mentally Ill? In: W. H. Fisher (Editor). *Community-Based Interventions for Criminal Offenders with Service Mental Illness.* New York: Elsevier.

Earley, P. (2006). *Crazy: A Father's Search Through America's Mental Health Madness.* New York: G. P. Putnam's Sons.

Ellis, R. (2003). Staff Services and Programs. In: T. J. Fagan, and R. K. Ax (Editors). *Correctional Mental Health Handbook*. Thousand Oaks, CA: Sage (pp. 219–36).

Fagan, T. J. (2003). "Mental Health in Corrections: A Model for Service Delivery." In: T. J. Fagan and R. K. Ax (Editors). *Correctional Mental Health Handbook* (pp. 3–19). Thousand Oaks, CA: Sage

Grob, G. (1991). *From Asylum to Community: Mental Health Policy in Modern America*. Princeton, NJ: Princeton University Press.

Haney, C. (1993). "Infamous Imprisonment: The Psychological Effects of Isolation." *National Prison Project Journal,* 8, 3–21.

Haney, C. (2003). "Mental Health Issues in Long-Term Solitary and 'Supermax Confinement.' " *Crime and Delinquency,* 49, 124–156.

Harrison, P. M., and A. J. Beck. (2005). *Prisoners in 2004*. Washington, DC: Bureau of Justice Statistics.

Hodgins, S. (1990). Presence of Mental Disorders among Penitentiary Inmates in Quebec. *Canada's Mental Health,* 3, 1–4.

Jemelka, R., S. Rahman, and E. Trupin. (1993). Prison Mental Health: An Overview. In: H. J. Steadman and J. J. Cocozza (Editors), *Mental Illness in America's Prisons*. Seattle: National Coalition for the Mentally Ill in the Criminal Justice System.

Kiesler, C. A. (1982). Public and Professorial Myths about Mental Hospitalization: An Empirical Reassessment of Policy-Related Beliefs. *American Psychologist,* 37, 1323–39.

Kondo, L. L. (2000). Therapeutic Jurisprudence, Issues, Analysis, and Applications: Advocacy of the Establishment of Mental Health Specialty Courts in Their Provision of Therapeutic Justice for Mentally Ill Offenders. *Seattle University Law Review,* 24, 373–464.

Lovell, D. and R. Jemelka. (1998). "Coping with Mental Illness in Prison." *Family and Community Health,* 21, 54–66.

Lurigio, A. J., and D. A. Lewis. (1987). The Criminal Mental Patient: A Descriptive Analysis and Suggestions for Future Research. *Criminal Justice and Behavior,* 14, 268–87.

Lurigio, A. J., and J. A. Swartz. (2000). Changing the Contours of the Criminal Justice System to Meet the Needs of Persons with Serious Mental Illness. In: J. Horney (Editor). *NIJ 2000 Series: Policies, Processes, and Decisions of the Criminal Justice System* (Vol. 3) (pp. 45–108). Washington, DC: National Institute of Justice.

Massaro, J. (2003). *Working with People with Mental Illness Involved in the Criminal Justice System.* Washington, DC: Substance Abuse and Mental Health Services Administration.

Metzner, J., and L. Hayes. (2006). Suicide Prevention in Jails and Prisons. In: R. Simon & R. Hales (Editors). *The American Psychiatric Publishing Textbook of Suicide Assessment and Management,* 1st Edition. Washington, DC: APA.

Munetz, M., T. Grande, and M. Chambers. (2001). "The Incarceration of Individuals with Severe Mental Disorders." *Community Mental Health Journal,* 37, 361–372.

Palermo, G., M. Smith, and F. Liska. (1991). "Jail versus Mental Hospitals: A Social Dilemma." *International Journal of Offender Therapy and Comparative Criminology,* 35, 97–106.

Parsons, S., L. Walker, and D. Grubin. (2001). "Prevalence of Mental Disorder in Female Remand Prisons." *The Journal of Forensic Psychiatry,* 12, 194–202.

Penrose, L. (1939). Mental Disease and Crime: Outline of a Comparative Study of European Statistics. *British Journal of Medical Psychology,* 18, 1–15.

Pinta, E. R. (1999). "The Prevalence of Serious Mental Disorders among U.S. Prisoners." *Correctional Mental Health Report,* 1, 44–47.

Pinta, E. (2001). "The Prevalence of Serious Mental Disorders among U.S. Prisoners." In: G. Landsberg & A. Smiley (Editors). *Forensic Mental Health: Working with Offenders with Mental Illness*. New Jersey: CVI.

Public Broadcasting System (PBS) (2006). *The New Asylums: Frequently Asked Questions.* Retrieved February 10, 2006 from http://www.pbs.org/wgbh/pages/frontline/shows/asylums/etc/faqs.html.

Rhodes, L. A. (2004). *Total confinement*. California: University of California Press.

Robins, L. N. and D. A. Reiger. (Editors). (1991). *Psychiatric Disorders of America: The Epidemiologic Catchment Area Study.* New York: Free Press.

Rotter, M. and M. Steinbacher. (2001). The Clinical Impact of Doing Time—Mental Illness and Incarceration. In: G. Landsberg and A. Smiley (Editors). *Forensic Mental Health: Working with Offenders with Mental Illness.* New Jersey: CVI (pp. 16-1–16-6).

Shadish, W. R. (1989). "Private Sector Care for Chronically Mentally Ill Individuals: The More Things Change, the More They Stay the Same." *American Psychologist,* 44, 1142–47.

Sharfstein, S. (2000). "Whatever Happened to Community Mental Health?" *Psychiatric Services,* 51, 616–26.

Singer, M., J. Bussey, S. Li-Yu, and L. Lunghofer. (1995). "The Psychosocial Issues of Women Serving Time in Jail." *Social Work,* 40, 103–113.

Smiley, A. (2001). Forensic Mental Health in the United States—an Overview. In: G. Landsberg and A. Smiley (Editors). *Forensic Mental Health: Working with Offenders with Mental Illness* (pp. 1-2–1-14).

Steadman, H., J. Cocozza, and M. Melick. (1978). "Explaining the Increased Crime Rate of Mental Patients: The Changing Clientele of State Hospitals." *American Journal of Psychiatry,* 335, 816–20.

Steadman, H., J. Monahan, B. Duffee, E. Hartstone, and P. Robbins. (1984). "The Impact of State Mental Hospital Deinstitutionalization on U.S. Prison Populations, 1968–78." *Journal of Criminal Law and Criminology,* 75, 474–90.

Swanson, J., S. Estroff, M. Swartz, R. Borum, W. Lachinotte, C. Zimmer, and R. Wagner. (1997). "Violence and Severe Mental Disorder in Clinical and Community Populations: The Effects of Psychotic Symptoms, Comorbidity, and Lack of Treatment." *Psychiatry,* 60, 1–22.

Swanson, J., J. Morrissey, I. Goldstrom, L. Rudolph, and R. Manderscheid. (1993). Funding, Expenditures, and Staffing of Mental Health Services in State Correctional Facilities: United States, 1988. *Mental Health Statistical Note 208.* Washington, DC: United Sates Department of Human Services.

Swartz, J. A. and A. J. Lurigio. (1999). "Psychiatric Illness and Comorbidity among Adult Male Detainees in Drug Treatment." *Psychiatric Services,* 50, 1628–30.

Swartz, J. and A. Lurigio. (1999). "Psychiatric Illness and Comorbidity among Adult Male Jail Detainees in Drug Treatment." *Psychiatric Services,* 50, 1628–30.

Swartz, M., J. Swanson, V. Hiday, R. Borum, R. Wagner, and B. Burns. (1998). "Taking the Wrong Drugs: The Role of Substance Abuse and Medication Noncompliance in Violence among Severely Mentally Ill Individuals." *Social Psychiatry and Psychiatric Epidemiology,* 33, S75–S80.

Teplin, L. (1983). "The Criminalization of the Mentally Ill: Speculations in Search of Data." *Psychiatric Bulletin,* 94, 54–67.

Teplin, L. and E. Voit. (1996). *Criminalizing the Seriously Mentally Ill: Putting the Problem in Perspective.* Durham, NC: Carolina Academic Publishers.

9

Cultural Roots of Violence in England's Prisons: An Exploration of Inter-Prisoner Conflict[1]

Kimmett Edgar

Head of Research, Prison Reform Trust
Oxford University

Prison life is a continuing series of close calls in which violence is narrowly avoided.
—Lee Bowker (1983)

Prison Violence

Dan[2] was a sentenced prisoner on a vulnerable prisoner wing. He borrowed a friend's radio. As borrowing is against prison rules, he carefully hid it under a blanket before going to education. Officer Kartner discovered the radio and charged Dan with an offence. Dan suspected that Officer Kartner had been tipped off by Lee, so he announced to his associates that he would take revenge. In the evening, Dan was watching television when a friend told him the coast was clear. Dan went to Lee's cell, accused him of grassing (snitching), and punched him in the face, knocking him down.

[1]My thanks to Ian O'Donnell for his perceptive comments on an early draft.

[2]All prisoners' names are pseudonyms. Further detail on these conflict situations is provided in the appendix.

Early one morning in a top-security prison, Paul wanted to play pool. Henry opened his cell door and told Paul to leave it until later. Paul went to his friend, Marvin, to complain that he'd been threatened. Henry went to Marvin's cell to argue, but a knife was produced and there was a scuffle. Henry went back to his cell and broke a bottle. Returning to Marvin's cell with the make-shift weapon, he was intercepted by officers and restrained.

In the gym at a young-offender institution, Andy and Tyrone argued about the way Andy was doing an exercise. Although they had been friends, their relations had become more competitive and were now volatile. Tyrone belittled Andy, who then offered to fight Andy. They decided to take the argument back to the wing. In the evening, by prior arrangement, a third prisoner cleared his cell to give them room to fight and left them to it. Tyrone hit Andy with an iron bar, but Andy overpowered him and beat him until Tyrone acknowledged that he had won.

The three situations have in common an ethos which suggests that prisoners need to deal with conflicts between them without recourse to staff and with physical force if necessary. This chapter is intended to explore the norms in prison that contribute to a social milieu in which the use of injurious force is accepted as a normal—if not always justifiable—response to interpersonal conflict.

Research on levels of victimization in prisons and young offender institutions in England and Wales by O'Donnell and Edgar (1998A) found that the vast majority of incidents in which one prisoner harms another go unreported. A victimization survey of over 1500 prisoners systematically measured the willingness of prisoners to report victimization to officers. Thefts from cells had been reported by over a quarter of adults and over one-third of young offenders. For all other types of victimization measured, the reporting rates were much lower (about 14 percent for assaults, 13 percent for threats, and 12 percent for verbal abuse).

Of course, officers can directly observe some verbal and racial abuse, threats, and even assaults among prisoners, but even then they play a reactive role, coming to the scene after the victimization has already occurred. In a study for the Economic and Social Research Council's Violence Research Program, Edgar and Martin (2000) interviewed 58 prison officers who responded to assaults and fights between prisoners. Asked what the fight or assault was about, the officers' answers were compared with the information that the prisoners directly involved had provided. One-third of the officers had a good grasp of the background circumstances; but another third either did not know or gave a completely wrong explanation of the conflict that led to the violent incident.

Question: What do you think the dispute was about?

Officer: *No idea. They both tell different stories.*

(Officer, four years' experience, local prison)

Two-thirds of the officers said that they had no prior security information that could have alerted them to the risk of violence by the prisoners involved. These figures are likely to overstate the intelligence officers have about the sources of prison violence. Yet they refer to prisons in which staff-to-prisoner ratios approach 1 to 10 (depending on the security category of the prison).

The lack of knowledge among officers and prison managers about the circumstances that result in violence seriously impedes the development of effective prevention measures. Violence comes to the attention of staff only after the incident has taken place. The sources of the violence remain hidden. Predictably, violence reduction strategies that draw on retrospective knowledge of fights tend to focus on:

- How staff can identify individual prisoners who have the potential for violence
- Techniques by which staff should employ physical force to minimize injuries
- Punishing perpetrators to try to deter future assaults

None of these strands addresses the underlying causes of prison violence, because they ignore the reasons people resort to injurious physical force. Further information about the nature and dynamics of situations that escalate into physical violence is needed to inform violence reduction strategies.

The Conflict-Centered Approach

The definition of violence by the Prison Service in England and Wales provides a useful starting point. The Violence Reduction Strategy definition explicitly includes emotional and psychological harm, defining violence as: "any incident in which a person is abused, threatened, or assaulted. This includes an explicit or implicit challenge to their safety, well-being or health. The resulting harm may be physical, emotional or psychological" (HMPS, Violence Reduction Strategy, para 3.1).

Conflict refers to a clash of interests, situations in which parties pursue competing interests and needs in uncompromising ways. In this sense conflict is endemic in prison. Conflict may lead to violence, or it may be resolved before it escalates. A conflict-centered approach to reducing violence builds on the recognition that prisons generate conflict, between prisoners and managers, between managers and staff, and among prisoners. Attention to the conflict-generating dynamics of prisons (the conflict-centered approach) provides an effective foundation for strategies to reduce violence.

In the ESRC study, six key components of interprisoner conflicts emerged from detailed analyses of 141 incidents. These components can be represented as a conflict pyramid (see Figure 9.1).

The Conflict Pyramid

Interests comprised material goods, such as tobacco, phonecards, and drugs. Values such as respect, privacy, honor, loyalty, and honesty consistently played an important role. Relationships referred to social distance (whether the parties were

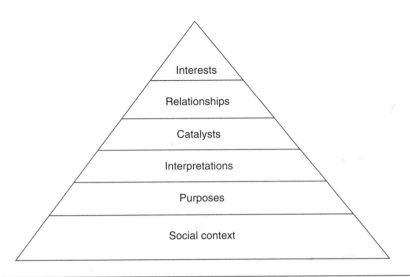

FIGURE 9.1   The conflict pyramid.

Source: Edgar, O'Donnell, and Martin, 2003.

strangers, acquaintances, or close friends), but also to the balance of power between the prisoners. Catalysts were the tactics which prisoners used when in dispute with other prisoners, such as threats, verbal challenges, accusations, and personal invasions of space. The course of disputes was strongly influenced by each person's interpretations. They inferred the meaning of the actions and words of their counterparts, and responded accordingly. But they also based their decisions about what to do on their understanding of the other party's intentions. In this study of prisoner conflicts, purposes refers strictly to the objectives the person who used force intended it to achieve. Finally, conflicts occur in a particular social and situational context, which have an impact on the likelihood of disputes resulting in physical violence.

Conflicts among Prisoners

The detailed sequences of the three incidents described in the appendix at the end of this chapter reveal some of the most common factors that contributed to the escalation from clash of interest (or dispute) to violence.

Interests—Material interests were important in only half of the violent incidents. Surprisingly—and against the expectations of many staff—drugs were involved in only about 13 percent of the conflicts. In this sense, Andy and Tyrone's dispute was typical, in that the interests that set off the dispute were about attitudes and values, rather than material goods.

Honor, loyalty, fairness, respect, or other nonmaterial interests were an important part of every conflict. Often, conflicts that began over an object in dispute became more intense and volatile when people felt affronted, at which point the original spark—the object—became unimportant. Henry and Marvin's dispute began about access to the pool table, but turned violent when Henry confronted Marvin about threatening his friend.

Catalysts—Andy and Tyrone's argument was aggravated by verbal abuse and threats of violence. Henry invaded Marvin's personal space to challenge him about his behavior toward Paul. Accusations or threats were the most frequently used tactics in disputes. Others were invasions of personal space, commands, verbal challenges, insults, and undermining behavior.

Many prisoners had some skills which could help to resolve conflicts. But these tactics (catalysts of violence) had the opposite effect, ratcheting up the tension and making violence more likely. Verbal challenges such as, 'What are you looking at?' or 'What are you going to do about it?' are widely recognized precursors to violence.

Interpretations—Tactics for dealing with conflict are mediated by each party's perceptions about the other. Paul and Henry saw Marvin's behavior as a threat to Paul. Andy inferred that Tyrone was failing to show him respect. Dan assumed that Lee wanted to gain favors from the officers. Lee believed that Dan had been manipulated by others into assaulting him.

Relationships—A lack of familiarity could exacerbate conflict when it contributed to misunderstandings. Loyalty to one's allies was another way that relationships influenced the course of disputes. For example, Henry did not know Marvin and the violent incident began when Henry decided to stand up for his friend, Paul.

However, the main influence of relationships on prison conflicts was when the dispute became a struggle for dominance (power contests). To introduce a theoretical distinction: In one type of conflict, the two parties can dispute whether A or B will have his interests met; in the second type of conflict, the focus shifts to determine whether A or B holds power over the other.

Practical outcomes at issue included whether Paul could play a game of pool or not; whether Marvin's early morning peace would be disturbed; and whether Andy or Tyrone could lift heavier weights. As long as the dispute remained at this level, resolutions of conflict were possible: Paul could make allowances for Marvin's desire for quiet; Andy and Tyrone could decide to exercise separately.

Tyrone and Andy's dispute highlights this dimension of interprisoner conflict. The exchange of insults and threats between them signaled that each wanted to intimidate the other person into submission. When Andy insulted Tyrone's mother, Tyrone felt a need to prove that he could not be humiliated, and carried an iron bar to the prearranged fight.

> *When he argues, he's used to people backing down. When he got angry,*
> *he thought he could just threaten and I would back down.*

Social/situational context—Prisons are a behavior setting that generates conflict. Dan's borrowing of a friend's radio would not have subjected him to punishment outside. Marvin's cell was next to the pool table, which meant that he was particularly sensitive to the noise early in the morning. One of the most obvious ways that prison settings foster conflict is in the competition it produces for basic human needs. For example, prisoners need to maintain contact with their families. A typical wing of 60 prisoners has two or three telephones operating, usually for about 2 hours per night. As the time for locking up approaches, the competing interests of prisoners who need to ring home raise tensions as some of them will be unable to use the phone. The prison restricts family contact, and disputes by the phone are one result.

Violence-Prone Characteristics of the Prison Environment

Four aspects help to show how prisons promote conflicts:

- Deprivation of material goods
- High risk of victimization
- Loss of personal autonomy
- Lack of nonviolent routes for resolving conflicts

Prisons control people's access to resources. As prisoners in England and Wales earn about 7£ per week, the perceived cost of material goods is amplified. For example, prisoners must pay about five times as much for a phone call as the rates outside. By controlling the provision of food, means of communicating with families, access to showers, goods from the shop, and games facilities, prisons create competition among prisoners.

> It sounds silly fighting over tobacco. But you can't let it go with losing your respect. You wouldn't fight about it on the out, but we are not on the out. We're in jail.

A second situational source of conflict is the risk of being victimized by other prisoners. The prevalence of theft and robbery puts personal possessions at risk. As a result, many prisoners believe that they must physically defend their possessions and personal security. There is a perverse cycle in prisons, when prisoners anticipate being assaulted and gain the will to defend themselves by force if necessary. Other victimization, including insults, racial abuse, and harassment exacerbate disputes and make violence more likely.

> I sat in my cell and thought I might as well do him before he can get to me, so I put a glass jar—peanut butter jar—in a sock and I saw him queue up for dinner and I attacked him.

A third source of conflict is the deprivation of personal power or self-determination. The actions of any prisoner are subject to the scrutiny and judgment of any staff member. With their autonomy so restricted, prisoners become sensitive to the balance of power between them and other prisoners.

> *I owed someone an ounce of burn. They came in at ten o'clock in the morning, demanding it. I said to him, 'Don't come in my cell acting like you're some total Yardie on the street.' He said, 'What are you going to do, make me get out of the cell?' I said, 'If I have to, yes.' He said, 'You won't be able to.' I kicked him in the bollocks and hit him with the jug.*

A prisoner's interest in maintaining autonomy while at risk of domination from other prisoners means that mutual intimidation is a frequent occurrence. Power contests arise when two prisoners, in opposition, define their dispute as a win-or-lose challenge. They are both anxious about being dominated by their opponent, and they test them to gauge their strength of will. They tend to believe that being open to compromise is a sign of weakness. They tend to be less concerned with what the "audience" will think of them and focused on making their opponent respect them. In power contests, both parties define their differences as a test of which of the two will hold power over the other.

A fourth factor is a lack of opportunities available to prisoners to resolve their conflicts nonviolently. In most prisons there are no wing forums, impartial mediators who are trained to intervene in disputes, or formal opportunities to negotiate win–win solutions.

Victimization

The inherent dangers in prison foster attitudes of distrust and suspicion. The high-risk milieu in which disputes develop colors the prisoner's assumptions about what the other person is trying to achieve. Prison life subjects prisoners to a pervasive risk of being intimidated, exploited, or injured. This effect of prisons can be described as psychological preparations for violent self-defense (cf., Lockwood, 1980).

Intimidation

O'Donnell and Edgar (O'Donnell and Edgar, 1998B: 24) found that about one in four adult males and half of young offenders had been threatened with violence in the previous month of custody. A common pattern of escalation—particularly among young offenders—was an exchange of insults, followed by threats, and then a fight. Intimidation was the central factor in power contests, as the following episode illustrates.

Evan and Ken were on the gardens working party. Evan felt that Ken was shirking his duties and expecting him to do all the hard work. When he accused Ken, Ken warned him not to criticize or there would be trouble. The next day, Evan again told him off for not doing his share of the work. They exchanged punches, and Evan was injured.

In his interview, Evan described Ken as . . . "bossy. He thought he could push me about." Ken felt that Evan was trying to achieve superiority over him by his aggressive tactics. "He was trying to intimidate me cos I wouldn't rise to his threats." Both interpreted the actions of the other person as evidence of a desire to intimidate and dominate him. As Evan said, "Once you allow someone to push you about, you've got troubles. If they realize you're weak, they'll pick on you all the time." By trying to deter their opponent with tough talk, they drove the argument toward a violent outcome. Depriving people of the power of self-determination, the prison social structure fosters the belief that might makes right, and this belief makes it much more difficult to find nonviolent solutions to conflict.

Exploitation

One-third of adults and over one-quarter of young offenders had been victims of cell theft in the previous month (O'Donnell and Edgar, 1998B: 30). Opportunities for one prisoner to take advantage of another are plentiful: jumping the queue for the phone, food, or a game, abusing the power invested in certain prison jobs, or winning a play-fight are other examples. The risk that someone might take advantage led to routine distrust of others.

Material deprivations may lead some people to improve their standard of living at the expense of others. However, there is a more important bridge between the deprivations inherent in prison and violence. Things like tobacco or food symbolize deeper personal needs. As a dispute grows, these needs become more important.

Sarah and Angie had come into the prison on the same day. Sarah asked Angie if she could use one unit of her phone card. When Sarah returned with the card she explained that she had used two units. Angie insulted her and said, "Get out of my face," Sarah retaliated by insulting Angie and cursing her mother. Angie stood face to face and warned Sarah not to speak about her mother. Sarah said it again. Angie headbutted Sarah.

Sarah's need to borrow a phone card reflects the way that deprivations create conflicts. As Sarah explained, their argument was . . . *"more serious, because it was in prison. It wouldn't have happened at all outside. I don't think it would have mattered. You get so little in here that small things matter."*

Although both women were jail-wise and were not anxious about being targeted as weak by other prisoners, Sarah and Angie believed that they had to stand up to the other. Angie interpreted Sarah's use of two units as a sign that Sarah thought Angie was someone who could be exploited. Angie stated. "She thought I was some new girl that's why she took advantage and used two units."

The high-crime environment inspired Angie's inference that, in using more units than they had agreed, Sarah had intentionally defrauded her. High rates of theft and robbery signal a failure to uphold prisoners' needs for distributive justice, consistency, and personal security. The belief that force restores order after norms have been transgressed leads some prisoners to manage these risks by inflicting punishment on suspected thieves.

Danger

Prisoners accept that there is a pervasive risk of being involved in physical violence. Eighty-nine percent of prisoners interviewed by Edgar and Martin (2000) believed that violence in prison was inevitable. Perceptions that prisons are risky settings were supported by the actual rates of assault. One in three young offenders and one in five adults said they had been assaulted in the previous month (O'Donnell and Edgar, 1998B: 26).

In the ESRC study, Edgar and Martin (2000) conducted a survey of 590 prisoners, including their views on the risk of sexual assault in a general discussion of prison violence. According to this survey, a small minority of prisoners had experienced sexual assault in prison (about 2%). Another study in England and Wales, with a more specific focus on sexual assault, also found less than 2 percent self-reporting that they had experienced coercive sexual intimacy (Banbury, 2004).

Physical assault was far more prevalent. Living with a constant risk of being assaulted affects how prisoners respond to conflict. When a dispute is becoming tense, prisoners must be aware of the distinct possibility that the other party will use aggressive physical force. Both parties are likely to infer hostility from their foe, leading each to feel justified in preparing a violent response.

Hal and Barry were on Basic regime, and spending most of their time locked in neighboring cells. When an officer opened their doors, Hal punched Barry in the mouth. He explained the background to the attack:

> Barry had taken some of my tobacco from someone else on the exercise yard so I felt annoyed about that. His window was broken and he tried to get me to take the rap for it. I said no. He threatened me through the pipe that evening and the next day that he'd cut me or throw hot water on me if I didn't agree. I decided to go for him at lunchtime. When they unlocked us for dinner I hit him.

Barry's threat to scald or cut Hal turned the dispute violent. The substantial risk of being assaulted in prison provided Hal with good reason to take Barry's threats as genuine. His expectation that Barry was planning to assault him led Hal to mount a preemptive attack.

Hal explained, "I'd thought I'd get the first punch in. I thought something was going to happen with the hot water so I'd get in first." Hal was reacting to an immediate threat from an individual. But prison life also presents a more vague risk from unknown others. Some prisoners voiced concerns about appearing vulnerable to inmates not involved in their dispute.

> *I wasn't really feeling aggressive. It was just something that had to be done in order to protect myself. If you don't do something against the first one in prison, you will have to do it with two. I wouldn't react the same way outside.*

Evidence does not support the belief that projecting a tough image achieves greater personal security. Those who had assaulted others were more likely than average to be assaulted. Prisoners who feel intimidated may believe that an aggressive response will force the other inmate to back down; the evidence suggests it is more likely to initiate a cycle of violence.

The cycle of physical violence is an example of contradictory consequences. One individual feels at risk, and believes that a show of force is needed to guarantee his safety. He assaults the person he fears, and in so doing, makes his environment more dangerous for everyone.

On the face of it, the code of violence in the high-security prison had the opposite effect. Prisoners were aware that if a dispute were to become violent, it would probably involve weapons and serious injuries would result. This assumption contributed to a widespread reluctance to resort to physical force and the appearance of a low rate of violent incidents. However, there was a high risk of retaliation when violence occurred, not only from the victim but also from his allies. It was widely considered that any use of violence had to be so extreme that the managers would be forced to transfer the victim away. The frequency of violent acts was low, while the intensity of the violence was high. The likelihood of serious injury seemed to reduce the frequency of events, but the risk of retaliation increased the degree of violence used.

Assaults and threats of violence undermine social order, denying prisoners a sense of personal security, rationality, and control over their lives. If they assume that potential predators will respect shows of force, prisoners are likely to grasp violence as a means of reasserting some control.

Mutual Harm

The prison disciplinary system tends to react to harm inflicted by one prisoner on another as transgressions of the rules. The disciplinary response is characterized by three basic steps. The duty of the authorities is to identify the guilty prisoner, decide on and impose a fitting punishment, and, if necessary separate the perpetrator from others in order to prevent recurrences of the behavior. Evidence about the nature and dynamics of prisoner-on-prisoner victimization suggests that each of these steps can have the effect of exacerbating conflicts between prisoners, thereby increasing the likelihood of interprisoner violence.

O'Donnell and Edgar's (2000) research demonstrated that, for some types of harm, victims and perpetrators were not distinct groups. Thefts, exclusion (e.g., forcing another prisoner off the games table or away from the phone), and robbery were "hierarchical" forms, with fairly distinct groupings of victims and perpetrators. For other types of harm there was a substantial overlap between the groups of victims and perpetrators. Excluding the prisoners who had been neither a victim nor a perpetrator in the previous month, the degree of overlap for assault was 36 percent (adult) and 42 percent (young offender); while for robbery, the overlap was 8 percent (adult) and 9 percent (young offender) (Edgar, O'Donnell and Martin 2003: 65–66).

A prisoner who is repeatedly forced off the pool table is unlikely to be able to intimidate another prisoner into backing away. Prisoners who robbed others were unlikely to be robbed, and those who were robbed were unlikely to rob others. Where the roles are distinct, the situations tend to match the prison's response; there is an identifiable perpetrator who should be held to account for the harm done to the victim.

The most common types of harm—verbal abuse, threats, and assault—exhibited much greater overlap between victims and perpetrators. Prisoners who assaulted others were very likely to have been assaulted. Although intimidation is sometimes understood as an exercise in domination, with a perpetrator and a victim, O'Donnell and Edgar (2000) reported that there was also a substantial overlap between victims and perpetrators of threats of violence (35 percent, young offender; 27 percent, adult).

The vast majority of the violent incidents analyzed in the ESRC study featured some degree of mutual harm. The conflict involving Dan and Lee had a clear perpetrator and victim. However, Dan believed that Lee had brought harm on him indirectly by alerting staff to the hidden radio in his cell. Lee stated that he had not told officers about Dan's radio, but conceded that if he had done so, he would have deserved his punishment. Henry said that he had been threatened with a knife before he went to his cell to get a weapon. According to Marvin's story, Henry came into his cell in a threatening manner. Tyrone and Andy exchanged verbal abuse, ridicule, and threats before meeting in the cell to fight.

Prison rules distinguish between unilateral violence (assaults) and mutual violence (fights). But because adjudications are designed to weigh up the evidence and decide on whether or not the rule was broken, they often fail to take mutual victimization into account, particularly if the prisoner chooses not to disclose it. When the victim's contribution to the incident is ignored by the disciplinary system, the outcomes are very often one-sided, arbitrary, and unjust. When mutual harm has contributed to the escalation of a conflict, the prison's reaction, to charge one party with an offence and punish him, often aggravates the conflict. This effect is magnified when, as reported above, officers do not know what problems between the prisoners led up to the incident.

Insights from Literature on Prison Violence

Richard Sparks, Anthony Bottoms, and Will Hay (1996) applied concepts of situational and social approaches to prison social order. The point of situational controls is to reduce opportunities that make it possible to commit a crime inside. More prison officers, providing more consistent surveillance; marking personal property so that it can be tracked; locked gates that divide vulnerable prisoners from would-be predators—these are situational measures.

Social measures are characteristics of regimes that promote a culture of nonviolence. For example, a wing for long-term prisoners contains people who know they are not moving on and therefore have an incentive to protect their social world from the uncertainties brought about by violence. On a wing with enhanced privileges, prisoners may feel that they have too much to lose, and hence be empowered to intervene to prevent two inmates from arguing.

There is no reason that situational and social measures cannot be applied in harness:

1. To seek a "social" crime prevention approach, aimed at enhanced legitimacy, to the maximum extent possible extent consistent with the adequate maintenance of order and supervision in each prison (and recognizing that prisons vary in the composition of their populations and their past histories of control problems) whilst;
2. within this framework, considering creatively how "situational" dimensions of the prison environment could be adapted to reduce opportunities for control problems, without destroying the legitimacy of social relations and trust necessary for effective *social* control. (Sparks et al., 1996: 322–3).

Sparks et al. (1995), perceived clear links between social order in prison, the exercise of power by the authorities, and legitimacy. In exceptional circumstances, authorities might need to exercise their superior power if it is the only way to reestablish order. But when the state resorts to the use of force, legitimacy is severely tested. Might does not make right; rather, when the state must use force, the central question is whether that force was used legitimately.

In performing their duties, working with prisoners, each prison officer represents the authority to run the prison. The prison authorities cannot claim the punishment imposed on the prisoner is legitimate unless officers are rigorously fair in their dealings with prisoners.

As Sparks and Bottoms (1995: 60) wrote:

Every instance of brutality in prisons, every casual racist joke and demeaning remark, every ignored petition, every unwarranted bureaucratic delay, every inedible meal, every arbitrary decision to segregate or transfer without giving clear and well founded reasons, every petty miscarriage of justice, every futile and inactive period of time—is delegitimating.

Power must be seen by prisoners as legitimate. Legitimacy is dynamic, not a permanent status. The tests of legitimacy extend beyond the use of force by officers to the entire regime. All aspects of the regime can contribute to (or can undermine) the legitimacy of the social order.

The benefits of situational controls have been explored by Richard Wortley. Early work in this tradition focused on opportunity reduction and target handling, including increased surveillance and CCTV. Although improvements in the architecture are important, they are unlikely to be effective if used in isolation from other approaches. For example, prisoners could have reasons to choose to fight directly in front of staff.

Wortley developed the concept by focusing on situational precipitators of violence. Aspects of the physical environment carry a range of behavioral cues. The prison setting affects the emotions, for example by inducing frustrations, that can be expressed in violence. The environmental influence can also reduce self-control and permit behavior that the individual would otherwise eschew. In other ways, the setting also causes pressures on the individual to use violence.

Situational violence reduction measures require prison managers to analyze the prison methodically to determine how it influences behavior. By identifying how the environment promotes violence, managers are better equipped to take effective prevention measures.

The example of prisoners actually choosing to fight in front of staff exposes the weaknesses of theories of prison management which fail to take into account the prisoners' autonomy. Hence, Bottoms stresses the importance of the interaction between the prisoner and the environment. The effectiveness of any measure to reduce violence—from social and situational approaches—depends on how it is received by prisoners, how they define its implications for them, and the choices they make about how to respond to it. Neglecting this dimension profoundly limits the options for reducing violence. Bottoms advocated an interactive framework, "focusing on the individual *and* the environment *and* on the way that the individual reacts to the specific environment" (Bottoms, 1999, 248).

Unfortunately, prisons have traditionally worked on the basis of coercive strategies—policies and practices predicated on an image of the prisoner as a malleable self, an object upon which the custodians inscribe a set of behavioral patterns. Foucault describes the intended impact of prison regimes in these terms:

> What one is trying to restore in [the] technique of correction is not so much the juridical subject, who is caught up in the interests of the social pact, but the obedient subject, the individual subjected to habits, rules, order, an authority that is exercised continually around him and upon him, and which he must allow to function automatically in him. (Foucault, 1979: 128–129)

This artificial construct of the malleable self shows how policies designed to reduce violence can have the opposite effect. Ross Homel and Carleen Thompson concluded a recent literature review on prison violence with the following summary:

> Although the picture is complex, and some inconsistent findings have emerged, generally the literature supports the notion that the more coercive the prison environment the greater the potential for violence. This is especially so where the prison management and treatment of prisoners are perceived by prisoners as illegitimate, as this strengthens prisoner solidarity in opposition to the authorities. (Homel and Thompson, 2005)

A prison regime that exercises control over prisoners but does not win the acceptance of most prisoners is likely to generate undercurrents that lead to violence. A strict regime strengthens the code against passing information to staff, provides a perverse incentive to engage in private justice, gives disruptive prisoners a status of martyrs for standing up to oppression, and fosters rebellious functions of violence.

One explanation for these outcomes is that coercive strategies are inherently divisive. Bottoms refers to research conducted by Mandaraka–Sheppard (1986) on the roots of violence among women prisoners. She found that prisoners whose position with regard to their imprisonment was defiant were more likely than compliant prisoners to engage in violence. But she also found that prisons could encourage defiance—even for those who had not previously felt this way—if the prison failed to ensure social order, stifled prisoner autonomy, or imposed severe punishments.

Suggested Solutions

Bottoms proposed seven areas that he saw as essential to maintaining social order in prisons:

1. *Legitimacy*—fairness of staff, fairness of regime features (visiting, jobs), and fairness of distribution (formal procedures such as discipline and complaints)
2. *Power and routine as structural constraints*—the visible presence of staff, routines that bring stabilizing predictability but also give structure to the prisoners' day
3. *Normative involvement in projects*—attracting the cooperation of prisoners through constructive activities such as education
4. *Incentives and disincentives*—these work better if they are linked to what is important to prisoners (e.g., parole as an incentive works best with prisoners for whom family ties are important)
5. *Degree of physical constraints*—the right balance of physical constraint (too much can encourage more violence—too little can allow too much violence)
6. *Specific incidents*—the private recent history of the particular establishment and the reverberations of the episode in that community's world view
7. *Staff*—deployment, approaches, and skills: If prisoners think staff are fair, they are inclined to accept aspects of prison life they regard as unfair (paraphrased, Bottoms, 1999: 257–260):

Edgar and Martin's ESRC research provided empirical evidence that would confirm the importance of each of these dimensions, and of building strategies that integrate all seven areas. For example, he advocates a balance of physical constraints. The ESRC study suggests that one of the key contributors to a violence ethos is an environment shaped by risks of victimization. Clearly, each time an officer protects a prisoner from theft or verbal abuse, there is a possibility that a violent incident has been prevented.

However, the conflict-centered approach was designed on the basis of a detailed study of situations as they unfolded prior to the violent outcome. Unlike Bottoms' seven dimensions, the conflict-centered approach proposes that the key to preventing violence is to focus on the roots of conflict. At this microlevel of prisoner interactions, ideas about how to prevent or reduce violence cannot be detailed and prescriptive. The origins of fights and assaults lie in conflicts which are embedded in the particular social context of each prison. A prison in which most people feel at risk requires a different solution from a more settled one, where violence is used to regulate the social interaction among prisoners.

In England and Wales, the Prison Service has developed a violence reduction strategy that is designed to be proactive, multidisciplinary, and inclusive. Consulting prisoners is a key part of the strategy. The strategy document (Prison Service Order 2750) sets out, in positive terms, to explain how prisons should approach the task of reducing violence:

> A safer prison is one where:
>
> - Early signs of conflict are recognized and acted upon sensitively.
> - Intervention is with a calm response, before any signs of physical threat arise.
> - Complaints and grievances are listened to.
> - The interests of all parties involved in a conflict are considered (win–win outcomes).
> - An ethos of care and respect is clearly and consistently demonstrated.
> - Personal responsibility for incidents is based on an understanding of the causes, rather than allocating blame.
> - Wherever possible, there is a responsive approach, rather than a reactive approach from the organization.
> - Intervention results in sustained, reasoned changes in behavior.
> . . .
> - The effect of verbal abuse, insults or threats is not under-estimated.
> . . .
> - Verbal abuse, insults or threats are consistently challenged in a constructive way, acknowledging the need for communication.
> (HMPS 2006, PSO 2750, Annex)

The conflict-centered approach drawn from the ESRC research fully supports this direction. The focus on the roots of conflict between prisoners sets out four spheres of action for promoting personal safety:

- Fulfilling prisoners' basic human needs;
- Ensuring personal safety;
- Providing opportunities for the exercise of personal autonomy; and
- Building in mechanisms for prisoner to resolve their conflicts.

Neglecting the sources of conflict and denying human needs is certain to increase levels of violence. Thus, the first step in reducing prison violence is to understand how the specific prison setting generates conflict. John Burton (1990: 29) posed the links between conflict and violence in terms of basic human needs:

> Do we assume that conflicts are due to human aggressiveness requiring and justifying authoritarian political structures and processes of punishment and containment as the

means by which to control conflict; or do we assume that there are inherent human needs which, if not satisfied, lead to conflictual behaviors?

Prisons inherently deny basic human needs. Prison governors should consider using a survey to establish the concerns that are most important to their specific population. One group of prisoners will have different priorities from another. For example, purposeful activity might be more important to young offenders, while stability and routine might be more highly valued by older, long-term prisoners (cf., Toch, 1992). There is no one-size-fits-all program for meeting prisoners' needs. When a prison has high levels of violence and other victimization, it will need to be resourceful in trying to learn from prisoners what their main concerns are about. For example, they might use a prisoner council to raise and resolve some of the basic conflicts.

Creating or enhancing opportunities for prisoners to exercise autonomy can produce a wide range of benefits for reducing violence. First, it reduces the conflicts that arise from the division between staff and prisoners by giving prisoners some responsibility for the prison community in which they live.

Elizabeth Edith Flynn has analyzed the ways that structural conflicts within prisons erupt in riots. She draws a link between silencing criticism from prisoners and the likelihood of violence:

> The [prison] administrator or researcher can . . . readily identify and evaluate structural conduciveness to violence in his institution by assessing whether or not the existing social structure encourages conflict and hostility; and whether or not the existing social structure prohibits the peaceful airing of grievances held by staff and inmates alike. (Flynn, 1980: 760–761)

But a second important benefit of enhanced prisoner autonomy is that they then have more options to resolve interprisoner conflicts. When prisoners do not see any legitimate avenue to resolve their differences, they may feel that they have no option but to use force. When prisoner councils or wing meetings function properly, disputes can be raised with the confidence that solutions can be found. In a Prison Reform Trust report on prisoner councils, a prisoner was asked about the effects of having regular wing meetings:

> You get anger in other prisons. You walk past another con and you feel the anger welling up. Soon you feel that with every other prisoner. You feel the tension all of the time. Here, you bring it up in the wing meeting, and settle it. (Prisoner, cited in PRT, 2003: 25)

This person's insight leads to a further problem that requires attention: prisoners' techniques for handling conflict. The effects of catalysts in exacerbating conflicts suggest that prisoners can benefit from learning skills of resolving conflict by nonviolent means. The Violence Reduction Strategy expresses the hope that this kind of support can go beyond a safer prison to enhancing the chances of successful reintegration:

> By constructively and consistently taking action to prevent violence and promote fairness and decency, prisons can offer a structured environment in which to influence future behavior, encourage positive communication and develop social skills that assist offenders with rehabilitation. (HM Prison Service, 2006: Annex)

The conflict-centered approach also has implications for changing the role of prison officers, from:

- the reactive (using force when fights break out, taking action to punish suspected "bullies") to the preventative, and from
- enforcing the rules to a broader, more engaged sense of dynamic security, in which they intervene to mediate in conflicts between prisoners.

In developing the skills which staff need, governors should focus on supporting officers in:

- developing methods of handling of inmates' disputes by focusing on the interests, values, and needs at stake
- identifying aggressive tactics and intervening to prevent prisoners from using behavior such as insults, threats, accusations, or hostile gestures
- improving communication between the parties
- searching for options for win–win outcomes
- striving to create a culture that favors negotiation and the fulfillment of basic needs over coercive controls.

To what extent could peacekeeping in prison be informed by restorative justice? What kind of strategies would a whole-prison commitment to restorative justice bring to bear on the prevention of violence? First, it would be inclusive. Picking up on the sources of conflict in deprivations, it would mean that representative groups of prisoners would regularly be consulted to gain an understanding of the most pressing deprivations and to decide, collectively, how some of these could be addressed. Second, it would focus on harm rather than rule-breaking. The whole prison would be focused on preventing victimization, and would respond to harmful behavior in a way that rejected the harmful acts while seeking the reintegration of the perpetrator. Third, in the aftermath of violence, it would promote a nonpunitive, problem-solving response. A fight or assault would be followed up by a conference, facilitated by external, trained mediators, and including each party's supporters. The conference would try to establish the sources and course of the conflict that led to the violence as a means of understanding how the problem escalated.

The conflict-centered approach advocates a pioneering change in the strategies prisons use to reduce violence. Its focus on conflict management and resolution, an inclusive response, and minimizing harm echo the principles of restorative justice. The links between needs, fears, conflicts, and violence strongly suggest that the prison that most successfully fulfils the basic needs of the people it holds will be seen as a place of legitimacy and safety.

References

Banbury, S. (2004). "Coercive Sexual Behaviour in British Prisons as Reported by Adult Ex-Prisoners." *The Howard Journal of Criminal Justice*, 43 (2), 113–130.

Bottoms, A. E. (1999). *Interpersonal Violence and Social Order in Prisons, Crime and Justice*, Chicago: University of Chicago Press.

Bowker, L. (1983). "An Essay on Prison Violence." *The Prison Journal*, LXIII, No. 1.

Burton, J. (1990). *Conflict Resolution and Provention*. New York: St Martin's Press.

Edgar, K and C. Martin. (2000). "Conflicts and Violence in Prison." Research Findings from the ESRC Violence Research Programme. Online: http://www1.rhbnc.ac.uk/sociopolitical-science/vrp/Findings/rfedgar.PDF.

Edgar, K., I. O'Donnell, and C. Martin. (2003). *Prison Violence: The Dynamics of Conflict, Fear and Power*. Devon: Willan Publishing.

Flynn, E. E. (1980). "From Conflict Theory to Conflict Resolution," *American Behavioral Scientist*, 23, 5, May/June, pp. 745–76.

Foucault, M. (1979). *Discipline and Punish*. New York: Vintage Books.

HM Prison Service. (2006). Violence Reduction Strategy, Prison Service Order 2750. Online: http://pso.hmprisonservice.gov.uk/PSO_2750_violence_reduction.doc.

Homel, R. and C. Thompson. (2005). "Causes and Prevention of Violence in Prison." Online: http://www.griffith.edu.au/centre/kceljag/director/causes.pdf.

Lockwood, D. (1980). *Prison Sexual Violence*. New York: Elsevier.

Mandaraka-Sheppard, A. (1986). *The Dynamics of Aggression in Women's Prisons in England*. Aldershot: Gower.

O'Donnell, I. and K. Edgar. (1998A). "Routine Victimisation in Prisons," *Howard Journal of Criminal Justice*, 37, August: pp. 266ff.

O'Donnell, I. and K. Edgar. (1998B). *Bullying in Prisons*. Occasional Paper No. 18, Oxford: Oxford Center for Criminological Research.

Prison Reform Trust. (2003). *Having Their Say: The Work of Prisoner Councils*. By E. Solomon and K. Edgar, London: Prison Reform Trust.

Sparks, R. and A. E. Bottoms. (1995). "Legitimacy and Order in Prisons." *British Journal of Sociology*, 46:45–62.

Sparks, R., A. E. Bottoms, and W. Hay. (1996). *Prisons and the Problem of Order*. Oxford: Clarendon.

Toch, H. (1992) *Living in Prison: The Ecology of Survival*. Washington, DC: American Psychological Association.

Appendix

Escalators—Moving from Conflicts to Violence—Three Case Examples

Case 1:

Dan	Lee	Officer Kartner
I borrowed a radio. Lee saw me take it to my cell. An officer accused me of having something. I said no, I didn't. The officer was satisfied.	Dan was on Education. He come out, went into somebody's cell. He obviously arranged to borrow somebody's radio. I watched him walk past and into his own cell. An Officer actually called him and said, "What have you got under your shirt?"	In the afternoon, they were coming out of Education. The teacher let them walk back on the landings. I called out to them to get their water and get back in. With this I saw Dan coming down the landing towards his cell with something under his shirt. I challenged him twice, asking him what he had got under his shirt. Both times he said, "Nothing." With that, I followed him into his cell and asked him again. Again he said, "Nothing." Whilst in there, I noticed his cell mate had two pillows. I ushered Dan back to Education.
Lee went to the office. Another inmate told me that Lee grassed. I told Lee he was getting a slap.		
Later, in association, I was in TV room. Someone said, 'Now's your chance.'	Then after that he was found to have somebody else's radio. He was nicked and the radio taken back off him. In the afternoon he was told that if it weren't for me he wouldn't have got nicked.	
I nipped into Lee's cell, and told the other guy to leave.		
I said to Lee, "Put that bowl down." He stands up, facing me and goes, "What's this all about?" I go, "You know what it's about."	Basically, the person whose radio it was told Dan. With that he stormed in here, told the person that was in here to get out and— whack! I was sitting on the bed. You see how tall he is,	Not being satisfied with his answer, I went back to his cell with the idea of getting the pillow out. After retrieving the pillow I noticed a black wire in Dan's bed. Under the bed covers were a radio
He lifted his hands up and sticks out his chest. I punched him in the face—		

198

Case 1: *(Continued)*

Dan	Lee	Officer Kartner
knocked him back onto the bed. Then I was out of there, down the steps and back in the TV room. Lee went to the office. I went to chapel. When I came back; I was taken down to Seg. Q: Why this particular person? Cause he's a screwboy. I'm not the first person he's grassed up. What does he got to have, a real bad kicking? Q: Did you disagree with something the other person had said? Yes, grassing me. He shouldn't have opened his mouth. He is taking time off me. If you grass, you expect a slap in the mouth.	yet he had to hit me when I was sitting down. He walked back out. My lip opened up about that much. It had gone right the way through. I had a stitch in it. Q: What was did you think Dan was trying to achieve confronting you in your cell? I couldn't think why he was here. I didn't connect with the radio whatsoever, till I learned the next day. Q: Do you think this happened because of his temper? I think it happened because he was given false information. He was used. We all know that.	and plug lead, which he'd taken from another inmate. That was what was under his shirt. I went to Education and pulled him out and told him that he was going to be nicked—not just for the radio, but for lying to me. I drew the adjudication up and as afar as I was concerned the case was closed.

Case 2:

Henry	Marvin
Paul was setting up the pool table. Marvin says, "Can't play pool now." I'm making a cup of coffee for me and Paul. Paul comes down. I say, "Come on, we'll go play." Paul, "No, we can't play. They told me no." I went down to Darrell's pad. I went in and said, "What you playing at?" Marvin [Darrell's mate] comes in behind me, so I hit Darrell. Darrell pulls a knife. He had in it in his pocket.	This guy [Paul] came on 3–4 weeks ago. On the weekend, in the morning, just after eight, he wants to play pool. I said, 'It's too early. Let's wait till about nine o'clock.' Polite. People like to lie in. When I said that, he just walked away. I carry on doing what I was doing. Didn't think it was nothing. I was coming back from the recess and Henry said, 'What was you trying to tell Paul what to

Continued

Case 2:   (Continued)

Henry	Marvin
I grabbed his arm and fought with the two of them. I've got one on the bed, pushed him away and walked out of the pad. They start following me down landing–still got the knife. [They were shouting,] "Get off the wing!"	do for?' I wasn't telling him. It's early in the morning.
	Henry went to Darrell next door and said the same thing to him. Henry had his hand in his pocket. "I don't like people telling me what to do."
I go in me pad. Get the sauce bottle and smash it. I walked out with it under a towel. They ran off. I tried to get into Darrell's door. But it was locked, so I walked into next door cell. I said something: "You got to come out sometime."	He was pulling a knife out. Darrell quick grabs his arm. A little rustle took place.
	Henry goes away for a couple of minutes and then run up with a broken bottle.
	Everyone just slammed their doors and he was going mad pushing at the door and the officers took him away.
Q: Did you disagree with something he said? Yes, that my pal couldn't play pool. Who was he to tell somebody they couldn't play pool?	Q: Did you disagree with something he said? Yeah, he said he don't like people telling him what to do, like he wanted to go for it. My reaction was very calm.
Q: What were you hoping to achieve when you broke the sauce bottle? Cut his throat. He'd be dead. No more problem.	Q: What did you think he was trying to achieve coming back with the bottle? He was trying to put out a point that he was not afraid of you. Don't think because I'm alone I'm easy.

Case 3:

Tyrone	Andy	Shawn
For 3–4 days, Andy was condescending to me. I took the piss out of him. Andy wasn't doing an exercise properly. I took the piss–"Doing them like a girl"–something like that. Andy got angry—stewing. I said, "We're supposed to be friends." In changing room, Andy said, 'What are you going to do about it?'	I was in the gym, doing exercises. Tyrone came over and told me I was doing it wrong. I told him to go away, shut up. In showers, Tyrone brought it up again—an argument developed. I was calling him names. Tyrone, "Come into my cell on the wing." I said Okay. Back on the wing, Shawn told Andy it	They had some stupid argument about exercises. It turned into some argument. Man said, "You're taking it too far." They just arranged to come in my cell. I tried to tell them not to fight.

Case 3: *(Continued)*

Tyrone	*Andy*	*Shawn*
I said, 'Come in my cell and I'll show you,' (offering him a fight). The whole changing room discussed it—they knew we would fight.	was on in his cell, on association.	My cell—I got an end one with the cabin out front hiding it—I moved my stuff out—open empty room. I tried to keep the door open.
Shawn offered to host the fight in his cell. On association, Andy called me to his cell door to try to make peace, but he was still condescending. I slammed his flap and called him a dickhead.	Association—I went straight to Shawn's cell and Andy was there. Fight started straightaway.	I saw Andy grab him by the neck. Andy got the better of him.
	Fighting in the cell, Andy produced an iron bar and hit me with it.	They were punching each other. Then the govs clocked it and we all got nicked.
He insulted my mother. He tried again, but there was no talking.	I was getting the better of the fight. Tyrone said: Okay, you win." We both stopped.	
Andy and I went to Shawn's cell and fought.	An officer came to the door. We were both nicked for being in the wrong cell, although the officers knew we had been fighting. My head was bleeding and the nurse came over.	
	I was banged up and we got nicked next morning.	
Q: What were you trying to achieve when you took the piss out of him? He's a strong guy. I'm laid back. A lot of people, when they don't feel you're a threat, then they want to threaten you. My laid back attitude meant he was starting to take me lightly and I resented that.	Q: What did you try to achieve by arguing in the shower? I called him a couple of names and other people heard. He wanted a fight and it achieved a fight.	
Q: What did you think he meant to achieve when he repeated asking, 'What are you going to do about it'? He's used to people backing down. When he argues, he's used to people backing down. When he got angry, he thought he could just threaten and I would back down.	Q: What did you think about his bringing an iron bar? I told him he took the piss. He said the way I was talking to him in the dinner queue—he'd better bring it. I told him I was going to hurt him. He was listening to Shawn.	

10

Prison Violence, Prison Culture, and Offender Change: New Directions for Research, Theory, Policy, and Practice

James M. Byrne
University of Massachusetts Lowell

Don Hummer
Penn State Harrisburg

Jacob Stowell
University of Massachusetts Lowell

Introduction

In this final chapter, we examine the utilization of prison both in terms of offender control and offender change, and then consider alternative mechanisms for controlling *and* changing offender behavior in institutional settings. Three related developments have renewed the public's interest in prison reform and prisoner rehabilitation. First, prisons represent a cost prohibitive crime control strategy; the 60 billion dollars spent on corrections last year in the United States could have been used elsewhere to benefit a larger proportion of our citizens (e.g., education, health care, housing, employment). There are a variety of ways to reduce the cost of corrections, but the one strategy receiving the most recent attention is *downsizing* our institutional corrections system (Jacobson, 2005). Secondly, criminal justice policy makers and practitioners are beginning to recognize that *prison* violence and disorder appear to be inexorably linked to *community* violence and disorder; what happens in prison doesn't stay in prison, which means out-of-site/out-of-mind responses to criminal misbehavior may only interrupt, and may actually exacerbate, the problems posed by these individuals in both prison and community settings (Clear, Rose, and Ryder, 2001; Stemen, 2007). And thirdly, the public appears to recognize the limitations inherent in control–based correctional systems, and they are beginning to call for the development of new initiatives that focus on offender change, rather than offender control, as the primary mission of our corrections system (Gilligan and Lee, 2004; Deitch, 2004).

We begin our assessment of the prison violence problem by highlighting "new directions" in research on the cause, prevention, and control of interpersonal, intrapersonal, institutional, and collective violence in prison, including: (1) new strategies for measuring prison performance and prison violence; (2) the recent application of evidence-based reviews to prison violence research, and (3) the development of innovative approaches to the study of person-environment interactions in institutional and community settings. We then review traditional perspectives on the causes of prison violence and identify recent theoretical developments, such as Sampson and Bean's relational theory of culture (Sampson and Bean, 2006) and Sparks and Bottoms "Tipping points" hypothesis (see also Clear, Rose, and Scully, 2005; Liedka, Piehl, and Useem, 2006), and discuss their implications for the study of prison violence. We conclude by examining the broad policy/practice implications of a variety of new inmate-centered, staff-centered, and management-centered prison violence prevention and control initiatives.

New Directions for Research: Prison Violence, Prison Performance and Evidence-Based Corrections

The authors of each of the chapters included in this book identify several avenues for the next wave of research on the cause, prevention and control of prison violence. In the following section, we present an agenda for research in three separate areas of inquiry: (1) prison violence research, (2) prison performance research, and (3) evidence-based research reviews of institutional corrections policies, practices, and programs.

(1) Prison violence research

Even a cursory review of the prison violence literature reveals the disjuncture between official and unofficial estimates of the extent of various forms of violence (and disorder) in prisons today (Byrne and Hummer, 2007). As we highlighted in our introductory chapter, researchers need to be allowed into prisons to study the prison violence problem using a variety of data collection methods (observations, personal interviews with inmates, staff, and management, self-report surveys, victimization surveys, and reviews of existing official data on incidents, grievances, and sanctions) and more rigorous research design strategies. Perhaps most importantly, the next wave of research needs to underscore the new era of *transparency* in our institutional corrections systems. Independent, external reviews of prison management and administration need to be conducted and the results presented to oversight commissions, thus providing the public with an objective view of "what actually happens" in prison (Gibbons and Katzenbach, 2006).

In terms of a specific research agenda, one area of inquiry that certainly needs further review is the purported link between institutional and community violence (Stowell and Byrne, *this volume*). There has been much debate on the effect (positive and negative) of recent immigration trends on community violence in this country. Recently, a number of research studies have been released highlighting the "Latino Paradox," the finding that "in many cases, compared with native groups, [Latino] immigrants seem better able to withstand crime-facilitating [neighborhood] conditions than native groups" (Martinez and Lee, 2000, p. 486). In fact, Sampson and Bean (2006) argue that the Latino Paradox offers perhaps the best explanation currently available for the decade-long violent crime drop in this country. Can increases in the proportion of Hispanics generally, and Hispanic immigrants in particular, sent to federal and state prison *also* explain the recent decline in official levels of prison violence? If so, what exactly does this tell us about the violence in both prison and community settings? Sampson and Bean (2006) argue that culture, in addition to social structure, may be a property of communities that helps us explain differences in racial/ethnic involvement in violence; a similar argument can be made about the role of culture in prison violence (Stowell and Byrne, *this volume*). Much more research needs to be conducted on the links between immigration, cultural norms, and violence in both institutional and community settings.

(2) Prison Performance Research

One of the questions that is being asked today about our reliance on incarceration for both violent and nonviolent offenders is: "What do we expect prisons to do?" The short answer to this simple question is that we expect prisons to separate them (inmates) from us (the public) for a period of time. However, serious questions are currently being raised about the techniques and technologies we use to control inmates while in prison (Stowell, in press; Byrne and Pattavina; in press; Gibbons and Katzenbach, 2006), focusing on the impact of control-based corrections policies, not only on preventing escapes, but also on preventing various forms of prison violence (interpersonal, intrapersonal, collective, and institutional violence). In addition, there has been a renewed interest in expanding treatment programming in prison, based on the notion that "offender change" is also a legitimate—and achievable—goal for institutional corrections (Byrne and Taxman, 2006). Finally, it has been suggested that in prisons, as in other "industries," cost effectiveness is another important outcome to measure (Jacobson, 2005). At a minimum, a national performance measurement system needs to be developed and fully implemented in order to provide the public with answers to questions about whether prisons are effective in each of the following areas (preventing escapes, preventing violence by and against inmates, rehabilitating inmates, cost/benefit of prison) (Wright, 2005).

More recently, it has been argued that a new set of outcome measures needs to be considered that attempts to quantify the "moral performance" of prison in such areas as inmate/staff relationships, procedural justice, access to various forms of treatment and services, and the general quality of life for both inmates and staff in the institution (Liebling, 2005; Edgar, *this volume*; Liebling, *this volume*). While this type of research has been conducted in England and Scotland in recent years, U.S. researchers have not yet attempted to measure the moral performance of American prisons.

(3) The Movement Toward an Evidence-based Corrections System

Much of the recent discussion of "what works" in corrections has been based on evidence-based reviews of the research on a particular topic of interest (e.g., prison-based treatment programs). The proliferation of "what works" reviews run the gamut from high-quality, well-designed "scientific" reviews on the one hand to low-quality, poorly designed unscientific reviews (otherwise known as nonsense) on the other. As we examine the available evidence on the impact of a wide range of violence prevention and control strategies, we need to distinguish the "science from nonsense" among the current wave of evidence-based reviews.

Essentially, there are three basic types of evidence-based reviews: (1) the "gold standard" focuses only on randomized, controlled experiments; (2) the "bronze standard" includes both experimental and (well-designed) quasiexperimental research (that includes comparison groups); and (3) the unscientific (or nonsense) approach of self-selecting a number of studies in an unsystematic manner, including experiments, quasiexperiments, and nonexperimental research. The unscientific reviews are typically written by advocates of a particular program or strategy. In the most extreme form, the authors of the review simply allude to an evidence-based review or "best practices," with no supporting documentation. Unfortunately, much of what is available in the area of institutional corrections falls into this last category.

For a variety of reasons, corrections managers have not supported the use of independent, external evaluations of corrections programs (and strategies) in their facilities. As a result, only a small number of external, independent evaluations have been conducted; and with only a few exceptions, these evaluations are often of such poor quality that they would *not* be included in the reviews of "evidence-based practice" that legislators and policymakers are now using as a blueprint for organizational change in a variety of police, court, and corrections systems across the country. Because of this long-standing resistance to external, independent evaluation, today's corrections managers are at a distinct disadvantage, because they are unable to cite "best practices" (or evidence-based reviews) either to support their request for new resources, (and programs) or to bolster their claim of organizational effectiveness (and, of course, good management).

The "gold standard" for evidence-based research reviews mandates that at least two randomized field experiments must have been conducted on a particular program/strategy before we can offer an assessment of "what works" (see, e.g., the reviews conducted for the Campbell Collaboration at www.campbellcollaboration.org). When applied to institutional corrections, the use of this gold standard results in a simple conclusion: We simply don't know what works (and what doesn't work) with offenders in correctional settings. Since 1980, only 14 randomized experiments have been conducted in corrections (Farrington and Welsh, 2005), including seven evaluations of *juvenile* corrections programs, [two evaluations of scared straight programs for male juveniles, four evaluations of boot camps for male juveniles, one evaluation of a juvenile treatment facility (Paint Creek)] and seven evaluations of *adult* corrections programs (three evaluations of therapeutic communities for adult drug-involved inmates, and four evaluations targeting male prisoners placed in one of the following four treatment programs: reasoning and rehabilitation, social therapy, moral reconation therapy, and cognitive behavior treatment). Obviously, much more rigorous evaluation research will have to be conducted before "evidence-based reviews" can be used to guide corrections practice in either adult or juvenile corrections facilities in the United States.

The lack of quality research in institutional settings on the impact of programs and strategies on offender change (upon release from prison or even within the prison setting) is not surprising, given the emphasis placed by prison administrators on controlling the level of violence and disorder *in* prisons and jails. However, it is surprising that more quality research has not been conducted on the effectiveness of various institutional control strategies on the behavior of inmates—and staff—while in prison. Recent reviews of the research on the effectiveness of various institutional control strategies (see Byrne and Hummer, *this volume*) highlights the paucity of research in this critical area. Regardless of whether your criterion of interest is short-term institutional control or long-term offender change, application of the "gold standard" to the existing body of evaluation research will lead to a simple conclusion: We don't know "what works" in prisons and jails, because the necessary evaluation research (independent, external, and using randomized designs) has yet to be completed.

One solution to the problems associated with applying the "gold standard" to the current body of corrections research is offered by both the University of Maryland and the Campbell Collaborative—lower your standards for including studies in your evidence-based reviews. Using what some have called a "bronze standard," members of the Campbell Collaborative have conducted evidence-based reviews of a wide range of criminal justice interventions. Based on this relaxed standard, both experimental and well-designed, quasiexperimental research studies [levels 3,

4, 5 on a quality scale ranging from 1 (low) to 5 (high)] would be examined. For a specific program or strategy to be deemed effective, at least two level 3 (or higher) studies would be needed, with supporting research from the majority of lower quality evaluations (level 1 or 2). Byrne and Hummer (*this volume*) utilized this research strategy in their review of the available research on a wide range of possible "causes" of various forms of prison violence and disorder. A summary of their key findings is included in Table 1 below. Definitive assessments of the link between these factors and various forms of prison violence could only be offered in *two* of the nine areas included in this evidence-based review: (1) treatment/programming and (2) prison classification systems.

Throughout the country, legislators and policymakers are incorporating evidence-based research reviews in new legislation and program initiatives for a broad range of criminal justice initiatives, including both institutional and community corrections. There are a number of recent comprehensive reviews of the effectiveness of various *prison-based* treatment (and control) programs on the behavior of inmates post-release (see, e.g., Farrington and Welsh, 2005; Latessa, 2004; and Cullen, 2005 for an overview). A much smaller number of research reviews examined the impact of various interventions on the institutional behavior of offenders (see, e.g., Liebling and Maruna, 2005; Edgar et al., 2003; Wortley, 2002; and Bottoms, 1999). In several states, legislation has been passed that *prohibits* the development of new initiatives unless they are based on a detailed "evidence-based" review. Although there is currently a debate over be standards to be established for such a review (e.g., gold vs. bronze standards), there is an emerging consensus on the need for more—and better designed—evaluations of criminal justice interventions generally, and corrections strategies in particular (Sherman, et al., 1997; Farrington and Welsh, 2005).

TABLE 10.1   *Summary of Evidence-Based Review*

1. Prison Culture: Unknown effect on prison violence
2. Prison crowding: Unknown effect on prison violence
3. Staffing levels: Unknown effect on prison violence
4. Treatment/programming in prisons: Direct link established between programming and reduction in interpersonal violence in prison
5. Classification/placement practices: No link established between classification and violence (risk) reduction in prison
6. Management practices: Unknown effect on prison violence
7. Facility design: Unknown effect on prison violence
8. Situational context (e.g., daily routines, autonomy): Unknown effect on prison violence
9. Offender profile (e.g., larger number/proportion of violent offenders in prison, gang affiliation): Unknown effect on prison violence.

Adapted from Byrne and Hummer (*this volume*)

New Directions for Theory: Emerging Perspectives on the Social Ecology of Violence

By focusing on the need to anchor prison policy and practice not on the latest fad or politically attractive reform, but rather on an evidence-based review of the empirical research, corrections managers in several jurisdictions are pursuing the same general strategy that has been used to reform policing (National Research Council, 2004), the courts (National Center for State Courts, 2003), prosecution (National Research Council, 2001), and probation (Center for Civic Innovation, 2000): *Focus on the cause, not the consequence, of the behavior in question*. But what do we actually know about the causes of violence and disorder in prison?

Most discussions of the problem of prison violence and disorder first identify likely "causes" of prison violence and disorder in U.S. prisons as jumping off points for recommendations for changes in the U.S. prison system's policies and practices (Gibbons and Katzenbach, 2006; Mushlin, 2004; Welch, 2004; Jacobson, 2005). According to a recent review by Welch (2004), there are two primary explanations to consider: (1) importation theory (focusing on characteristics of offenders sent to prison, such as prior offense history, gang affiliation, and/or community culture); and (2) deprivation theory [focusing on the negative consequences of the prison "experience," including the use of segregation and isolation (supermax prisons), as well as access to treatment, staff violence, etc].[1] Since theories of the cause of prison violence and disorder based on either importation or deprivation suggest different solutions to the problem, there is certainly good reason to briefly consider the link between/among theory, research, and policy on prison violence and disorder, based on each of these perspectives.

Deprivation theory is based on the premise that prison violence and disorder occur not because of the characteristics of the individuals we incarcerate, but because of how these inmates are required to live in prison. When applied to prison problems, this approach invariably begins with an examination of prison culture and its effect on prison order. Prison (or institutional) culture has been defined in a variety of ways by researchers, but typically, it refers to "the values, assumptions, and beliefs people hold that drive the way the institution functions and the way people think and behave" (National Institute of Corrections' working definition of institutional culture, 2003). While some researchers have focused their attention on *staff* culture (see, e.g., Carroll, 2003), much of the research on this topic emphasizes *inmate* culture (see, e.g., Edgar, O'Donnell, and Martin, 2003 for an overview of this literature). If deprivation theory is correct, it is something about the prison experience that causes negative inmate and staff culture to emerge, resulting in changes in how both inmates and staff view violence and disorder in prison (Toch, 1992).

---

[1]*Note:* In addition, others have suggested that a "popcorn" theory may actually apply, particularly to riots and disturbances (focusing on watershed incidents, and/or the implementation of new policies and practices at an institution that may exacerbate levels of violence and disorder).

If importation theory is correct, negative (inmate and staff) culture is simply a reflection—albeit in a new setting—of values, assumptions, and beliefs found in the home communities of both inmates and staff. From this perspective, it could be argued that prison violence and disorder are a direct consequence of whom we put in prison and whom we hire as corrections officers and administrators, rather than the negative consequences of the prison experience itself. Let us present this argument in its simplest form: If you put more violent offenders in prison, then expect a rise in prison violence; similarly, larger proportions of drug offenders and mentally ill offenders in prison will result in more drug problems/drug overdoses, and higher levels of intrapersonal violence (e.g., self-injury, suicide) in prison; and finally, hiring poorly educated and poorly trained line staff will inevitably lead to higher levels of institutional violence.

There appears to be an emerging consensus that both importation and deprivation explanations need to be integrated in a single, unified perspective. Research on the *community* context of violence suggests that the most likely explanation includes the independent effects of both sets of factors, and emphasizes the need to understand the importance of person–environment interactions in community settings (Pattavina, Byrne, and Garcia, 2006). Although less extensive, research on the *institutional* context of violence appears to support the notion that person–environment interactions also offer the best explanation for prison violence and disorder (see and Stowell and Byrne, p. 204 *this volume*; Fleisher and Krienert, 2006). From a policy perspective, this suggests that any new initiatives need to incorporate both theories—importation and deprivation—into their intervention plan.

A number of the chapters in this volume have studied the problem of prison violence from what can broadly be described as a social ecological perspective (Byrne and Sampson, 1986; Toch, 1992), examining the consequences of person-environment interactions for inmates involved—as both offenders and/or victims—in various forms of prison violence and disorder. A similar strategy has been employed by the Centers for Disease Control and the World Health Organization (2004) in their assessment of the cause of *community* violence. The challenge for those who argue that the causes of both institutional and community violence are found in person-environment interactions will be to explain the *reciprocal* nature of interactions that occur in these two "unique" settings.

One area of inquiry that needs to be developed further is the study of the role of culture in explaining violence in both institutional and community settings (Stowell and Byrne, *this volume*). Sampson and Bean's new relational theory of culture, based on Swindler's "culture in action" paradigm, appears to offer one possible explanation of violence in prison and in the community. In a similar vein, Sparks and Bottoms' (*this volume*) discussion of the importance of *legitimacy* in maintaining order in prison, and the need to identify the optimal "tipping point" between the use of formal and informal social control mechanisms to reduce prison violence, can also be applied to the community violence problem, especially in light of the recent emphasis on the impact of both collective efficacy and legal cynicism on violence in structurally disadvantaged "poverty pocket" neighborhoods (Sampson and Bean, 2006).

New Directions in Policy and Practice: Inmate, Staff, and Management-Focused Change Strategies

There are three broad categories of responses to the prison violence and disorder problem: (1) *inmate*-focused strategies designed to resolve the ongoing conflicts among inmates using restorative justice and conflict resolution techniques; (2) *staff*-focused strategies designed to change the "negative" staff culture that exists in many U.S. prisons today; and (3) *management*-focused strategies designed to change the "situational context" of prisons (e.g., daily routines, access to programs, staffing patterns, crowding reduction) in order to reduce violence and disorder in these facilities. Although the empirical research evaluating the effectiveness of these strategies is limited, there appears to be an emerging recognition of the need for high-quality, independent evaluations of the effectiveness of each of these problem-oriented intervention strategies.

In terms of *inmate*-focused strategies, recent research on the application of (restorative justice-driven) conflict resolution strategies to the prison violence problem in England appear particularly promising (Edgar, *this volume*; Edgar, 2005; Edgar, et al., 2003), although they have yet to be rigorously evaluated. According to Edgar (2005), "social order" in prisons can be promoted by the following: (1) fulfilling prisoners' basic human needs, (2) working to ensure personal safety, (3) providing opportunities to exercise personal autonomy, and (4) building in mechanisms (e.g., restorative justice panels) to resolve conflicts. The results of ongoing research on the impact of this conflict-centered approach on prison violence and disorder should be available soon.

In addition to Edgar's conflict-centered approach, a second inmate-centered approach that needs field testing and independent, external evaluation is the Lifers Public Safety Steering Committee's proposal to utilize current and former inmates who have completed the "transformation" process to change the culture of street crime by targeting the three distinct populations perpetuating the cycle.

> This includes *former* perpetrators who are presently confined and are likely to return to the culture when released, unless they undergo a substantial philosophic change accompanied by economic or occupational alternatives. It also includes *current* perpetrators who are presently engaged in the illicit drug trade, violence, and crime. In addition, it includes *future* perpetrators, those youth who will be attracted to, and/or recruited by, current perpetrators of the culture of crime (2004:59s).

Unlike other inmate-focused strategies, this proposal emphasizes the link between community and institutional culture and appears to embrace the notion that "what happens in prison doesn't stay in prison." According to The Lifers Public Safety Steering Committee (2004:60s), "[The transformation] process, to be effective, must be peer led, directed, and facilitated. Those released will further internalize this knowledge [transformation] through the perpetual practice of reforming others who exhibit criminal tendencies. In this way, one ensures personal change by assisting in the efforts to change others." While intriguing, we once again must emphasize the need for independent, objective research on the implementation and impact of this inmate-centered strategy.

In addition to inmate-centered strategies, a number of promising staff and management strategies can also be identified. In the United States, the National Institute of Corrections (NIC) has developed a *staff-* (and *management-*) centered institutional culture change initiative to address the myriad prison problems related to offenders, staff, and management in state prisons. We have recently conducted a multisite evaluation (9 prisons) of the implementation and impact of the NIC culture change initiative on prison violence and disorder. NIC program developers focused much of their attention on assessing (and changing) staff culture, based on the assumption that "if you change staff culture, inmate culture will follow." However, they also developed strategies to work directly with prison management on both "strategic planning" and "leading and sustaining change" initiatives. Our preliminary analyses of the impact of the four-part NIC initiative (assessment, promoting a positive corrections culture, strategic planning, and leading and sustaining change) revealed that although the level of violent incidents did *not* change at intervention sites, a short-term "announcement effect" on the overall level of incidents was identified (see Byrne, Taxman, and Hummer, *this text*). Given the modest scale of the NIC effort, it is certainly possible that a more intensive culture change strategy would yield more positive results, particularly if it was combined with the inmate-centered strategies discussed above.

Finally, Wortley (2002) recently completed a detailed review of the research on *management*-centered strategies aimed at reducing the level of violence and disorder in prison, focusing in particular on a number of promising situational prison control strategies (e.g., changes in physical environment, size of prison, crowding level, staffing levels and staffing characteristics, sanctioning practices, protection of vulnerable prisoners, program/treatment availability). Similarly, our own review of this body of research has linked higher levels of prison violence and disorder with the following factors: (1) inadequate programming in prisons (access and quality), and (2) ineffective classification/placement practices (Byrne and Hummer, *this text*).

Perhaps not surprisingly, existing prison research (although limited in scope and quality) on the causes of violence and disorder in prisons is *consistent* with a much larger body of research on the causes of violence and disorder in our communities (see, e.g., Sampson, MacIndoe, McAdam, and Weffer–Elizondo, 2005; Pattavina, et al., 2006 for an overview), which emphasize the importance of person–environment interactions and the breakdown of informal social controls.

While there is some evidence that the inmate-, staff-, and management-centered strategies just described can reduce prison violence and disorder, it appears that further research on each of these three broad approaches to the prison violence problem is needed before we can assess "what works" in this area. However, we do have a mounting body of evidence that in prisons—as in our communities—informal social control mechanisms are more effective than formal social control mechanisms in reducing levels of violence and disorder. We need to consider strategies for strengthening these informal control mechanisms, while simultaneously reducing our reliance on formal control technology. The key is to identify the optimal "tipping point" in violence prevention and control strategies that attempt to utilize both formal and informal social control mechanisms in prison settings.

Concluding Comment: Visions of Prison Reform

Our examination of the cause, prevention, and control of prison violence has revealed a prison system in need of reform. We recognize that for many observers, the question is not how to *reform* the prison, but rather how to drastically downside it, or even abolish it altogether (Jacobsen, 2005). However, our perspective is that prisons—if targeted correctly—provide opportunities not only for short-term control over individuals, but also for longer term changes in their behavior. We agree with Michele Deitch's recent assessment that it is possible to present a "vision of the transformed prison" (Deitch, 2004 as summarized by Mushlin, 2004, p. 415), managed by individuals who (1) recognize the critical importance of offender rehabilitation, (2) understand the need to find an optimal "tipping point" between formal and informal social control mechanisms, and who (3) believe that legitimacy (and the moral performance of prisoners) is a product of a prison's (and a community's) moral performance.

The features of a "transformed" prison were eloquently described in a recent review by Deitch (2004, p. 848 as quoted in Mushlin, 2004, p. 415–416):

> [The transformed prison] "includes a prison system which incarcerates far fewer prisoners and those who are incarcerated have shorter sentences and are housed in prisons where the culture is entirely different: inmates and staff would treat each other with dignity and respect, offenders would not be psychologically or physically harmed by their prison experience; and institutions would be open and transparent, . . . rehabilitation would be stressed above all: there would be strong efforts made to sustain bonds between inmates and the outside world; facilities would be smaller and located closer to urban communities and families; programs would be offered that help offenders treat their addictions, become educated, learn meaningful work skills, and learn to be responsible citizens. And prisons would be held accountable for meeting the needs of prisoners and rehabiliting them."

It seems reasonable to anticipate that prison violence would be drastically reduced if these reforms could be achieved; but we suspect that until similar transformation strategies are developed and implemented in community settings, prison-based reform efforts will have only modest effects on the levels of violence and victimization in prison.

Ultimately, our examination of the prison violence problem has led us to a simple conclusion that is at the core of criminal justice policies based on the social ecology of crime: *you cannot change offenders without simultaneously changing the communities in which offenders reside*. It is for this reason that we believe that much of the current debate about prison policy—for example, (1) whether the use of prison will incapacitate some offenders and deter others, thus lowering the crime rate (Levitt, 2004), or (2) whether there is an incarceration "tipping point" that can be identified at the neighborhood and state level, beyond which incarceration actually increases the crime rate (Clear, Rose, and Ryder, 2001; Liedka, Piehl, & Useem, 2006)—is largely beside the point.

The question we need to ask ourselves is what can and should we be doing at the *individual* level (in terms of addressing the healthcare, education, employment, mental health, housing, and victimization needs of individuals) and also at the *community* level (in terms of addressing the causes and consequences of living in structurally disadvantaged "poverty pocket" neighborhoods, where collective efficacy is low and legal cynicism is high) to reduce the risk of both individual and community-level violence and victimization? When viewed from a social ecological perspective, recent projections of continued increases in prison populations (e.g. Austin, 2007) are disconcerting, because they suggest that we are moving in the wrong direction (increasing our prison capacity) for the wrong reason (a mistaken belief that more incarceration will lead to less crime).

In *Reconsidering Incarceration: New Directions for Reducing Crime*, Don Stemen (2007, p. 16) offers a similar assessment of the need to move beyond prison and consider other strategies to address the individual and community context of violence.

> "Public safety cannot be achieved only by responding to crime after it occurs; research shows that it may also depend on protecting people against those factors that have been shown to be associated with high crime rates, such as unemployment, poverty, and illiteracy. By pursuing crime reduction chiefly through incarceration, states are forgoing the opportunity to invest in these other important areas. As state policymakers continue to feel pressure to introduce measures to keep crime rates low, they would therefore do well to look beyond incarceration for alternative policies that not only may be able to accomplish the important task of protecting public safety, but may do so more efficiently and more effectively."

It appears that the problems of prison and community violence are inexorably linked. We cannot expect to make progress in the area of prison reform (and the reduction of prison violence) unless we also change the community context of violence by utilizing a variety of community-level reform strategies designed to improve community resources (e.g., availability of treatment services), increase collective efficacy, strengthen informal social control mechanisms, and reduce legal cynicism in "high crime" neighborhoods (Pattavina, Byrne, and Garcia, 2006; Byrne and Taxman, 2006; Sampson and Bean, 2006).

References

Adams, K. (1992). "Adjusting to Prison Life." In *Crime and Justice: A Review of Research*, Vol. 16. Chicago, IL: University of Chicago Press.

American Correctional Association (ACA). (2004). *A 21st Century Workforce for America's Correctional Profession: Part One of a Three-Part Study Commissioned by the American Correctional Association.* Baltimore, MD: American Correctional Association.

Armstrong, T. A. (2002). "The Effect of Environment on the Behavior of Youthful Offenders: A Randomized Experiment." *Journal of Criminal Justice,* 30:19–28.

Austin, J. (2007). *Public Safety, Public Spending: Forecasting America's Prison Population 2007–2111.* Philadelphia, PA: Pew Charitable Trust available at URL: www.pewpublicsafety.org.

Austin, J. (2003). *Findings in Prison Classification and Risk Assessment.* Washington DC: U.S. Department of Justice, National Institute of Corrections.

Baro, A. (1999). "Effects of a Cognitive Restructuring Program on Inmate Institutional Behavior." *Criminal Justice and Behavior,* 26:466–84.

Beck, A., Hughes, and Harrison (2004). "Data Collections for the Prison Rape Elimination Act of 2003." *Bureau of Justice Statistics Status Report* (June 30, 2004) Washington, DC: U.S. Department of Justice, Office of Justice Programs.

Bench, L. L. and T. D. Allen (2003). "Investigating the Stigma of Prison Classification: An Experimental Design." *Prison Violence,* 83 (4): 367–82.

Berk, R. A., B. Kriegler, and J. Baek. (2006). *Forecasting Dangerous Inmate Misconduct.* Berkeley, CA: University of California, California Policy Research Center.

Borrill, J., A. Maden, A. Martin, T. Weaver, G. Stimson, M. Farrell, T. Barnes, R. Burnett, S. Miller, and D. Briggs. (2003). "Substance Misuse among White and Black/Mixed Race Female Prisoners" *Prisoners' Drug Use and Treatment: Seven Research Studies (Home Office Research Study 267).* London: Home Office Research, Development and Statistics Directorate.

Bottoms, A. E. (1999). "Interpersonal Violence and Social Order in Prisons." In M. Tonry and J. Petersilia (Editors). In: *Prisons.* Chicago, IL: The University of Chicago Press.

Braswell, M. C., R. H. Montgomery, Jr., and L. X. Lombardo (Editors). (1994). *Prison Violence in America,* second edition. Cincinnati, Anderson.

Briggs, C. S., J. L. Sundt, and T. C. Castellano. (2003). "The Effect of Supermaximum Security Prisons on Aggregate Levels of Institutional Violence." *Criminology,* 41:1341–76.

Bullock, T. (2003). "Changing Levels of Drug Use Before, During and After Imprisonment." In: *Prisoners' Drug Use and Treatment: Seven Research Studies (Home Office Research Study 267).* London: Home Office Research, Development and Statistics Directorate.

Bureau of Justice Statistics (BJS). (2000). *Correctional Populations in the United States, 1997.* Washington, DC: U.S. Department of Justice, Office of Justice Programs, Bureau of Justice Statistics.

Byrne, J. M. (2006). Testimony before the Commission on Safety and Abuse in America's Prisons. Public Hearing #4: Oversight, Accountability, and Other Issues. Los Angeles, CA, February 8–9.

Byrne, J. M. and D. Hummer. (2007). "Myths and Realities of Prison Violence: A Review of the Evidence." *Victims and Offenders* 2: 77–90.

Byrne, J. M. and A. Pattavina. (2007). "Institutional Corrections and Soft Technology" in J. M. Byrne and D. J. Rebovich (eds.) *The New Technology of Crime, Law and Social Control.* Monsey, NY: Criminal Justice Press.

Byrne, J. M. and R. Sampson, Editors. (1986). *The Social Ecology of Crime* New York: Springer Verlag.

Byrne, J. M. and F. S. Taxman. (2006). "Crime Control Strategies and Community Change: Reframing the Surveillance vs. Treatment Debate." *Federal Probation,* June 2006: 3–12.

Byrne, J. M., F. S. Taxman, and D. Hummer. (2005). *An Evaluation of the Implementation and Impact of NIC's Institutional Culture Initiative: Year 2 Update.* Prepared for the National Institute of Corrections, Federal Bureau of Prisons, U.S. Department of Justice. Project #S10002750000006.

Camp, S. D. and G. G. Gaes. (2005). "Criminogenic Effects of the Prison Environment on Inmate Behavior: Some Experimental Evidence." *Crime and Delinquency,* 51:425–42.

Camp, S. D., G. G. Gaes, N. P. Langan, and W. G. Saylor. (2003). " The Influence of Prisons on Inmate Misconduct: A Multilevel Investigation." *Justice Quarterly* 20(3): 501–33.

Carroll, L. (2003). "Institutional Culture." Unpublished Paper.

Center for Civic Innovation. (2000). *Transforming Probation Through Leadership: The Broken Windows Model.* New York: Center for Civic Innovation at the Manhattan Institute and the Robert A. Fox Leadership Program at the University of Pennsylvania.

Clear, T. R., D. R. Rose, and J. A. Ryder. 2001. "Incarceration and Community: The Problem of Removing Offenders." *Crime and Delinquency* 47: 355–51.

Commission on Safety and Abuse in America's Prisons. (2006). *Confronting Confinement.* Washington, DC: Vera Institute of Justice.

Cooke, D. J. (1989). "Containing Violent Prisoners: An Analysis of the Barlinnie Special Unit. *British Journal of Criminology,* 29:129–43.

Corrections Compendium. (2002). "Riots, Disturbances, Violence, Assaults, and Escapes." *Corrections Compendium,* 27:6–19.

Cullen, F. T. (2005). "The Twelve People Who Saved Rehabilitation: How the Science of Criminology Made a Difference." *Criminology,* 43:1–42.

Cunningham, M. D., J. R. Sorensen, and T. J. Reidy. (2005). "An Actuarial Model for Assessment of Prison Violence Risk among Maximum Security Inmates." *Assessment,* 12:40–49.

Dietch, M. 2004. "Thinking Outside the Cell: Prison Reform Litigation and the Vision of Prison Reform." *Pace Law Review* 24 (2): 847–55.

Dietz, E. F., D. J. O'Donnell, and F. R. Scarpitti. (2003). "Therapeutic Communities and Prison Management: An Examination of the Effects of Operating an In-Prison Therapeutic Community on Levels of Institutional Disorder." *International Journal of Offender Therapy and Comparative Criminology,* 47:210–23.

DiIulio, J. J. (1991). *No Escape: The Future of American Corrections.* New York: BasicBooks.

DiIulio, J. J. (1987). *Governing Prisons: A Comparative Study of Correctional Management.* New York: Free Press.

Duguid, S. (1997). "Confronting Worst Case Scenarios: Education and High Risk Offenders." *Journal of Correctional Education,* 48:153–59.

Dumond, R. (2000). "Inmate Sexual Assault: The Plague that Persists." *The Prison Journal,* 80:407–414

Edgar, K. "A Culture of Violence in England's Prison System: An Assessment of Causes and Solutions." *Journal of Offender Rehabilitation, this issue.*

Edgar, K. A. (2005). "Bullying, Victimization and Safer Prisons." *Probation Journal,* 52:390–400.

Edgar, K., I. O'Donnell, and C. Martin. (2003). *Prison Violence: The Dynamics of Conflict, Fear and Power.* Devon, UK: Willan Publishing.

Ekland–Olson, S. (1986). "Crowding, Social Control, and Prison Violence: Evidence from the Post-*Ruiz* Years in Texas." *Law and Society Review,* 20:389–422.

Farabee, D. (2005). *Rethinking Rehabilitation: Why Can't We Reform Our Criminals?* Washington, DC: AEI Press, American Enterprise Institute.

Farrington, D. P. and B. C. Welsh. (2005). "Randomized Experiments in Criminology: What Have We Learned in the Last Two Decades?" *Journal of Experimental Criminology,* 1:9–38.

Ferrell, S.W., R. D. Morgan, and C. L. Winterowd. (2000). "Job Satisfaction of Mental Health Professionals Providing Group Therapy in State Correctional Facilities." *International Journal of Offender Therapy and Comparative Criminology,* 44:232–41.

Fischer, D. R. (2001). *Arizona Department of Corrections Security Threat Group Program Evaluation: Final Report.* Washington, DC: Department of Justice, Office of Justice Programs, National Institute of Justice.

Fleisher, M. (2006). "The Culture of Prison Sexuality and Rape." Unpublished Paper.

Foucault, M. 1977. *Discipline and Punish: The Birth of the Prison.* New York: Vintage Books.

French, S. A. and P. Gendreau. (2006). "Reducing Prison Misconducts: What Works!" *Criminal Justice and Behavior,* 33:185–218.

Gaes, G. G. and A. Goldberg. (2004). *Prison Rape: A Critical Review of Literature.* Working Paper, National Institute of Justice, Office at Justice Programs, Washington, DC.

Gaes, G. G. and W. J. McGuire. (1985). "Prison Violence: The Contribution of Crowding versus Other Determinants of Prison Assault Rates." *Journal of Research in Crime and Delinquency,* 22:41–65.

Gaes, G. G., S. Wallace, E. Gilman, J. Klein-Saffran, and S. Suppa. (2002). "The Influence of Prison Gang Affiliation on Violence and Other Prison Misconduct." *The Prison Journal,* 82:359–85.

Gendreau, P., C. E. Goggin, and M. Law. (1997). "Predicting Prison Misconducts." *Criminal Justice and Behavior,* 24:414–31.

Gendreau, P. and D. Keyes. (2001). "Making Prisons Safer and More Humane Environments." *Canadian Journal of Criminology,* 43:123–30.

Gesch, C. B., S. M. Hammond, S. E. Hampson, A. Eves, and M. J. Crowder. (2002). "Influence of Supplementary Vitamins, Minerals and Essential Fatty Acids on the Antisocial Behaviour of Young Adult Prisoners." *British Journal of Psychiatry,* 181:22–28.

Gibbons, J. J. and N. B. de Katzenbach. (2006). "Confronting Confinement: A Report of the Commission on Safety and Abuse in America's Prisons." Vera Institute of Justice, New York, NY. http//www.prisoncommission.org/pdfs/Confronting_Confinement.pdf

Gillespie, W. (2005). "A Multilevel Model of Drug Abuse Inside Prison." *The Prison Journal,* 85:223–46.

Gilligan, J. (1996). *Violence: Reflections on A National Epidemic.* New York: Random House.

Goffman, E. (1961). *Asylums: Essays on the Social Situations of Mental Patients and Other Inmates.* Oxford, UK: Doubleday (Anchor).

Gordon, J. A., L. J. Moriarty, and P. H. Grant. (2003). "Juvenile Correctional Officers' Perceived Fear and Risk of Victimization: Examining Individual and Collective Levels of Victimization in Two Juvenile Correctional Centers in Virginia." *Criminal Justice and Behavior,* 30:62–84.

Hardyman, P. L., J. Austin, and O. C. Tulloch. (2002). *Revalidating External Prison Classification Systems: The Experience of Ten States and Model for Classification Reform.* Washington, DC: U.S. Department of Justice, National Institute of Corrections.

Harer, M. D. and N. P. Langan. (2001). "Gender Differences in Predictors of Prison Violence: Assessing the Predictive Validity of a Risk Classification System." *Crime and Delinquency,* 47:513–36.

Harrison, P. M. and A. J. Beck. (2006). "Prison and Jail Inmates at Midyear 2005." *Bureau of Justice Statistics Bulletin, May 2006.* Washington, DC: U.S. Department of Justice, Office of Justice Programs.

Hensley, C., M. Koscheski, and R. Tewksbury. (2003). "The Impact of Institutional Factors on Officially Reported Sexual Assaults in Prisons." *Sexuality and Culture,* 7:16–26.

Hensley, C., R. Tewksbury, and T. Castle (2003). "Characteristics of Prison Sexual Assault Targets in Male Oklahoma Correctional Facilities." *Journal of Interpersonal Violence,* 18: 595–606.

Jacobson, M. (2005). *Downsizing Prisons.* New York: New York University Press.

Jiang, S. and M. Fisher–Giorlando. (2002). "Inmate Misconduct: A Test of the Deprivation, Importation, and Structural Models." *The Prison Journal,* 82:335–58.

Johnson, B. R. (1987). "Religiosity and Institutional Deviance: The Impact of Religious Variables upon Inmate Adjustment." *Criminal Justice Review,* 12:21–30.

Kinlock, T. W., K. E. O'Grady, and T. E. Hanlon. (2003). "The Effects of Drug Treatment on Institutional Behavior." *The Prison Journal,* 83:257–76.

Langan, N. P. and B. M. M. Pelissier. (2001). "The Effect of Drug Treatment on Inmate Misconduct in Federal Prisons." *Journal of Offender Rehabilitation,* 34:21–30.

Latessa, E. J. (2004). "The Challenge of Change: Correctional Programs and Evidence-Based Practices." *Criminology and Public Policy,* 3:547–59.

Lawrence, C. and K. Andrews. (2004). "The Influence of Perceived Prison Crowding on Male Inmates' Perception of Aggressive Events." *Aggressive Behavior,* 30:273–83.

Liebling, A. (2006). "Why Prison Staff Culture Matters." *Journal of Offender Rehabilitation,* present issue.

Liebling, A. (2005). *Prisons and Their Moral Performance: A Study of Values, Quality, and Prison Life.* New York: Oxford University Press.

Liebling, A. (1999). "Prison Suicide and Prisoner Coping." In: M. Tonry and J. Petersilia (Editors). *Prisons.* Chicago, IL: The University of Chicago Press, pp. 283–359.

Liebling, A. and S. Maruna. (2005). "Introduction: The Effects of Imprisonment Revisited." In: A. Liebling and S. Maruna (Editors). *The Effects of Imprisonment* Devon, UK: Willan Publishing, pp. 1–29.

Liedka, R., A. Piehl, & B. Useem, 2006. "The Crime Control Effect of Incarceration: Does Scale Matter? *Crime and Public Policy,* 5(2): 245–76.

Lifers Public Safety Steering Committee of the State Correctional Institution. (2004). "Ending the Culture of Street Crime." *The Prison Journal,* 84 (supp.):48s–68s.

LIS, Inc. (2000). *Sexual Misconduct In Prison: Law, Agency Response, and Prevention.* Washington, DC: U.S. Department of Justice.

MacKenzie, D. L. and J. W. Shaw. (1990). "Inmate Adjustment and Change During Shock Incarceration: The Impact of Correctional Boot Camp Programs." *Justice Quarterly,* 7:125–50.

Mair, J. S., S. Frattaroli, and S. P. Teret. (2003). "New Hope for Victims of Prison Sexual Assault." *The Journal of Law, Medicine & Ethics,* 31:602–06.

Martinez, R. Jr. 2002. *Latino Homicide: Immigration, Violence, and Community.* New York: Routledge Press.

Martinez, R. Jr. and M. T. Lee. (2000). "On Immigration and Crime." In: G. LaFree and R. Bursik. (Editors). *Criminal Justice 2000: The Changing Nature of Crime, Volume I.* Washington, DC.: National Institute of Justice.

Maruna, S. and H. Toch. (2005). "The Impact of Incarceration on the Desistance Process." In: J. Travis and C. Visher (Editors). *Prisoner Reentry and Public Safety in America.* New York: Cambridge University Press.

McCorkle, R. C., T. D. Miethe, and K. A. Drass. (1995). "The Roots of Prison Violence: A Test of the Deprivation, Management, and 'Not-So-Total' Institution Models." *Crime and Delinquency,* 41(3): 317–31.

McShane, M. D. and F. P. Williams III. (1990). "Old and Ornery: The Disciplinary Experiences of Elderly Prisoners." *International Journal of Offender Therapy and Comparative Criminology,* 34:197–212.

Moos, R. (1968). "The Assessment of the Social Climates of Correctional Institutions." *Journal of Research in Crime and Delinquency,* 5:174–88.

Morgan, R. D., C. L. Winterowd, and D. R. Fuqua. (1999). "The Efficacy of an Integrated Theoretical Approach to Group Psychotherapy for Male Inmates." *Journal of Contemporary Psychotherapy,* 29:203–22.

Mushlin, M. 2004. "Forward, Prison Reform Revisited: The Unfinished Agenda." *Pace Law Review,* 24 (2): 395–417.

National Center for State Courts. (2003). *Health Insurance Portability and Accountability Act of 1996; Standards for Privacy of Individually Identifiable Health Information. Applicability to the Courts: An Initial Assessment.* Denver, CO: National Center for State Courts in conjunction with the National Governors Association Center for Best Practices.

National Institute of Corrections (NIC). (2003). Institutional Culture Initiative, Program Meeting, Washington, DC.

National Research Council. (2004). *Fairness and Effectiveness In Policing.* Washington, DC: National Academy Press.

National Research Council. (2001). *What's Changing in Prosecution? Report of a Workshop.* Washington, DC: National Academy Press.

O'Donnell, I. and K. Edgar. (1998). "Routine Victimization in Prisons." *Howard Journal of Criminal Justice,* 37: 266–79.

Patrick, S. (1998). "Differences in Inmate-Inmate and Inmate-Staff Altercations: Examples from a Medium Security Prison." *Social Science Journal,* 35:253–63.

Pattavina, A., J. M. Byrne, and L. Garcia. (2006). "An Examination of Citizen Involvement in Crime Prevention in High-Risk versus Low-to-Moderate Risk Neighborhoods." *Crime and Delinquency,* 52:203–31.

Pelissier, B. (1991). "The Effects of a Rapid Increase in a Prison Population: A Pre- and Posttest Study." *Criminal Justice and Behavior,* 18:427–47.

Pelissier, B., S. D. Camp, and M. Motivans. (2003). "Staying in Treatment: How Much Difference Is There from Prison to Prison?" *Psychology of Addictive Behaviors,* 17:134–41.

Porporino, F. J. (1986). "Managing Violent Individuals in Correctional Settings." *Journal of Interpersonal Violence,* 1:213–37.

Porporino, F. J., P. D. Doherty, and T. Sawatsky. (1987). "Characteristics of Homicide Victims and Victimizations in Prisons: A Canadian Historical Perspective." *International Journal of Offender Therapy and Comparative Criminology,* 31:125–35.

Prendergast, M. L., D. Farabee, J. Cartier, and S. Henkin (2002) "Involuntary Treatment within a Prison Setting: Impact on Psychological Change during Treatment." *Criminal Justice and Behavior,* 29:5–26.

Reisig, M. D. (2002). "Administrative Control and Inmate Homicide." *Homicide Studies,* 6:84–103.

Reisig, M. D. (1998). "Rates of Disorder in Higher-Custody State Prisons: A Comparative Analysis of Managerial Practices." *Crime and Delinquency* 41(2): 229–44.

Riveland, C. (1999). "Prison Management Trends, 1975–2025." In: M. Tonry and J. Petersilia (Editors). *Prisons.* Chicago, Illinois: The University of Chicago Press, pp.163–203.

Ruback, R. B. and T. S. Carr. (1993). "Prison Crowding over Time: The Relationship of Density and Changes in Density to Infraction Rates." *Criminal Justice and Behavior,* 20:130–48.

Ryan, T. A. and K. A. McCabe. (1994). "Mandatory versus Voluntary Prison Education and Academic Achievement." *The Prison Journal,* 74:450–61.

Sampson, R. J. and L. Bean. (2006). "Cultural Mechanisms and Killings Fields: A Revised Theory of Community-Level Racial Inequality." In: R. Peterson, L. Krivo, and J. Hagan (Editors). *The Many Colors of Crime: Inequalities of Race, Ethnicity, and Crime in America.* New York: New York University Press, pp. 8–36.

Sampson, R. J., H. MacIndoe, D. McAdam, and S. Weffer–Elizondo. (2005). "Civil Society Reconsidered: The Durable Nature and Community Structure of Collective Civic Action." *American Journal of Sociology,* 111:673–714.

Sampson, R. J. and W. J. Wilson. (1995). "Toward a Theory of Race, Crime, and Urban Inequality." In: J. Hagan and R. Peterson (Editors). *Crime and Inequality.* Stanford, CA: Stanford University Press, pp. 37–56.

Sherman, L. W., D. Gottfredson, D. MacKenzie, J. Eck, P. Reuter, and S. Bushway. (1997). *Preventing Crime: What Works, What Doesn't, What's Promising: A Report to the United States Congress.* Washington, DC: U.S. Department of Justice, Office of Justice Programs, National Institute of Justice.

Snacken, S. (2005). "Forms of Violence and Regimes in Prison: Report of Research in Belgian Prisons." In: A. Liebling and S. Maruna (Editors). *The Effects of Imprisonment.* Portland, OR: Willan Publishing, pp. 306–37.

Sparks, R. (1995). "Situational and Social Approaches to the Prevention of Disorder in Long-Term Prisons." In: T. Flanagan (Editor). *Long Term Imprisonment: Policy, Science and Correctional Practice.* Thousand Oaks, CA: Sage.

Sparks, R., A. Bottoms, and W. Hay. (1996). *Prisons and the Problem of Order.* Oxford: Clarendon Press.

Stemen, D. 2007. *Reconsidering Incarceration: New Directions for Reducing Crime.* New York: Vera Institute of Justice.

Stephan, J. and J. Karberg. (2003). *The Census of State and Federal Correctional Facilities.* Washington, DC: U.S Department of Justice.

Struckman-Johnson, C. J. and D. L. Struckman-Johnson. (2000). "Sexual Coercion Rates in Seven Midwestern Prison Facilities for Men." *Prison Journal,* 80: 279–390.

Swindler, A. 1986. "Culture in Action." *American Sociological Review* 51: 273–86.

Sykes, G. M. (1958). *The Society of Captives: A Study of Maximum Security Prison.* Princeton, NJ: Princeton University Press.

Tartaro, C. (2002). "The Impact of Density on Prison Violence." *Journal of Criminal Justice,* 30:499–510.

Toch, H. (1977). *Living in Prison: The Ecology of Survival.* New York: Free Press.

Toch, H. (1992). *Living in Prison: The Ecology of Survival.* Washington, D.C.: The American Psychological Association.

Useem, B. and A. M. Piehl. (2006). "Prison Buildup and Disorder." *Punishment and Society,* 8:87–115.

Useem, B. and M. D. Reisig. (1999). "Collective Action in Prisons: Protests, Disturbances, and Riots." *Criminology,* 37:735–59.

Walrath, C. (2001). "Evaluation of an Inmate-Run Alternatives to Violence Project." *Journal of Interpersonal Violence,* 16:697–711.

Walters, G. D. (1998). "Time Series and Correlational Analyses of Inmate-Initiated Assaultive Incidents in a Large Correctional System." *International Journal of offender Therapy and Comparative Criminology,* 42(2): 124–32.

Walters, G. D. (1999). "Short-Term Outcome of Inmates Participating in the Lifestyle Change Program." *Criminal Justice and Behavior,* 26:322–37.

Walters, G. D. (2003). "Changes in Criminal Thinking and Identity in Novice and Experienced Inmates: Prisonization Revisited." *Criminal Justice and Behavior,* 30:399–421.

Warren, J. I., S. Hurt, A. B. Loper, and P. Chauhan. (2004). "Exploring Prison Adjustment among Female Inmates: Issues of Measurement and Prediction." *Criminal Justice and Behavior,* 31:624–45.

Welch, M. (2004). *Corrections: A Critical Approach* (2nd Edition). New York: McGraw-Hill.

Welsh, B. C., and D. P. Farrington. (2000). "Monetary Costs and Benefits of Crime Prevention Programs." In: M. Tonry (Editor). *Crime and Justice: A Review of Research, Vol. 27.* Chicago, IL: University of Chicago Press, pp. 305–361.

Welsh, B. C., and D. P. Farrington. (2001). Toward an Evidence-Based Approach to Preventing Crime. *Annals of the American Academy of Political and Social Science,* 578:158–73.

Wener, R. (2006). "Effectiveness of the Direct Supervision System of Correctional Design and Management." *Criminal Justice and Behavior,* 33:392–410.

Williams, J. L., D. G. Rodeheaver, and D. W. Huggins. (1999). "A Comparative Evaluation of a New Generation Jail." *American Journal of Criminal Justice,* 23:223–46.

Wilson, D. B., L. A. Bouffard, and D. L. MacKenzie. (2005). "A Quantitative Review of Structured, Group-Oriented, Cognitive-Behavioral Programs for Offenders." *Criminal Justice and Behavior,* 32:172–204.

Wooldredge, J. D. (1998). "Inmate Lifestyles and Opportunities for Victimization." *Journal of Research in Crime and Delinquency,* 35:480–502.

Wooldredge, J., T. Griffin, and T. Pratt. (2001). "Considering Hierarchical Models for Research on Inmate Behavior: Predicting Misconduct with Multilevel Data." *Justice Quarterly,* 18:203–31.

World Health Organization. 2004. *Preventing Violence: A Guide for Implementing the Recommendations of the Worlds Report on Violence and Health.* Geneva: World Health Organization. http://whqlibdoc.who.int/publications/2004/9241592079.pdf

Wormith, J. S. (1984). "Attitude and Behavior Change of Correctional Clientele." *Criminology,* 22:595–618.

Wortley, R. (2002). *Situational Prison Control: Crime Prevention in Correctional Institutions.* Cambridge, UK: Cambridge University Press.

Wright, K. N. (1986). *Improving Correctional Classification Through a Study of the Placement of Inmates in Environmental Settings.* Binghamton, NY: Center for Social Analysis, State University of New York at Binghamton.

Wright, K. N. (2005). "Designing a National Performance Measurement System." *The Prison Journal,* 85:368–93.

Wright, K. N., with J. Brisbee and P. Hardyman. (2003). *Defining and Measuring Corrections Performance: Final Report.* Washington, DC: U.S. Department of Justice.